WORRY-FREE
RETIREMENT LIVING

Choosing a Full Service Retirement Community

WORRY-FREE RETIREMENT LIVING

Choosing a Full Service Retirement Community

❊❊

BY RALPH AND LONI SMITH

PublishAmerica
Baltimore

First printing

ISBN: 1-4137-2621-6
PUBLISHED BY PUBLISHAMERICA, LLLP
www.publishamerica.com
Baltimore

Printed in the United States of America

To the hard-working, caring men and women of the American Association of Homes and Services for the Aging and the American Seniors Housing Association,

for their spirit of sharing ideas and information to further the quality and raise the standards of care for our elders.

CONTENTS

FOREWORD

by Jennie M. Forehand
Maryland State Senator

Knowledge is power.

—Sir Francis Bacon
English Philosopher, Essayist,
and Statesman, 1561-1626

As a Maryland State Senator, I understand and appreciate the value and assistance that this book will bring to my aging constituents and their families. I have first-hand knowledge of the problems they might face when they choose to stay in their own homes. Everyday life becomes more difficult and loneliness and depression frequently overtake them. The solution for many seniors lies with the full service retirement community (FSRC), also known as the continuing care retirement community (CCRC). It provides independent living for vibrant retirees and a safety net with assisted living, skilled nursing, and Alzheimer's/dementia care on the same property.

If you are thinking about retirement, but are not sure about the how, where, or when, *Worry-Free Retirement Living: Choosing a Full*

Service Retirement Community is a treasure designed with just these questions in mind. The authors have visited and studied hundreds of communities and interviewed more than a thousand residents and scores of administrators to find the answers, while searching for a community for themselves. In the process, the authors became well informed and wanted to share their knowledge with other potential residents and their families.

Practical and enjoyable, the book is an interesting read, written in an easy informative style. It gives the reader a very specific method for shopping for a full service retirement community. I immediately caught myself saying, "Oh, yes—why didn't I think of that?" The authors give suggested questions to ask yourself and to ask staff and administrators at the FSRCs you visit. In addition, you will find advice on the kind of answers you might or should receive at communities you might be seriously considering.

How I wish I had been able to read this book fifteen years ago! My mother, a recent widow, had found it necessary to make a similar transition from her longtime home and left the decision up to me, her only child. Luckily, I had friends with contacts at most of the places that I had chosen to check out for Mom. I didn't have the luxury of having this book to guide me, as you have. After reading this book, you will be armed with info on the specifics of many topics, such as grounds, buildings, amenities, services, health care, occupancy fees, entrance requirements, contracts, ownership, management, and so on.

Because I served for six years on the Board of Trustees of an excellent CCRC, I thought I knew it all. Nothing could be done better anywhere than at the community I knew so intimately. Well, I learned more from this book than I did as an active trustee. In fact, this should be required reading for CCRC trustees, board members, management, marketing representatives, and service providers as well.

This book could have answered many of my inquires and, in addition, given me the questions I should have been asking. If you want a guidebook on how to pick out an FSRC for yourself, a friend, or a parent, you need look no farther than Loni and Ralph Smith's gem. *Worry-Free Retirement Living: Choosing a Full Service Retirement Community* will help you make an educated, lifelong decision for yourself, a friend, or a loved one and even enjoy the process!

PREFACE

They who have curiosity will find adventure;
they who have wisdom will see the truth.

—Anonymous

Worry-Free Retirement Living is addressed to retirees and to everyone who has retired parents or relatives. Good news greets those of you who are concerned about your future well-being or that of your relatives.

The full service retirement community (FSRC), also known as a continuing care retirement community (CCRC), solves many of life's problems before they start. Living in such a community is like living on a stationary cruise ship or in a country club community—and it is not as financially elusive as you would think.

Communities offer a variety of mentally and physically stimulating activities. Meals are served in a dining room for residents who wish to dine without cooking and doing the dishes. All interior and exterior maintenance is included. When the community bus takes the residents to the mall or the theater, they do not have to deal with parking hassles. The icing on the cake is that, in the background, personal and medical care is available for residents who might need it.

Heretofore, we, as a society, have managed to do all these things for the elderly. Mostly women have been the caretakers of the aging and the ill. Churches and other social programs supported the efforts of families who undertook this responsibility. Commercial care consisted of rest homes or nursing homes and they were dreary places—surely a last resort for those who had no other choice.

The Baby Boom Generation is the first where working women with careers—not just jobs—are commonplace. These women are not in a position to be full time caretakers anymore, even if their hearts are willing. Church membership is down drastically and those who do belong are not so free to aid others as they were in the past because of their own busy lives. Federal, state, county, and city governments cannot afford to pick up the slack.

We citizens are being charged ever more with having to make our own long-term plans to assure safe and healthy futures for ourselves and our relatives in our retirement years. The marketplace is providing choices in several forms. Their pros and cons are clearly outlined in easy-to-read charts.

The 3500 plus[1] full service retirement communities (FSRCs) are the most promising answers to meeting the continuing needs of a large segment of the retired population. Transportation, prepared meals, housekeeping, and maintenance of the residences relieve the residents of the burdens of running a home, thus, giving them the time and freedom to pursue treasured interests. The opportunities for many friendships and a broad range of activities combat loneliness, isolation, and depression. The assisted living, skilled nursing, and Alzheimer's/dementia care serve as a safety net for residents who might need these services on a temporary or permanent basis and allow for residents to age in place.

Shopping for just the right community for yourself or your relative can be confusing because the choices are many and some call themselves full service retirement communities or continuing care retirement communities that really are not. This book is designed to help you investigate FSRCs so that you can make your own judgments based on what you see and on what the community does, not on how it labels itself. We give you the tools to analyze FSRCs to

---

[1] This is a rough estimate according to a source at the American Association of Homes and Services for the Aging (AAHSA).

determine if they are well managed, looking toward the future, and offering the quality care and lifestyle that you are looking for amid amenities that fit your personal preferences.

This book is divided into two parts. Part I tells you what choices seniors have and what an FSRC is all about. It is liberally sprinkled with charts that summarize, clarify, and simplify complex, voluminous information. It also helps you find the one that suits you or your relative.

Part II is the workhorse of the book. It organizes what we've been discussing in Part I into a checklist of questions and observations to note during your visits. It is designed so that you can record the answers to the questions quickly. In addition, the most important issues are highlighted so that you can easily find them. The Appendices give you resources to find additional help.

Chapter 1, "Senior Housing Options," outlines the three choices that seniors have for getting the help that they will need as they age. The pros and cons of staying at home, living with others, and moving to a full service retirement community are explored.

The many choices of residential communities are described in Chapter 2, "Residential Communities." The pluses and minuses of independent living, dependent living, and combination living arrangements are thoroughly covered. Many charts summarize the points.

"Lifestyle," Chapter 3, looks at the benefits of an FSRC. A checklist helps you to zero in on what your expectations, wants, and needs in retirement might be. Future trends in the industry are extremely important in the selection of a full service retirement community. New residents will want to move into a community whose financial stability will be assured far into the future. These details will be discussed more fully in subsequent chapters.

Chapter 4 gives you a detailed discussion of available options with respect to grounds and buildings. Entrance fees can vary from $20,000 to over a million dollars, depending on the size of the home, how posh the community is, and how many amenities and services are offered. The communities can be in high-rise buildings or situated on rambling acreage.

Chapter 5 delves into the details of a wide range of amenities and services. The amenities vary widely, but all should offer some sort of space for activities, hobbies, and sports/fitness. Commercial amenities can range from a visiting bank representative to small self-contained villages comprising a full service bank, country store, café, and other shops.

The many services allow residents freedom to pursue their interests. These services typically include maintenance, housekeeping, meals, flat linen laundry, transportation, and more.

At the core of the FSRC is the care and, as such, all of Chapter 6 is devoted to an in-depth discussion of the various ways the care is delivered to residents. A full service retirement community (FSRCs), as a matter of definition, should include health care, personal care, and medical care. This should translate into a minimum of independent living (IL), assisted living (AL), skilled nursing (SN), and Alzheimer's/dementia (A/D) care.

More complicated information is presented in Chapter 7, "Occupancy Options and Fees." Legal technicalities and their implications are explained in layman's terms. In order for FSRCs to be competitive, they have a myriad of pricing and payment plans and each has variations with its pros and cons. It continues with explanations of what the basic formats are and how to evaluate them for the near- and long-term. Comparisons of costs for several more popular payment options are condensed into easy-to-read graph charts. Basic tax implications are interpreted with Internal Revenue Service (IRS) references for your accountant and others who are savvy about taxation.

Chapter 8 explains the entry requirements of communities and dives into the contracts new residents must sign. Charts clearly explain what clauses the contracts should contain.

The ownership, sponsorship, and management of the community heavily influence the quality of life. The policies, challenges, and accreditation issues are explored in Chapter 9. Each of these points and others are examined from both the viewpoints of the management, current residents, and future shoppers. A detailed chart summarizes and the text explains what items should be covered in contracts that residents must sign. Instructions on what to look for when considering a community under construction are also included.

Each FSRC has its own personality. It is not always readily discernable at first glance. Suggestions on how to determine if a community is appropriate for you are discussed in Chapter 10.

The quest for your new home begins in Chapter 11. Hints on how to find communities through searches with and without the Internet are presented in easy-to-follow charts. Instructions on how to read between the lines of the information packets and how to phone screen the communities finish the chapter.

Part II begins the first of the checklists of questions to ask when evaluating communities. You do not have to take notes while reading Part I; the questions address the points discussed there. Workbook spaces are set up to record information received for three communities to make comparisons easier. Guidelines are provided for ascertaining whether an answer is a positive, neutral, or negative one.

With many points to observe and ask about, the process can be readily condensed to questions about deal breakers and red flags. The evaluation process can take from one to three hours, as you choose. The importance of why many questions are being asked will be lost without your having read Part I.

Chapter 12 supplies a detailed explanation of how the questions are organized. They begin with the screening format discussed in Chapter 11.

Observation can yield a tremendous amount of information. Tips on what to look for in and around the community are listed in Chapter 13.

The bulk of your visit is spent in the office of the marketing representative. This is your opportunity to ask the hard questions. They are presented in Chapter 14. Entrance and financial requirements, policies, and legal structure can provide some details that might make or break a deal.

Walking through an FSRC is not only interesting, but revealing. Here the personality and level of commitment by management to its residents can become evident. The points in Chapter 15 illuminate possible trouble spots.

Of course, no one knows the community the way the residents do. Dining with them can give you an entirely different slant on things. Suggested questions to ask are in Chapter 16.

For those of you who are independent researchers, many outside sources can uncover other facts about the community. For instance, the police will know whether it is in a safe part of town, if you are not familiar with it. Past newspaper articles tell tales a marketing rep might not. How the laws of the state might affect you is important to know if you move to a new state. See Chapter 17 for other items to check out.

As a potential resident, you will surely want to talk to the top executive of the communities you are seriously considering. Their titles vary; they might be executive directors, chief operating officers, chief executive officers (CEOs), or others. We will refer to them hereinafter as CEOs. Chapter 18 covers topics to ask about. They can reveal information that will tell you how well the management runs the community. The ratio of staff to residents and the cost of raw food per plate will give you a picture that other sources cannot.

Chapter 19 provides a space for you to record your overall impressions and conclusions. By the time you have evaluated the facts you will be able to make a reasoned decision. It ends with the most important question: "Is this retirement community for me?"

❧❦

Together we shopped for a community for ourselves and helped several others in their searches. In the process we gained a body of information that has proved helpful to many. It is our hope that this book will become as invaluable in your quest for a community as it has been to ours.

We bring many diverse skills and different bodies of knowledge to this endeavor. Loni's familiarization with her parents' living in an FSRC for eighteen years gave her an insider's perspective of one community. She observed first hand just how well the concept works. Since her mother and father were in one of the first communities that was helping to redesign the industry in the 1980s and 1990s, she saw the FSRC's growing pains and lived through the ins and outs of a lawsuit against the board of directors.

As an attorney and professor of business law and business management, Loni's legal and business knowledge gave her the background to delve into the complex legal structures and management of full service retirement communities. She is also the award-winning author of the best-selling *The Needlepoint Book*, written under the pen name Jo Ippolito Christensen. Her skills in research, writing, and teaching enabled her to organize voluminous information into book form for lay readers.

Ralph's inquiring, philosophical mind was the basis for multiple probing questions that spawned many of our deal-breaker and red-flag issues. His lifelong study of social sciences allowed him to tour communities with a perspective that many of us do not have, thus, uncovering and later verbalizing and quantifying the ingredients for a desirable quality of life.

Ralph's experiences in serving on the Commission on Aging for our city introduced him to government's difficulties in providing increasingly more services for a growing segment of the population and funding them from a shrinking tax base. In addition, he is absolutely ruthless with the editor's blue pencil!

꙾꙾

In writing this book, it has been our intention to be fair to both the consumer who is shopping for a community and to the FSRCs. As consumers ourselves we know what it takes to make us comfortable. We have sought out the advice of dozens of others who were also looking for a new home. In addition, we interviewed more than a thousand current residents.

We have made it a point to find out what issues the industry faces by attending the conferences of the American Association of Homes and Services for the Aging. Many chief executive officers, chief financial officers, and marketing representatives have graciously helped us comprehend their obstacles in pleasing the residents, the staff, and the board of directors, while complying with the law and keeping expenses within the budget. One very helpful CEO gave us an extended tour. For six hours he showed us, explained to us, and guided us through his challenges in running an FSRC.

We like to think that every FSRC is run by capable, caring people—indeed, that has been our experience in traveling to vast numbers of them. Although aspects of some FSRCs might be less than ideal, we do not mean for our comments to be in any way critical of the good faith effort that is being made to better each community.

We fully understand that running such a complex enterprise requires smoothing out a few wrinkles. Any problem can be fixed while the iron is still plugged in. The checklist is designed to help you find out who has the hot iron.

A WORD OF THANKS

*One can pay back the loan of gold,
but one dies forever in debt
to those who are kind.*

—Malayan Proverb

No book is ever written without the help of a myriad of people. It was Gaye and Jerry Kirkpatrick who started us on this venture. We are very grateful to them. Jerry aptly told their story in the Introduction, which follows.

Maryland State Senator Jennie Forehand lent a different perspective, encouragement, and sage words of advice to the project. She shared her experiences not only from a personal and legislative viewpoint, but also from her position on the Board of Trustees at Asbury Methodist Village in Gaithersburg, Maryland. She graciously wrote the Foreword.

Professionals in the industry were very hospitable to us. Doug Pace, Director of Assisted Living and Continuing Care for the American Association of Homes and Services for the Aging (AAHSA), helped us in a number of ways. Not only did he offer much information, but he introduced us to others whose help was invaluable. He was also instrumental in facilitating our admission to the AAHSA's semiannual conferences so that we could attend countless educational classes.

Sue Matthieson, Director of Strategic Projects of the Continuing Care Accreditation Commission, generously allowed us to sit in on training courses for the evaluators of CCRCs. It was there that we learned to look at the industry from the viewpoint of management.

We are grateful for the words of wisdom from Roger Stevens, Senior Vice President and Chief Operating Officer of Westminster Services in Orlando, Florida. He spent many hours of his valuable time proofreading our manuscript and commenting at length.

Gary Selmeczi is Executive Director of Goodwin House, a premier full service retirement community in Alexandria, Virginia, just four blocks down the street from where we live. The tour of his community was most enlightening. He has been an e-mail and phone buddy who cheerfully answered miscellaneous questions all along the way. He also diligently proofread the final manuscript, keeping the contents true and accurate.

Doug Halvorsen, the President and Chief Operating Officer of The Evergreens, graciously invited us to spend the day learning his challenges in running his beautiful upscale community in Moorestown, New Jersey. He generously gave us his time and patiently answered our many questions.

Star Bradbury, Marketing Representative of Oak Hammock at the University of Florida, Gainesville, Florida, was most obliging in gathering information. She went out of her way to help us with our research and to refer us to other resources.

Tye Campbell, Senior Vice President of SFCS, Inc.: Architecture, Engineering, Planning, and Interiors in Roanoke, Virginia, graciously allowed us to reprint some of his company's excellent photos of full service retirement communities. Louisa Brancati, Marketing Manager, waded through thousands of images to give us a well-balanced pool of shots from which to choose. Thanks also to photographers Tim Schoon and Louisa Brancati, whose quality images aptly illustrate that the full service retirement community is not the rest home of yesteryear. More of Tim's impressive photography may be seen at www.timschoon.com. Developer of full service retirement communities, Praxeis of Jacksonville, Florida, kindly provided their rendering of atrium apartments.

A Word of Thanks

Paul Gordon is an attorney and partner with the San Francisco law firm, Hanson, Bridgett, Marcus, Vlahos, & Rudy. Since 1975, he has represented more than 200 senior housing and care facilities. Besides writing the book that is considered the bible of the industry, *Senior's Housing and Care Facilities: Development, Business, and Operations,* published by the Urban Land Institute, he serves on the boards of many national associations that represent the industry. He kindly gave Loni his time and expertise by answering a multitude of her legal questions on several occasions.

Our attorney, the late Alan Winterhalter, was our sounding board for reason. In his inimitable style of wit and humor, he pointed out weaknesses and urged us onward. In addition, he backed Loni up on the legal issues.

Lynne Lumsden is the former Editor-in-Chief of Spectrum Books and Vice President and Editorial Director, General Publishing, Prentice-Hall and Executive Vice President and Publisher of Dodd Mead. She was the editor for Loni's best-selling book, *The Needlepoint Book*, published by Prentice-Hall. She spent many hours advising us, reviewing contract terms, and encouraging us in our endeavor.

Our agent, Al Zuckerman of Writer's House, believed in this book and its value to all retirees. We thank him for his persistence and dedication to the concept of the full service retirement community.

Jeff Lubin, Regional Sales Manager, Southeast Region, Merrill Lynch, guided us through various financial planning scenarios. He encouraged us to continue with our research and book writing, citing that his clients could benefit from learning about FSRCs. He and his industry, he said, needed such a tool.

Loni is a professor at Northern Virginia Community College, which is the second largest community college in the nation; it enjoys a fine reputation for academic excellence. Loni's colleagues in the Business Technologies Division of the Alexandria campus are among the best and brightest educators that Virginia has to offer. Each of them generously shared their knowledge and skills in his or her areas of expertise for the betterment of this book.

Business Technologies Division Dean, Jenny Graves, and Assistant Dean, Joyce Fairchild, generously gave us the support of the department. Joyce Fairchild, as the marketing professor, guided us through the latest ideas in marketing.

Professors who are proficient in business management shared their knowledge on the wide range of topics that affect the smooth running of an FSRC. These specialists are Bob LeRosen, Lynn Pape, and Rieann Spence-Gale.

Accountants Jim Gale, Jim Gray, and Bill Petersen lent their expertise to the tax sections of the text. They even doubled checked our math! Statistics professor Mike Palguta patiently advised us as to the best way to translate numeric information into graphs and charts. Jim Lock, finance professor, helped with the sources needed in checking on the financial strength of an FSRC, among other things.

Anne Marie Klinko, professor in Administrative Support Technology, kept us abreast of the latest official word in the ever-changing grammar rules. She also poured over the final version of the manuscript, correcting everything from commas to syntax.

Ali Soleymani, computer hardware professor, adeptly took our computer apart and put it back together again so that it would stop crashing, taking valuable data with it. He also upgraded its memory and speed. He was ably assisted by professors of Information Systems Technology, Pablo Ibar and Kevin Reed. Computer security specialist Dennis Stewart gave advice on the management of our computer on this huge project. Professors Barbara Holt and Dale Wurzer kept us straight on correct terminology. Suzanne Stevenson cheerfully aided us with software.

The Business Technologies Division enjoys a very competent and congenial administrative staff. Alessi Bland, Brenda Robinson-Baptist, and Bea Curtis graciously helped in so many of the little ways that only secretaries can.

The human mind is a funny thing when it comes to reading printed words on a page, particularly when you are the author. Sometimes they seem to say what we want them to say and not what they do say. Many people generously proofread our manuscript. We are grateful to Bob Benedict, Randy Falk, Gaye and Jerry Kirkpatrick, Andi McKinsey, Annette McQueen, Melinda Mosbey, Dave and Helen Naley, Martha Naley, Don Taylor, and Eleanor Young.

We offer a special thanks to Don Taylor, Colonel, United States Air Force, Retired, our good friend and neighbor. We spent countless hours with him discussing the topic at length over a period of several years. His acute listening skills allowed him to form astute questions that identified areas of confusion and omission. This, in turn, allowed us to see the subject matter from the point of view of one who was seeking in-depth knowledge of FSRCs. Under starry, moonlit summer skies and in front of a cozy fire in the cold weather, we debated with him and his many friends about what was important to various people with differing values. We, then, refocused, reorganized, and rewrote much of the text and many questions. We are grateful for his time, insight, and continued interest and support.

Martha Naley was a regular attendee at the debate sessions at Don's house. Her ideas were valuable in forming questions to pose to others and were treasured for their breadth. She also proofread the final manuscript, interjecting many constructive comments.

Terry Travers, President and CEO of Interactive Planet, is a whiz at the computer and in graphics. She put together a few sample designs for the cover and performed other computer tricks that are greatly appreciated. Her computer and Internet services Website can be seen at www.ia-planet.com. Terry also ably designed and now hosts our Web page, www.worryfreeretirementliving.com.

Barbara Fossum, another computer whiz, patiently taught us how to make graph charts on the computer. Elza Daniel contributed to the cover by skillfully taking photographs of us for the back cover.

Equally dedicated to the goal of getting the word out to seniors about the best kept secret in senior housing is publisher Larry Clopper of PublishAmerica. We are very grateful to him for his vote of confidence in us and this book.

It takes an exceptional individual to be a supervising editor. Jaime Polychrones was incredible! After we and many others had proofread our manuscript a zillion times, she zeroed in on missing words, mismatched plurals, superfluous commas, and a whole host of other errors. Her talent, patience, and flexibility made putting this book to bed a joy rather than a chore. Our hats are off to her.

In the six years that this book was in the making, we met many kind and generous people throughout the industry whose names are endless. Without the efforts of all those involved, we could not have brought you this timely and informative book.

INTRODUCTION

by Gerald J. Kirkpatrick, J.D., LL.M.
Captain, U.S. Navy (Retired)

It wasn't raining when Noah built the ark.

—Howard Ruff
American Author and Editor

My wife, Gaye, and I started visiting FSRCs in the early 1990s, when we were barely 50 years of age. I wasn't at all ready to begin thinking about our retirement. However, my wife is a long-term planner, so I went along as a dutiful husband, but not with much enthusiasm. After visiting several communities and talking with marketing representatives and many residents, I started to become interested in the subject, and then I began to think about the benefits of the FSRC model, with independent living, assisted living, and skilled nursing care all located within the same community. This thought process was helped along by my wife's reminder that I not think of us as we were then, but instead to picture us in our 70s and 80s. Reflecting upon the assistance my widowed mother required from family and friends helped me to do this.

INTRODUCTION

I began to think that when it came time for us to retire and settle down for good, I would definitely want to reside in an FSRC, as opposed to living on our own among the general population or in an over-55 residential community with no provisions for assisted living or skilled nursing care should we need these services as we age.

As we visited additional FSRCs, I realized two important things: 1) that the people who benefit most from living in an FSRC are those who enter the community earlier rather than later, while they are young enough to enjoy a physically active lifestyle, and 2) there is wide diversity among FSRCs in terms of setting, building style, cost to residents, quality of management and care, amenities, programs, and policies. Because we began our search for the "perfect" FSRC well before our actual retirement, we were able to proceed at a leisurely pace. We took mini-vacations visiting communities across the country. We made notes of our impressions, but later realized that our approach to evaluating these communities wasn't very organized or efficient. Enter Loni and Ralph Smith, the authors of this book.

We met Loni and Ralph socially. In general conversation that first evening, we mentioned our interest and experiences in searching for a retirement community. To our surprise, Loni and Ralph were quite knowledgeable about the FSRC concept (Loni's parents had lived in one for many years) and began giving us tips on things to look for in evaluating a community—everything from financial soundness to the appearance of happiness among the residents as indicated by laughter and lightheartedness in the dining room.

That very night we took the bold step and asked our new friends if they would consider accompanying us on our next trip to visit a few FSRCs. To our delight, they accepted our offer, and what followed was an educational experience we could not have imagined.

During two earlier visits, we had been impressed by a particular FSRC that appeared to us to be almost "perfect." It had a great location, was aesthetically pleasing in architecture and furnishings, had inviting amenities, and offered reasonable entrance and monthly fees; but when we returned with Loni and Ralph to visit the same community, our eyes were opened. On the surface, the community looked great, and its financial footing appeared sound, but we had overlooked its lack of long-term planning for continued financial viability and its ill-advised policies on several important issues affecting the quality of life for an aging population. This particular community was new, so there weren't residents of longstanding to question about their experiences while living there, and even if there had been long-term residents, we didn't know many of the right questions to ask.

For example, we did not know to ask how long one spouse would be permitted to remain in the couple's independent living home if the other spouse required placement in the assisted living or skilled nursing area or whether a resident who is able to live independently, except for requiring a wheelchair, would be welcome to take his or her meals in the community's main dining room. When we began asking these questions, we found that, in some communities, residents in wheelchairs were welcome in the main dining room, while at other communities they were not. This could be especially important for a couple when one spouse requires a wheelchair and the other spouse is fully ambulatory. The couple might never enjoy a meal together in the social atmosphere of the main dining room. These issues might or might not be important to you; however, we never even thought to ask these questions. Also, we never asked community representatives about their strategic planning, which is vital to the long-term success of all communities, particularly for a new community or one whose ownership or management has changed.

Loni and Ralph helped us to realize that while we had enjoyed the experience of visiting a number of FSRCs and listening to and reading the marketing presentations, we had not acquired the requisite knowledge to make an intelligent and informed choice of a community in which to spend our retirement years. Actually, this had been our feeling for some time. We had visited more than twenty communities, but we perceived an information vacuum. We knew something was missing, but we didn't know exactly what it was. We were soon to find out.

Before we made our first FSRC visit with Loni and Ralph, they wanted to know the details of our previous trips. Did the marketing representatives tell us this? Did we ask about that? Loni and Ralph helped us to realize that our previous trips had not been very effective, except for providing an overall orientation to the world of full service retirement communities.

Introduction

Loni and Ralph had us prepare a list of issues and items that were important to us in selecting an FSRC; so when the four of us embarked on our future journeys, we were armed with a long list of questions for the marketing representatives and residents. As we visited additional communities, the list grew and we began keeping track of responses and adding new questions. Before long, it was apparent that we had acquired more knowledge about FSRCs than that possessed by most community marketing representatives, and that was just the beginning.

Loni and Ralph continued to visit many more FSRCs coast to coast, asking probing and challenging questions. They compiled data and acquired additional knowledge, both for themselves in planning their own retirements and, potentially, for the benefit of others. Gaye and I were privileged to have benefitted from their research, experiences, and insights to the point of their calling us and announcing excitedly that they had found "the right community" for us, one that we had never even heard of before in a state we had summarily ruled out as a retirement destination.

They were right. Their research had turned up a community whose campus, programs, and policies provided exactly the right mix for us. We researched further, visited the community several times, researched some more, and then made our choice.

The beauty of this book is that Loni and Ralph have done years of work in evaluating FSRCs and are passing on the fruits of their labor to you. It is not only an excellent primer on FSRCs; it is also a valuable resource as a workbook for doing your own evaluation of full service retirement communities. All the issues Gaye and I failed to address, and all the questions we did not ask in our early FSRC visits, plus much, much more are in this book. Charts, graphs, checklists, and suggested methodologies all make this book a practical, useful tool in your search for the right FSRC. Loni and Ralph have done an incredible amount of groundwork that you can use as a platform and "in-flight" guide for launching and conducting your own search for the FSRC that will be your perfect choice.

PART I

THE FACTS

We all go through life on a tightrope;
some use a safety net and others do not.
Only those who do can climb back up.

—Anonymous

1

SENIOR HOUSING OPTIONS

Long-term planning is not about
making long-term decisions,
it is about understanding the future
consequences of today's decisions.

—Gary Ryan Blair
American Author

The times have changed dramatically since the parents of today's seniors retired. Heretofore, planning for retirement has not been necessary. Their parents' employers paid pensions they could actually live on until their children took them in, when they could no longer care for themselves.

Today, many seniors now live well for an extended number of years. Long-term planning is necessary to turn that extra time into quality time.

In the middle of the twentieth century the American Dream was to buy a house in the suburbs, have 2.5 children and a dog, eventually have a mortgage-burning party, and live there for the rest of our lives. Society would reward those who worked hard.

We've seen the concept in action. When Mrs. Jones was sick, her extended family who lived in town stepped up their visits to her, ran her errands, cooked her meals, did her laundry, and cleaned her house. The leader of her religious institution and ladies' group organized visits, taking stews to help her out. The neighbors would check on her often. When Mrs. Jones could no longer cope in her own home, family took her in for the rest of her days.

Every generation adapts the American Dream to the changing times of their youths. Those of us who embraced the American Dream of the 1950s turned around in the twenty-first century only to find that dream is radically different from today's reality. The social structure that our elders relied on is now gone.

We don't have to accept that new program so long as we are self-sufficient. But what happens when we reach out to the community resources that we grew up with and find that they aren't there?

When we come to that point, we must determine whether to stick with or rethink our positions. As a result, we opt for the consequences of these decisions. Each has its pros and cons. Each choice is individual.

Our children are caught up in their generation's own aspirations. They have organized their lives around the achievement of goals that are new and, sometimes, quite foreign and meaningless to us. Behind our children are their children, building their own views of the American Dream. Society, as a whole, reflects the newest version.

The purpose of this book is to give you the facts that will help you make your own decision for tomorrow's society. We—and millions of others—believe the full service retirement community offers the best solution to the most problems for a large segment of our society.

We will look at all of the options for vibrant, active seniors who are looking ahead. The pros and cons of each of these choices are discussed. This book will delve into the full service retirement community (FSRC), also known as a continuing care retirement community (CCRC), in great detail. Hopefully you will be able to select your path from a wide variety of options before your health narrows the choices for you.

STAYING AT HOME

When seniors stay in the home where they have lived for many years—even decades—they mirror the American Dream of a half century ago. Others have chosen a senior community with a golf course, but with no medical care. That community is no different from staying in the house they have lived in for many years except that all of their neighbors are over a certain age. In either case, these seniors are choosing to stay at home. It has its benefits and its detriments.

THE PLUSES FOR STAYING AT HOME

Many dream of living the rest of their days at home. They have devoted their energies and resources to making it come true.

Responsibilities

There is plenty to be happy about. The house is probably paid for or at least has a low house payment. Many seniors who have lived in a house for years have a lot of equity in their homes. The responsibilities of rearing children and working every day might have dwindled to just caring for the house, themselves, and, perhaps, a spouse.

Comfort

Everything is familiar. Family and friends are in town, maybe even in the same neighborhood. It is reassuring to see doctors and dentists who know their patients and their histories. The house holds many fond memories of good times. It is emotionally comforting and soothing to stay put.

Some people have extended family who are ready, willing, and able to care for them if and when the time comes. These caretakers need to be the primary caregivers. They will need plenty of resources: money, time, energy, education, and space in their homes.

Community Services

The local area, hopefully, has services for seniors. Many have a senior center; some serve hot meals at noon. County or city government might underwrite discounts for retirees for taxi service. Home health care (HHC) is probably readily available.

Many feel secure in thinking that all the services they will need as they age and become less independent will surround them. Everything might go very well.

THE MINUSES OF STAYING AT HOME

All too often everything does not go well for those who wish to age at home. Today, the reality of getting the goods and services that they need to live in their own homes is far more complex and costly than they anticipated. In addition, the environment must be altered to accommodate the needs of the aging, *e.g.* walk-in showers, grab bars, wider doorways, pullout shelves, and so on.

Many make emotional decisions to stay at home rather than viewing the practical assessment of their current and future situations. This is not always in their best interests for the long run.

Changing Needs

Historically, as people age, energy and flexibility dwindle, making getting around more demanding. The stairs might become obstacles that are too difficult to manage several times a day. Doing the cleaning, repairs, and maintenance around the house will become more difficult and expensive to accomplish as time goes by.

Senses will become less acute; vision and hearing might diminish; and reaction times will slow. All these things could impair the ability to drive a car, get groceries, and prepare meals.

The Need for Personal Care

Illness might make it difficult for the elderly to bathe or dress themselves safely. Retirees who live with a spouse will have some help, but over time this situation could become too taxing for the healthier spouse. The problem is more acute for those who live alone.

At some point a caregiver is necessary. It is possible to hire an aide to come and help with bathing and dressing. The cost of hiring this assistant ranges from $20-50[2] an hour for a minimum number of hours, usually four. The prices go up for service on nights, weekends, and holidays.

It is a difficult chore to find someone who is honest and competent. Caretakers might arrive late or not show up at all. They have been known to steal everything from food to jewelry from their employers. A personality clash could make the day unpleasant.

The more help a person needs, the fewer unlicensed individuals there are who are willing and/or able to assume the liability of caring for ill or disabled people. This is especially true if medications need to be given or treatments performed. Having a licensed practical nurse (LPN) will cost from $80-150 an hour for visits that are most commonly one hour long. Registered nurses (RNs) cost more.

This seems like a suitable remedy for this need, but like everything else, it has its downsides. At first, infrequent visits might suffice, but all too often, the health conditions of ill or frail seniors escalate far faster than one might think. Medicare and some long-term care insurance policies only pay for skilled care. Unskilled (custodial) care is often what is needed, especially in the beginning.

Because of the enormous expense, getting help all day is out of the question for many middle income workers. Some long-term care insurance policies pay partly for this aid. Home health care (HHC) is really intended to be assistance for the primary caregiver, and not a substitute. In addition, without someone else to monitor the personnel coming in, managing schedules and payments for caregivers will become more difficult for seniors as time goes on.

Relying on one caregiver to aid a senior while a spouse works or to administer care to relieve an elderly spouse is risky. Should that one person become sick, arrive late, or quit at the last minute, an ill person is left in a lurch without a back-up system.

---

[2] Metropolitan Life Insurance Company sponsors an information and policy resource center. The staff geriatricians study aging, long-term care, and retirement. Their yearly study on costs can be found at www.maturemarketinstitute.com. It will tell you up-to-date figures on the costs of home health care, assisted living, and nursing homes. They can also be reached at MetLife Mature Market Institute, 57 Greens Farms Road, Westport, CT 06880, 203-221-6580, Fax: 203-454-5339.

When a home health care agency is hired, these caretakers come into seniors' homes and help them with personal care, physical and other therapies, nursing services, counseling, and social services. The agency is responsible for covering for the aide, nurse, or therapist that doesn't show up. That system is usually designed for visits of one to four hours.

Sometimes an agency will provide around-the-clock care. It handles schedules, screens and bonds their employees, and replaces caregivers who don't work out in a timely fashion. They also carry liability insurance. Consequently, hiring help through a home health care agency is more expensive than hiring an individual. Once care at home is no longer a practical choice, an assisted living facility becomes the only alternative.

The Need for Medical Care

Previous generations did not live so long as we do today because medical science is prolonging our lives. Too often today's forty- and fifty-somethings are left with loved ones to take care of with little medical knowledge and fewer family and community resources. The influx of the retiring Baby Boomers will only worsen this situation. The elderly who receive professional monitoring will enjoy richer, fuller lives. Once the senior who is living alone at home needs medical care, the only options are moving in with someone else or into a nursing home.

The Need for Socialization

The one thing that does not change is our need for socialization. We, no matter how old we are, still need to be around people and have interactive relationships with them. While we all enjoy being around people of all ages, we make our best friends from among our peers.

The disability of a spouse can isolate seniors. Alzheimer's and dementia can become more of a problem than caring for someone with a physical ailment. The person who once provided comfort and companionship and made a contribution to the union becomes someone the other partner must care for. While a loving spouse will want to undertake this responsibility, it can be an enormous physical and emotional drain on him or her, which leads to even more diminished energy and, perhaps, declining health for the caregiver. The loss of a spouse can also isolate him or her to the point of depression.

Housebound seniors who stay in their own homes all too soon become separated from their friends. The friends, like the spouses, pass away, leaving them in a position that makes it harder to make new friends. When they cannot get out like they used to, depression all too often sets in; the quality of life diminishes.

Changing Families

More social changes have taken place in the twentieth century, especially in the latter half, than any other century in history. Many of our elderly do not have the same hope for care from family that their ancestors did in the early to mid-1900s.

Distant Families

We have seen the widespread development of electricity, indoor plumbing, cars, electronic products, air travel, and a whole host of other inventions. These things have made our daily lives easier in many ways, but, at the same time, more complex.

Social changes have profoundly affected the way we conduct ourselves. The post-World-War-II prosperity gave families enough extra money to send the children to college and to buy a second car.

This newfound mobility enabled people to travel farther for activities and support outside the small circle that they had once relied on. Technology produced highly specialized jobs that employed but an educated few in select locations of the country. People traveled far from their hometowns to take these jobs and to have new experiences.

Family planning has made it possible for women to have careers outside the home. Lifestyle choices and education have resulted in smaller, widely scattered families.

Overcoming the problems of daily life and celebrating their solutions together strengthens the bonds among family. However, the farther we roamed from our small circle of support, the less we had family members to help us with the responsibilities of rearing children, taking care of a home, and/or coping with illnesses and life overall. So our faraway families wouldn't worry, many of us managed to keep our problems to ourselves. Faster paced lives also left little time for extended family. Consequently, our family ties weakened. Soon relatives became distant.

Changing Structure

Even if families are not distant, their structures have changed dramatically. The once common intact family, where the wife stays at home with the children, is not the norm anymore. Women also used to be the caretakers of the elderly; but with women in the workplace, they simply do not have the time and the energy to do that anymore. In addition, there are many single parents whose resources are also limited.

Changing Responsibilities

Today, many people, particularly women in their forties and fifties, are still raising teenagers, putting young adults through college, and then having to cope with returning twenty-something children who cannot support themselves on entry-level salaries. At the same time they are confronted with older relatives who are facing a decline in their abilities to care for themselves. This so-called Sandwich Generation is encumbered with dual responsibilities at the same time that no preceding generation has ever had to endure.

Changing Neighborhoods

When people lived and worked in one town all their lives, they were members of a traditional extended family, a church, and a community. They worked together and they played together. When they had problems or they became ill, many pitched in to help. The neighbors brought soups and casseroles. When the elderly could no longer take care of themselves, someone in the family took them in.

Neighborhoods change in character. Once retirees probably lived among neighbors who were of similar lifestyles, age, race, and ethnic background as themselves. Many of today's neighborhoods are more diverse. They are no longer as cohesive a unit as they once were. Today, many homeowners do not know the names of the people who live next door or across the street.

Other times, people might find themselves surrounded by aging neighbors. This happens when the original owners of a subdivision still live in their homes. A retirement community of sorts is naturally created. Unfortunately, these neighbors are having such a hard time taking care of themselves that they cannot devote as much time to helping others as they might like.

Changing Society

Families and neighbors are running their own rat races. While their hearts might be in the right places, their time, energy, and resources are focused on meeting the needs of their immediate families. Their elderly relatives and neighbors still need help. This is the time that the seniors turn to local governments for community resources. Even the best of areas can provide only so much support.

Although local governments are stepping up their programs for seniors, they are meeting resistance from the taxpayers who must pay for these increased services. As we Baby Boomers age, our county and city resources will be even more diluted. The generation behind us has fewer taxpayers to support all of the required services.

STAYING at HOME	
Pros	**Cons**
• independence, based on health • familiar surroundings • retain the homestead • home health care • some community services	• isolation • limited transportation • grocery shopping, cooking • housecleaning, maintenance, repair • stairs, perhaps • home health care • unresponsive to changing needs of the aging • varying levels of support from family & neighbors • changing neighborhoods • not enough community services • forced from home for assisted living or skilled nursing in later years

Figure 1-1

❧❦

These factors have profoundly affected the way we take care of our elderly and should impact on the way we expect to be taken care of in the future. These elements in our evolving society have resulted in a need for changes to the American Dream.

Many people make the choice to stay at home a successful and happy one. We include this information only to point out what is happening to too many people who neither expected nor deserved the bad years due to lack of competent and consistent care. See the advantages and disadvantages of staying at home in Figure 1-1.

LIVING WITH OTHERS

Another choice for aging retirees is moving in with someone else. This might be a relative (usually one of the children) or a friend. It could mean actually sharing the same living space. It could also refer to living in a mother-in-law suite in the same house or in a cottage on the same property.

THE PLUSES OF LIVING WITH OTHERS

Should seniors move in with their children or someone else, many of the minuses of staying in their own homes will disappear. Several are discussed below.

Responsibilities

The responsibility for buying groceries and preparing meals will no longer fall entirely on the shoulders of the seniors. They will likely help with the chores while the homeowners will assume the primary burden of the care and maintenance of the house. Retirees will probably chip in to share costs, but the difficult tasks of caring for a home all by themselves is gone.

Comfort

Residing with their children or friends will fill their lives with activity and familiar people. No longer will they be isolated. Depression is less likely to overtake them.

Living with different generations will keep elders up to date with the changing times. They will learn, perhaps, to appreciate different outlooks on life.

As their health changes, support will be under the same roof. Someone will be available to take them to the doctor or for medical treatments. Loved ones who live with them might be able to help with at-home therapies and other medical needs. The neighborhood is less likely to be all elderly and its residents might be able to help out.

Community Services

Retirees who live with others might not need to rely on community resources for seniors. Senior centers are an option for those who do not require personal or medical care during the day. Some of them serve delicious hot meals and plan desirable activities. Many attendees are lively, interesting people.

The Minuses of Living with Others

Living with others creates another set of problems for seniors that living alone in their own houses did not. This situation involves adapting to the schedules and different ways of others. As a rule, the house will not be equipped with the walk-in shower, grab bars, and other features that aid an unsteady person.

Changing Needs

Seniors will most likely want to help in cleaning and cooking. But when these chores become overwhelming and the seniors are no longer able to help, guilt might overtake them. They could come to think of themselves as a burden.

As the elder's needs change, the family might not be able to keep up with his or her needs. These retirees who are left home alone with no other social outlets than the family could become depressed. In spite of everything, we all still need relationships with our peers.

Changing Health

Care for many medical conditions is often beyond the expertise of people without training. Even if family members can and are willing to learn, the responsibility can be intensely burdensome.

Should the seniors' conditions deteriorate to the point where they cannot stay home safely while the family members work or go to school, the family might be forced to hire caregivers. When these caretakers come into the seniors' homes, the family is faced with the same problems of absenteeism, questionable skill of the worker, and dishonesty that the seniors have when living alone. Should that prove not to be a viable option, the only other answer is moving to an assisted living or nursing facility.

Changing Families

The children are likely to be caring for their own children as well as their parents. It now takes two wage earners to support lower- and middle-income families. Sometimes they are so strapped for money that another person to feed and clothe becomes financially burdensome. This is minimized if the elder can make a monetary contribution to the family.

LIVING with OTHERS	
Pros	**Cons**
• companionship • some help with health matters • familiar surroundings, maybe • help with grocery shopping & cooking • help with care of the house • freedom from chores • some community services	• less independence • less privacy • isolation from peers • stairs, perhaps • limited transportation, perhaps • unresponsive to changing needs of the aging • varying levels of support from family & neighbors • not enough community services • must leave home of many years • forced from home for assisted living or skilled nursing in later years

Figure 1-2

On occasion, housing another person can be difficult due to lack of sufficient space. The seniors might not have the degree of privacy that they once had.

Younger generations see things differently from their parents and grandparents. The generation gap can get even wider as elders witness at close hand values and morals that differ widely from their own. Often a variety of personality differences causes friction within the family, particularly with the in-laws.

Caring for an older relative is even more difficult for single parents. Living space, money, time, and energy are all reduced when the family has only one breadwinner.

Changing Neighborhoods

Younger neighbors will be busy with their own lives and are not likely to be a significant source of help in caring for their neighbor's live-in grandparent. They might not be available in the daytime while the family is at work and school to join the senior for a cup of coffee or to run an errand for him or her.

Changing Society

Although many counties and cities offer senior services, they are not comprehensive. They do not provide the variety of amenities and services that many FSRCs do. Some are available only for retirees who qualify by income. Others are continued only at the whim of the voters, from whom the funds come.

Too often seniors feel dumped when sent to adult day care. These facilities are sometimes little more than babysitters who prop the elders in front of a television. Others do better. The cost ranges from $50 per day to well over $100 a day.

Isolation can be a problem, even for seniors who live with their families or friends. The few people that they meet at a senior center might not have anything in common with them.

※※※

For many people, living with others works very well. Only you can decide if this arrangement will work for you. The pros and cons of living with others are summarized in Figure 1-2.

LIVING IN AN FSRC

Just as our changing society has taken away the old support services, it has provided new forms of help through the marketplace, which is taking up the slack. Huge numbers of active seniors have chosen to move into full service retirement communities (FSRCs). These are essentially like any number of active retirement communities (page 21) across the nation, except that they include a safety net of care.

Seniors may move into residential living accommodations in one of two ways: 1) as a planned decision into the independent living portion of a full service retirement community of their choice or 2) as a crisis-driven response to their changing health needs. In the latter, seniors might no longer be eligible for admission to the independent living accommodations of an FSRC or they might find a waiting list with no immediate occupancy available.

THE PLUSES OF LIVING IN AN FSRC

The hallmark of a continuing care retirement community has always been the independent living, assisted living, and skilled nursing, all on the same premises. This full service retirement community assures seniors and their families of the independence that they need today and the care they might need tomorrow. No longer will anyone have to worry.

Many of the objections of living with someone else will be erased because seniors will have their own homes plus services and amenities. Meals will be provided. Housecleaning, repairs, and maintenance will be a thing of the past. In most communities, in-house transportation will take residents shopping and to doctors' appointments.

Amenities, such as hobby and fitness rooms, banks, and beauty/barber shops, abound. Residents delight in extras, which might include guest rooms, storage areas, community rooms, and private dining rooms, because they expand their living space.

Residents will no longer have to rely so heavily on the senior services from family, friends, church, city, and/or county. Most, if not all, of these services are provided by the FSRC, plus others. Quality activities, in particular, are common.

The likelihood of depression from isolation and loneliness is greatly minimized amid the support of an active and vibrant community. Opportunities for friendships are everywhere.

❧❀❧

In reading this book, you will find that the most promising answer for seniors is in the full service retirement community. It can provide a higher standard of living than many seniors are used to. Much more about its advantages is presented in the following chapters.

THE MINUSES OF LIVING IN AN FSRC

Nothing in life is perfect; therefore, any residential living arrangements will have drawbacks. The younger seniors are when they elect to move into an FSRC, the more reduced or nonexistent these imperfections will be.

The biggest drawback for some people is an emotionally wrenching move from the house where they have lived for decades. It is human nature to cling to the familiar. Leaving their present homes and moving into a full service retirement community (FSRC) could be difficult at first, because everyone might seem a stranger. These people are actually friends we haven't met yet.

As we Baby Boomers start to move into FSRCs, this reluctance to move might diminish, because we, unlike most of our parents, have been quite transient. We are, thus, more likely to believe we can make a home from any house.

Moving into independent living, where the residents are vivacious, will make this an easier transition. Making friends when the residents are not at their best, as in moving into a freestanding assisted living or skilled nursing facility, is difficult.

In independent living, residents can live in a home much like the one they left. Although most downsize, living in a house of a few thousand square feet is possible. Whether it is an apartment, cottage, or a single family house, they will find that their home extends itself to all the common areas of the community.

An FSRC allows its residents to live a more worry-free lifestyle than they might have had they remained in the home they lived in

LIVING in an FSRC	
Pros	**Cons**
• worry-free living • independence • age in place • possible guaranteed care for life • freedom from chores • companionship • privacy • responsive to changing needs of the aging • personal & medical care standing by • sense of community • convenience services • activities • transportation	• many strangers, at first • some rules • must leave home of many years

Figure 1-3

for so many years. While the move might be difficult now, it will become even more difficult in later years. The pluses and minuses of choosing a full service retirement community are in Figure 1-3.

All of the major types of residential living, including the FSRC, are compared in the next chapter. The rest of this book is devoted to the details of the FSRC and its component parts.

2

RESIDENTIAL COMMUNITIES

*Some people change their ways
when they see the light,
others when they feel the heat.*

—Caroline Schroeder
Author

Today we need to plan for our own care. If we move now, we have our choices. If we wait, our health will make the choice for us—we will go wherever they have a bed.

You will find many fine communities in the traditional style that might suit you just fine. You will only know once you visit several full service retirement communities (FSRCs), also known as continuing care retirement communities (CCRCs). This book will help you determine what you want for yourself or for your relative.

SENIOR CARE OPTIONS

Seniors have options. They can stay in their homes and have caregivers bring them the assistance they need. They could live with the children, other relatives, or friends. Maybe, in their later years, go to adult day care while the children work.

If we want to be independent and enjoy a longer, healthier, and carefree retirement, we will want to avail ourselves of one of the many types of alternatives. The decisions in opting for one of these choices are quite personal. They reflect lifestyles, values, religious and ethnic topics, money, and many other subjective and personal issues.

How will we get the care we will *need*? What do we *want*? Are our choices *practical*? How do we know if it's any *good*? Tens of thousands of facilities exist to help us. They don't all use the same names to refer to who they are and what they do. They offer varying combinations of independent living (IL), assisted living (AL), and skilled nursing (SN) care in varying levels of quality, style, comfort, and size.

SINGLE-FOCUS FACILITIES

Retirement housing often delivers just one level of living. It can be independent living or dependent living, which includes single-focus assisted living, or single-focus nursing homes (NH). Each type is vastly different from the others.

Independent Living

Independent living is for reasonably healthy people who are capable of living on their own. The lives of these residents continue much the same as they did before they moved into the retirement community. Retirees who select this form of housing are, essentially, staying at home, as discussed in Chapter 1.

Age Restricted Housing

Sometimes called independent living housing, age restricted (AR) communities are, as the name implies, only for residents over a certain age, most commonly 55. Residents who are healthy and active like this lifestyle. Usually the youngest of retirees choose this type of housing. This is the commercial version of staying at home, discussed in Chapter 1. See Figure 2-1 for the advantages and disadvantages of age restricted housing.

AGE RESTRICTED and RESORT RETIREMENT COMMUNITIES	
Pros	**Cons**
• independence • companionship • some sense of community • activities • convenience services • amenities • usually nearby health care & shopping	• limitations on resale • pay for services not used • possible narrowed perspective from living with the same age group • some rules • unresponsive to changing needs of the aging • must leave home of many years
This is the same as staying at home. See Figure 1-1.	

Figure 2-1

Often only the majority of residents in the whole community need be of the minimum age; as a rule just one of a couple needs to be of the designated age. Once in a great while, management expects the younger spouse to be over a certain age, as well—sometimes within ten years of the older spouse.

In a few jurisdictions, the law requires only the builder to sell to seniors. It does not restrict resales and a community can quickly become something entirely different from what the original residents expected.

AR: Housing facilities can vary from apartments in high-rise buildings to townhouses, duplexes, cottages, or single family houses. Occasionally structures are mobile homes or recreational vehicles, located in parks for seniors only. This category also includes subsidized municipal housing projects for low income elderly. Their homes are sometimes boardinghouse style.

The residences can be elder friendly, which means that there are elevators, ramps, handrails in bathrooms, levers for faucet handles and door knobs, and so on.

AR: Convenience services might be nonexistent or they could include grounds maintenance and, rarely, interior maintenance of the homes. Some age restricted communities usually provide security and planned activities. They seldom, if ever, provide meals, flat linen laundry, and housekeeping.

AR: Amenities are sometimes found in independent living facilities. How extensive they are depends upon how luxurious the community is. Activities rooms are common. These resort communities, sometimes called active adult communities or master-planned retirement communities, are facilities that revolve around active recreational activities, such as golf, tennis, and swimming.

AR: Personal care includes help with tasks, such as bathing, dressing, and eating (page 24). It is not a part of age restricted housing.

AR: Health/medical care is minimally available. When it is, it is usually in a nurse's office where the staff takes residents' blood pressures, tests for blood sugar levels, and draws blood for cholesterol tests. Very often age restricted housing projects are located near assisted living facilities and nursing homes, as well as doctors' offices and hospitals.

AR: Occupancy is often by purchase, although rentals are available. Ownership might be fee simple, condominium, co-op, or membership (page 121).

Congregate Care

The residents of congregate care (CC) housing are a bit older than most independent living facilities. They are usually not so mobile as those in other independent living situations, but certainly are able to care for themselves. This choice is the commercial version of living with others, as discussed in Chapter 1. Figure 2-2 lists the advantages and disadvantages of congregate care.

CC: Housing is usually a mid- or high-rise building, much like an old fashioned college dormitory or a boarding house. Residents in congregate housing, most often, have a bedroom with a private bath, but some do share bedrooms and/or bathrooms in older facilities.

CONGREGATE CARE	
Pros	**Cons**
• independence • companionship • sense of community • activities • accommodations suited to the elderly • convenience services • some subsidized rents	• less privacy • rigid schedules • possible narrowed perspective from living with the same age group • many rules • unresponsive to changing needs of the aging • must leave home of many years
This is the same as living with others. See Figure 1-2.	

Figure 2-2

Together all residents have access to the rest of the rooms in the building.

CC: Convenience services include meals that the group eats together in the dining room, housekeeping, laundry service for bed and bath linen, bus service, an activities area, maintenance, and others.

CC: Amenities might be found in such a facility, but they are not usually the hallmarks of congregate care. There should be, however, at least an activities room.

CC: Personal care is not a part of congregate housing.

CC: Health/medical care might consist of a registered nurse (RN) who provides minimal health care.

CC: Occupancy is usually all rentals. The Department of Housing and Urban Development (HUD) sets aside Section 8 and Section 202 monies for congregate care for the elderly. The federal government also funds congregate care housing across the country through the Congregate Housing Services Program. Potential residents must meet specific financial qualifications before they are eligible for a subsidized rent program.

Nonprofit groups, such as churches, also sponsor congregate housing. As one might expect, the waiting lists are long and occupancy rights are sometimes offered only to members.

Dependent Living

Seniors who need help with the everyday activities of taking care of themselves will benefit from a living arrangement where they can depend upon others daily. These activities include personal care, such as bathing and dressing, among others, and medical care for chronic conditions that cannot be managed at home.

Single-Focus Assisted Living Facilities

Assisted living (AL) facilities give residents needed help beyond the convenience services. This personal care covers the Activities of Daily Living and Instrumental Activities of Daily Living, as described by the General Accounting Office in a report to the United States Congress in 1994. The first group consists of physical activities such as eating and bathing. The second group addresses cognitive undertakings, such as balancing a checkbook; planning, shopping for, and cooking meals; and using the phone (Figure 2-3).

PERSONAL CARE	
Activities of Daily Living (Physical Impairments)	**Instrumental Activities of Daily Living (Cognitive Impairments)**
• getting in/out of bed & chairs • using the toilet (continence) • bathing • dressing • eating • getting around inside the house	• housekeeping • shopping • meal planning & preparation • using the phone • making & keeping appointments • taking medications as prescribed • balancing a checkbook • getting around outside the house

Figure 2-3

Many of these residents are the oldest of the old and are often quite frail. Some, however, are mobile enough and healthy enough to participate in outings to shopping malls, restaurants, and theaters in the facility's bus. Many residents are widowed or single. Statistically, they are mostly women, who outlive men.

The federal government does not regulate assisted living facilities. States vary widely as to how much regulation they impose on this level of living. The state bodies that license assisted living facilities would be the ones to inspect them. See Appendix C. Figure 2-4 enumerates the pros and cons of assisted living.

SINGLE-FOCUS ASSISTED LIVING	
Pros	Cons
• some independence • companionship • activities • accommodations suited to the elderly • convenience services • personal care • health care • responsive to changing needs of the residents, to a point	• some loss of privacy • schedules • rules • surrounded by disability • no skilled nursing (medical) care standing by • usually no payment from Medicare/Medicaid • must leave home of many years

Figure 2-4

AL: Housing in newer buildings is usually in the form of unfurnished studio or one bedroom apartments. Two bedroom apartments are becoming more common. These have their own bathrooms and, often, their own kitchens. Older living areas could be just rooms that might or might not share a bathroom. Some even require sharing of bedrooms.

This lifestyle more closely resembles apartment living than nursing home living where the staff comes and goes freely. Sometimes management removes the stove, coffee pot, and/or sharp knives if the residents have the potential to harm themselves because of a disability or some other medical problem.

The building and the residents' bathrooms and kitchens, in particular, should be elder friendly. This means that there should be ramps, grab bars and railings, pullout shelves, and levers instead of knobs.

AL: Convenience services are similar to facilities that house independent living residents, except that the emphasis is on giving personal care. Residents can expect meals in a central dining room, personal and linen laundry, housekeeping, and scheduled activities.

AL: Amenities are not usually found in abundance in assisted living facilities. There should be at least an activities room and a beauty/barber shop. Amenities increase in number as the facilities' size and budget do.

AL: Personal care is the main thrust of assisted living facilities. Residents can receive help with the functions listed in Figure 2-3. These are the physical and cognitive impairments. Not all assisted living facilities are set up to accommodate mentally impaired residents. Some will keep residents who develop dementia; others will try to place them in outside facilities that do care for Alzheimer's/dementia sufferers.

AL: Health/medical care is kept on the health side rather than on the medical side. Law prohibits the staff of an assisted living facility from giving skilled nursing care. They are, however, available twenty-four hours a day. In some facilities, doctors and therapists of all kinds routinely visit the premises to administer care. Medication administration is a common service.

AL: Occupancy is on a rental basis. At this writing, Medicare has not paid for assisted living facilities. In some states, Medicaid pays for this care with Medicaid waivers. Through long-term care policies, many private insurance companies do cover assisted living. Rents are less costly than nursing homes, but service- and/or amenity-rich facilities might cost as much as nursing homes.

Assisted living facilities offer a variety of personal services. Not all residents need the maximum level of care. So that residents do not pay for services they do not use, some facilities bundle services into packages. Each package has an increasing number of services for which management charges residents escalating fees.

Single-Focus Nursing Homes

The nursing home (NH) is probably the most well-known form of senior housing. The residents require nursing care twenty-four hours a day. Those who are not so ill are usually not admitted. Most of the residents are over age sixty-five. Sometimes younger people will need nursing care for chronic illnesses or conditions. See Figure 2-5.

NH: Housing is not so homelike as the other forms of senior housing. Nursing homes look more like hospitals, although most allow residents to bring some of their own furniture. Architects, builders, and interior designers are making serious efforts to make these places cozier. Many new or newly renovated facilities reflect innovative design.

SINGLE-FOCUS NURSING HOME	
Pros	**Cons**
• companionship • activities • accommodations suited to elderly • convenience services • personal care • health/medical care • responsive to changing needs of residents • Medicare, Medicaid, or insurance might pay partially for a limited time	• loss of privacy • schedules • rules • surrounded by disability • must leave home of many years • expensive

Figure 2-5

Rooms are private or semiprivate. Each should have its own half bath, with central bathing facilities down the hall. Newer nursing homes have more private rooms.

NH: Convenience services are reduced from the other types of senior housing. Nursing homes serve three meals a day in a dining room or at the bedside of residents who are not able to join others. Laundry services include linens and personal items. Housekeeping and maintenance are a given as well. Residents enjoy limited activities on a regular basis and often an activities director plans them. The monthly fee (based on a *per diem* rate) might include local phone service, with long distance and cable TV at an additional charge.

NH: Amenities are not a usual component of nursing homes. Multi-purpose rooms that switch between dining and activities are common. Other amenity spaces might include a chapel, beauty/barber shop, visiting areas, and, perhaps, a private dining room for small gatherings.

NH: Personal care is provided for all of the Activities of Daily Living. Care for mental impairments (Instrumental Activities of Daily

Living) varies from place to place. Many nursing homes accept Alzheimer's/dementia (A/D) residents; however, the care for them is different from those with physical ailments. Separate facilities are sometimes provided to care for persons with such diseases.

NH: Health/medical care is the paramount concern of a nursing home. The staff cares for residents around the clock. Care levels generally fall into three categories: intermediate, skilled, and subacute (page 104). The majority of facilities provide intermediate and skilled care. Only skilled care is covered by Medicare.

Registered nurses (RNs), licensed practical nurses (LPNs), and therapists (who are often contracted) deliver care. The therapists work in the fields of physical, occupational, and speech therapy. Some facilities also employ recreational therapists to conduct meaningful activities and programs for the residents. Certified nursing assistants (CNAs) deliver the personal care and have more interaction with the residents than the rest of the staff.

NH: Occupancy is classified as rental, rather than ownership. Medicare and Medicaid pay for nursing homes under certain conditions. Private long-term care insurance policies will also pay if policy holders meet their prerequisites.

❋

For-profit corporations may own nursing homes, known as proprietary facilities. Civic groups, churches, and fraternal organizations frequently own not-for-profit facilities. State or local governments fund public nonprofit corporations that own still other nursing homes. Taxes or municipal bonds also fund these facilities and entry is limited to local taxpayers.

MULTI-FOCUS FACILITIES

The marketplace for senior housing is growing rapidly to meet the demand. Many developers are finding that combinations of the common forms of senior housing are more practical to run and allow the residents to age in place.

The line between the types of housing is blurring rapidly. The coming generation of retirees has different wants and needs from the previous generations. To meet these new requirements, developers of senior housing are rising to the challenge.

Of the multi-focus facilities, one is getting increasingly more attention. For the seniors who want to remain independent as long as possible and avoid a traumatic move when they need help or care, one innovative solution addresses almost all of the problems inherent to aging. It is the full service retirement community (FSRC), which is becoming ever more the popular choice. According to the research of a prominent builder, interest in FSRCs has tripled in the last five years.

Full Service Retirement Communities

Full service retirement communities (FSRCs) incorporate at least three levels of living: independent, assisted, and skilled nursing—in the same location. There are thousands of such communities and the number is growing rapidly. Figure 2-6 lists their advantages and disadvantages.

This form of senior housing is often confused with facilities where residents must turn over all of their assets to the management or impoverish themselves in order to move in. Those residences were often called "life care communities" and were run by churches and fraternal organizations. While the roots of the FSRC or continuing care retirement community (CCRC) lie in these types of facilities, this turn-over-the-assets policy is rare today. What has held over is the name "life care." Today, this usually refers to the extensive contract of an FSRC. See Chapter 7 for a full discussion of this plan.

FSRC: Housing for independent living (IL) comes in as many forms inside an FSRC as it does outside one: apartments, duplexes, townhomes, cottages, and single family homes. The assisted living (AL) arrangements are usually studio or one bedroom apartments. Two bedroom homes are on the rise in new or newly renovated communities. Skilled nursing (SN) has private and semi-private rooms with at least a half bath.

FSRC: Convenience services are designed to allow the residents the time to indulge in their own interests. Services include security, meals, laundry, housekeeping, indoor and outdoor maintenance, transportation, recreation, and on-site entertainment. The FSRC might offer many others, depending on how luxurious the community is.

FSRC: Amenities include a multitude of activities and improvements designed to meet the changing needs of the FSRC's population. Usually, the more upscale the community is, the more amenities will be available, although very large, moderately priced FSRCs will have many, as well. They include a variety of in-home improvements such as dishwashers and ice-makers and commercial attractions such as banks and cafés. Common areas might be enhanced with spaces for many hobbies and fitness rooms.

FULL SERVICE RETIREMENT COMMUNITY	
Pros	**Cons**
• quality of life • independence • possible guaranteed care for life • privacy • friendship • sense of community • amenities • activities • accommodations suited to elderly • convenience services • transportation • reduced chances of permanently needing AL &/or SN • personal care standing by • health/medical care standing by • responsive to changing needs of residents • seamless transition through the stages of life	• many strangers, at first • some rules • must leave home of many years

Figure 2-6

To accommodate the coming generation of more active seniors, some of these communities are adding indoor and outdoor athletic activities that were previously found only in age restricted independent living senior housing. Unlike single-focus facilities, residents in assisted living and skilled nursing should have access to these amenities.

FSRC: Personal care is available for residents who are in need. The methods by which the staff gives the care depend on how much care, what kind of care, and how often and for how long the residents need help. The approach also depends on the policies of the community. Some communities allow limited care, called home health care (HHC), to be delivered in the independent living quarters. This permits residents to delay the move to assisted living. Others require the resident to move directly into the assisted living areas as soon as help is needed.

FSRC: *Health/medical care* is readily available at all times. Skilled nursing is usually on the same premises and treats minor emergencies, as well as providing for short- and long-term care. Many offer accommodations for Alzheimer's/dementia residents.

FSRC: *Occupancy* can be had by either endowment, equity, or lease (page 109). The fee structures vary widely. They are outlined in detail in Chapter 7.

A large entry fee is required for the overwhelming majority of full service retirement communities. The costs and payment plans can vary within the same community. Rentals might or might not charge an entry fee, but when they do, it is a mere fraction of the entry fee of endowment and equity communities.

CCRCs (FSRCs) in Transition

The continuing care retirement community (CCRC) has been redefining itself lately. No longer is the old folks home a place to sit in a rocking chair for the rest of one's life. Many CCRCs have transformed themselves into full service retirement communities and are being described as country club or resort communities. They have *more* amenities and services than country clubs and most resorts do, yet they are affordable to a wide range of seniors—more so than ever before.

If you have not visited a **second generation** CCRC, you are in for a treat! With a focus on service and wellness, professionals in many fields run these communities and are making it their objective to give residents an abundance of quality time. When you visit, you will find small, nearly self-contained villages full of vibrant people who are discussing current events, learning a new language, playing tennis, or planning trips to faraway places. Like the Old Grey Mare, the old folks home "she ain't what she used to be."

The emphasis is on life, not death; on ability, not disability; on individuality, not conformity; and on service, not care. Although care is an integral and essential part of the mix, it is not the only part.

Choices in each community abound. Whether you choose an apartment, penthouse, cottage, or large house, it can become your home. No longer must all residents select from the same menu at the same time. At FSRCs residents may dine during a range of times; they choose what they want from several entrées and side dishes on a menu or at a buffet table. No longer does everyone play bingo at 10:00 a.m. Residents might be visiting a new exhibit at the museum in town, taking an aerobics class, playing golf, volunteering in the local area, or learning how to make something artistic from a hunk of clay.

The industry is in transition, preparing for the Baby Boomers by creating a new style of CCRC—one with more emphasis on maximizing the quality time that CCRCs traditionally provide. This novel type of retirement community is so new it doesn't have a universally accepted name yet. "Full service retirement community" is more descriptive than "continuing care retirement community." Whatever it is called, one thing is for sure—**It is not the old folks home of yesteryear.**

Other Multi-Focus Facilities

Because this book is specifically about the full service retirement community (FSRC), other multi-focus facilities have not been discussed individually. Those that we have not addressed offer two levels of care. They are very similar in services and attributes to full service retirement communities (page 29).

The choice for a two-level facility should be for the combination of assisted living and skilled nursing. The marketplace, however, is fond of combining independent living (IL) with assisted living (AL). The reason for this is that with the addition of skilled nursing (SN) comes a whole lot more legal regulation and expense.

The independent/assisted living arrangement, though financially and legally practical for the owner, is not true aging in place for those who will temporarily or eventually need nursing care. The advantages and disadvantages of two-level communities are essentially the same as for the FSRC—except for one BIG difference: **Once a resident's physical or mental condition is beyond the scope of the community, the resident must move out.** Such a move for a frail, elderly person can be traumatic.

✺✺

The many types of residential housing break down into independent and dependent living. A comparison of the above discussed types is summarized in Figure 2-7.

TYPES of SENIOR HOUSING and THEIR SERVICES and AMENITIES					
Features	**Levels of Independence**				
	Independent		**Dependent**		**Both**
	Age Restricted	**Congregate Care**	**Assisted Living**	**Nursing Home**	**FSRC/ CCRC**
Independent — Housing	yes	yes	yes	yes	yes
Convenience services	*very few*	yes	some	some	yes
Amenities	yes				yes
Dependent — Personal care			yes	yes	yes
Health/ medical care	*very limited*	*very limited*	limited	yes	yes

Figure 2-7

✺✺

This chapter has given you an overview of senior housing options. The next chapter discusses how you might benefit from a full service retirement community.

3

LIFESTYLE

There are two things to aim at in life:
first, to get what you want;
and, after that, to enjoy it.
Only the wisest of mankind achieve the second.

—Logan Pearsall Smith
American Essayist and Critic, 1865-1946

The senior-care industry is offering many attractive choices to retirees today. The full service retirement community (FSRC), also known as a continuing care retirement community (CCRC), has everything we will ever need—and then some—in one neat package. While it is not the only choice for seniors, it is *the* innovative option in retirement living. It is the one that will give you the time to enjoy your interests.

Rest homes of yesteryear are closing their doors, giving way for active living for seniors. Today's full service retirement communities

(FSRCs) give residents independence and freedom with a host of activities and entertainment plus the safety net of health care—if and when it is needed. As a result you will already find younger retirees (and some not yet retired) taking advantage of this opportunity to live the good life.

Instrumental in making this change is the American Association of Homes and Services for the Aging (AAHSA). This nonprofit entity expertly sets industry guidelines for nonprofit organizations; educates developers, managers, and financiers of FSRCs; and lobbies Congress and state legislatures for more senior-friendly laws. See page 194.

The American Seniors Housing Association (ASHA) serves both for-profit and nonprofit communities in a similar way that AAHSA does. Though smaller, they still serve a valued purpose.

The Commission on Accreditation of Rehabilitation Facilities and the Continuing Care Accreditation Commission (CARF/CCAC), a newly merged independent certifying body furthers AAHSA's mission by accrediting communities (page 195). This process requires stringent scrutiny of the financial and managerial procedures and of resident life, health, and wellness in retirement communities.

These three prominent organizations and others provide strong leadership. Consequently, the senior-care industry is offering a multitude of financially secure, well-managed, attractive full service retirement communities to choose from.

WHO NEEDS AN FSRC?

You might be reading this book to find solutions for your own situation. The waiting lists at the more popular FSRCs can run as long as five to ten years. Surely you would rather make your own choices than have someone else do it for you when the situation is dire.

If you are reading this book to find care for an older loved one, it will help you discover just what type of community will be in the best interest of your relative and how to choose a desirable one. Hopefully, you are not at the point where the situation has become so urgent, as it all too often does, that the sole criterion for choosing a community becomes a matter of which one has a bed for him or her—tomorrow.

WHAT WILL AN FSRC DO FOR YOU?

The truth is that an FSRC provides everything you will need to enable you to stay in your own home, independently, happily, and safely far longer than you would be able to stay in the home that you live in now. You will live longer, studies show,[3] because of the continuous socialization, improved nutrition, health care, and worry-free living.[4] In addition, you will most likely experience an upgrade in lifestyle.

FREEDOM

No longer will you have to shovel snow and climb a tall ladder to clean the gutters. There will be no more household emergencies such as a dead air conditioner in the middle of a hot summer. Cleaning house, doing flat linen laundry, and making repairs will be long past. If you choose, you can go out to dinner every night at the community center. You will not have to worry about paying for major repairs or finding an honest repairman who might or might not show up. Living

---

[3] Social activities add an average of two and one half years to our lives. Harvard University study by Thomas Glass, Assistant Professor of Health and Social Behavior at Harvard's School of Public Health; published in the *British Medical Journal*, August 1999.

[4] Scanlon, W. and B. D. Layton. (1997) *Report to Congressional Requesters: How Continuous Care Retirement Communities Manage Services for the Elderly*, Washington, D.C.: U.S. General Accounting Office.

Sanders, Jacquelyn. (1997) *Continuing Care Retirement Communities: A Background and Summary of Current Issues*, Washington, D.C.: U.S. Department of Health and Human Services, Office of Disability, Aging and Long-Term Care Policy.

in a full service retirement community will allow you to spend your energy and time pursuing more enjoyable activities.

SECURITY

If you want to leave for months on end, security will watch over your home. No longer will you have to worry about theft, vandalism, the lawn, flooded basements, and frozen pipes. You can feel free to visit the children, cruise the Mediterranean, or drive to all of the National Parks across the country.

ACTIVITIES

Many have compared life in an FSRC to living on a stationary cruise ship or in a country club community. You can participate as much or as little as you like in a variety of activities—alone or in a small group of residents who share like interests. Most FSRCs welcome residents' enthusiasm in starting an activity that does not yet exist.

TRANSPORTATION

Unfortunately, many of us lose our ability to drive safely in the later years. Without a personal chauffeur, our independence is severely limited. The FSRC solves that problem in that almost all provide transportation as part of the basic monthly fee; others charge a nominal fee.

CARE

Full service retirement communities deliver health, personal, and medical care to their residents. Often health concerns of the seniors are greatly minimized by doctors who often do not take their complaints seriously. They chalk up too many of their ailments to "old age," which medical science now knows is not necessarily true. For instance, our friend Jean developed severe confusion quite rapidly. Her family doctor told her children, "Too bad; she's getting old." Her FSRC has a geriatrician (a doctor who specializes in the care of aging people) who keeps office hours there. He found that she had fluid on the brain, not so rare a condition in the elderly as one might think. Surgery brought her back to her own sharp self in short order.

FSRCs are known for their assisted (personal) care and skilled nursing (medical) care. We might tend to think of these areas as places where we go and they don't let us out. That is far from reality. The greater majority of residents use this care on a temporary basis only.

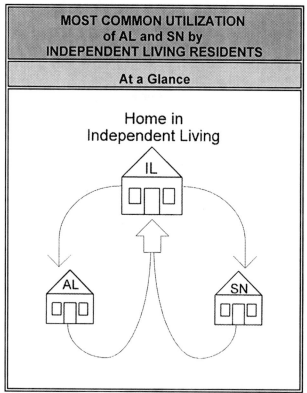

Figure 3-1

The beauty of an FSRC is that it is a community where there is care for times of need. Most commonly, residents will spend a short time in assisted living (AL) and/or skilled nursing (SN) after a too-short hospital stay. They then return home to their independent living apartments or cottages when they are stronger. (See Figure 3-1.) In the situation where care is needed on a long-term basis, it is readily available.

WHY WOULD YOU WANT AN FSRC?

You will find many services and features that will meet your needs. You will also delight in the prospect of not having to do some things that might be chores to you. You will receive the gift of time and energy to pursue interests you don't have time for now.

When you are considering where you or your relative will live during retirement, ask the following questions:

What do I want out of retirement?
- ☐ Independence
- ☐ Security
- ☐ Worry-free living
- ☐ Friendship
- ☐ Quality time
- ☐ Care when needed
- ☐ Financial stability
- ☐ Activity
- ☐ Solitude

What resources will I most likely need help with as I age?
- ☐ Transportation
- ☐ Cleaning
- ☐ Chores
- ☐ Cooking
- ☐ Health care
- ☐ Personal care
- ☐ Medical care

In reality, where will I be able to find ALL of the above resources?
- □ Family
- □ Friends
- □ Neighbors
- □ City/county programs
- □ Businesses
- □ Age restricted retirement communities
- □ Single-focus assisted living facilities
- □ Single-focus nursing homes
- □ FSRCs

If I can find all these resources, how do they rate against the criteria below?
- □ Reliable
- □ Available twenty-four hours/day, seven days/week (24/7)
- □ Infinite source of help
- □ Financially affordable
- □ Flexible
- □ Comprehensive

WHICH STYLE SUITS YOU?

There are FSRCs to suit every taste and lifestyle. They can be elegant and sophisticated or warm and cozy, formal or casual, urban or suburban, large or small. All FSRCs offer a variety of things to do; the larger the community, the broader the scope of interests. Some are oriented toward artistic undertakings; others stress more physical endeavors such as golf, tennis, and swimming; still others focus on intellectual pursuits or nature. If you want to play bridge, bingo, poker, or pool and read in your retirement, a host of FSRCs await you. If you want to indulge in other pursuits, there are many communities to fit your interests. Most have a balance of all sorts of things to do.

The atmosphere varies from one community to another. In some communities everyone knows everyone and the residents are like one big, happy family. In other communities, the resident populations encourage more independent living. Very large FSRCs are usually divided into neighborhoods, each of which functions like a small community.

MOVING IN

If you are still on the fence about whether you want to move in, keep in mind that you can stay where you are and hire all of the services you might need. But, of all the things that FSRCs offer, the singularly most important feature is continuous socialization[5]. Friends and meaningful activities are very hard to come by as one's circumstances change. The FSRC provides opportunities for both.

Another important feature is having a single contact point for all the services you might need to arrange. These include wellness programs, housekeeping, maintenance, transportation, meal delivery, and health care. In addition, the amenities that you need, such as beauty/barber shop, bank, and exercise facilities, are just outside your front door.

The transition of moving to a full service retirement community is much more easily accomplished when it is done in the spirit of adventure rather than out of necessity or to please someone else. Shopping for a community several years before you retire will give you more choices. In addition, it takes time to become familiar with the many options, to decide which will work best for you, and to select your future home.

Many of the more popular FSRCs have waiting lists of up to five years—some as long as ten years. *There are some quality communities with shorter waiting lists. Some even offer immediate occupancy, particularly those that are new or expanding.*

So many residents told us that they delayed moving in because they weren't "ready." Few could actually define what "ready" meant. Looking back, virtually all told us that they really did not comprehend just what a good thing they were missing. Later, they

---

[5] See Footnote 3 on page 36.

wondered why they weren't "ready" to be free from cleaning and repairing the house, free from cooking (if they chose), free from worry about future security, therefore, free to pursue their interests—and live the good life. Hundreds of residents confessed to us that they wished they had moved in ten years sooner, when they had more energy to take advantage of all the activities in the community.

WHEN TO MOVE IN

There really is no wrong time to move into a full service retirement community. Just remember that you need to be able to live independently to move into a life care community and the independent living portion of a fee-for-service community (page 136).

Before Retirement

Some people choose to move into a community before retirement. This is feasible if your resources are sufficient to do so. Many of these younger residents choose communities that offer a more active lifestyle. They might seek activities such as golf, tennis, and/or boating.

Usually new residents must meet age requirements, although some communities will make exceptions. Many such communities have a minimum age as low as 55. Some of these residents continue to work until they retire, if they do retire at all.

At Retirement

Retirement is a major life transition. Because you no longer work full time, a new routine must be created and self-entertainment may be pursued. New friends would be welcome if one's current friends were still working and were less available for daytime activities. New residents must make the same adjustments as new retirees, plus getting accustomed to different surroundings. Moving into an FSRC is a change in lifestyle—but a *positive* one.

It is our opinion that moving into an FSRC at retirement is the ideal time for four reasons. First, it eliminates one major life transition. Second, you will be young enough to really enjoy the catered lifestyle that allows residents the freedom to indulge life's passions. Third, the younger we human beings are the more readily we adapt to new places, activities, and ways. Fourth, the entry fee will be amortized over an extended period of time, due to a longer term of residency. This makes the FSRC's entry fee a better value. See Figure 8-3.

After Retirement

Many retirees move in after ten or twelve years of retirement. While this is not wrong, the residents we met invariably wished that they had made the move "ten years earlier."

❧※❦

No matter when you make the transition, communities will usually give new residents ninety days after signing the contract before the monthly fees begin to accrue. If residents have a house to sell, some communities offer a bridge loan at reasonable rates to help make things go more smoothly. It is in their best interests to support the new residents in this step.

❧※❦

Whenever you are ready to live the good life, there is an FSRC for you! It will have what you need, when you need it, the way you want it, and for a price you can afford.

FUTURE TRENDS

Soon, the retirement industry is going to explode. Why? First, beginning in 2008, the population over 62 will be larger than ever before. Second, and most important, the younger retirees want something different out of retirement than their parents did. The marketplace is scrambling to meet the demands of future residents.

We Baby Boomers, the new retirees, will expect more services and amenities from retirement than our parents did. The industry is gearing up for the changes. Progressive FSRCs are in various stages of this transition.

Larger living spaces with more bedrooms and dens will be in demand. The focus is going to be on more amenities. Many will be retiring at an earlier age than their parents and will be healthier. Since Baby Boomers value active lifestyles, FSRCs are feeling the competition from the age restricted communities that offer golf courses and tennis courts. Many are adding these features to compete in the marketplace.

The college connection is becoming increasingly more important to FSRCs. Growing numbers of communities will integrate their activity programs with local colleges or universities. Seniors will likely be able to take courses on the college campus for free or at a reduced cost. Some colleges are setting up student internship programs with FSRCs. Other creative facets to this new relationship are yet to emerge.

Assisted living quarters are becoming more homelike. They are moving toward larger homes; some communities are even building assisted living apartments that are exactly like those in independent living. This enables spouses to move in together, should they so choose.

Private skilled nursing rooms are increasingly more common. Some share a bathroom, while others do not. Some are adding full baths, rather than the typical half bath, to each room. Many encourage residents to bring a few pieces of furniture and home decorating accessories.

Many nursing homes evolved to nonprofit full service retirement communities. Nonprofit communities have dominated this market in the past—and still do. Now, *for*-profit developers are emerging with competitive communities. They were mostly born in the hospitality industry. They each bring many positive aspects of their own approaches to serving seniors.

Because Baby Boomers, as a group, value ownership, demographic experts predict that the number of communities that offer occupancy by ownership (equity), rather than endowment or rental, will increase. (See page 109.) The reality is that the Baby Boomers want choices. The market is responding; no longer do retirees need to go to the "rest home."

❊❊

The decision to move into a full service retirement community (FSRC) is very personal. Many situations in your life might have caused you to consider this option. It is encouraging to know at this point that there is an FSRC for everybody.

❧❦

This chapter has given you some idea of what an FSRC is and what qualities it can add to your lifestyle. The next chapter will paint a picture for you of what an FSRC's grounds and buildings might look like.

4

GROUNDS AND BUILDINGS

Charms strike the sight, but merit wins the soul.

—Alexander Pope
English Poet, 1688-1744

Full service retirement communities (FSRC), also known as continuing care retirement communities (CCRC), come in all sizes and shapes, just like any neighborhood. They can range from fewer than 100 residents to more than 2,000. They are in urban, suburban, and rural settings. They can vary from one high-rise apartment building on a city block to numerous buildings inside a gated community situated on many acres.

Your preference might be different from someone else's. You will need to visit a few FSRCs before you know exactly what you want. For example, Sherry was *sure* she wanted a single family home until she saw the atrium apartment (page 57-8) that she eventually moved into.

GROUNDS

FSRC properties come in three basic styles: high rise, small campus, and large campus. We are using these terms specifically to mean three different styles of living quarters. They are set in three types of locations: in the hearts of cities, on their fringes, and in the country.

High-rise FSRC.

HIGH RISE

The typical mid- or high-rise (hereinafter high rise) FSRC is a multistory apartment building that has underground parking and/or parking lots with few or no grassy areas. Trees are usually limited in number, if there are any at all.

The high rise can sit in the middle of a city or in suburbia. Rarely will this style of FSRC be found in rural areas. It might be a gated, walled, secure community with a guard on duty twenty-four hours a day, seven days a week (24/7). Some have security only after dark. Should the community consist of a high-rise building(s) with acreage, then it becomes a small or large campus, depending on other features.

The dining rooms, activities rooms, commercial areas, medical offices, and other public spaces are typically located on the lower floors of the high-rise building. Administrative offices are there, as well.

The hustle and bustle of city life speaks to many who love that lifestyle. If this describes you, you might never consider anything else in an FSRC.

Small Campus

The small campus FSRC can be a mixture of many types of buildings, including one or more low-, mid-, and/or high-rise buildings. You might find some duplexes or single family homes with small yards. There will be parking at curbside and/or in parking lots; there might be carports or garages. The property could resemble a residential suburban neighborhood and might be walled and/or gated. The amount of security varies, as mentioned above.

The grassy areas are somewhat limited, but there are usually trees. Hedges, grass, and/or flower beds dress up front doors and in the islands between the parking lot rows. Courtyards might contain a fountain or a very small body of water.

Sometimes a small campus will have a centrally located community center that houses all activities. It might have several small buildings for dining, woodworking, arts and crafts, and so on. Others will designate portions of the main apartment building for these activities.

This kind of campus is reminiscent of living in a subdivision with surrounding shopping and other services. Suburban living might be your ideal.

Photo by Tim Schoon © 2004. Courtesy of SFCS, Inc.

Courtyard with a fountain and duplexes in the background.

LARGE CAMPUS

The large campus FSRC has any number of acres. This property could also be surrounded by a wall or fence and have a gate at the entrance. It might sit in the heart of a city, in its suburbs, or in a rural setting.

The homes are probably a combination of single family, multifamily housing (cluster), apartment building(s), and garden or atrium apartments. The cottages could look much like a suburban neighborhood.

The large campus is even more likely to have a separate community center where all the activity takes place. The acreage supports more than just the buildings, parking areas, and roads. Many have a combination of the following: large expanses of grassy areas, wooded areas, natural terrain, room for expansion, and a natural buffer between the campus and neighboring properties.

The recreational areas might include a body of water, nature trails, paved walking or bike paths, and spaces for outdoor activities, such as swimming, croquet, or lawn bowling. The campus style is becoming increasingly more popular to younger retirees, in that it has the room to offer many choices of outdoor activities that are so appealing. See the summary of types of grounds in Figure 4-1.

Aerial view of a large campus.

A quality FSRC will maintain the whole community well, including the roads, driveways, and parking lots. Landscaping that is well planned and maintained adds to the overall charm of the community. Flowers always brighten the mood. Look for colorful varieties throughout the grounds, not just at the entrances to the public areas.

BUILDINGS

While FSRCs all perform essentially the same basic services, they look very different. The architecture usually blends with that of the local area. For instance, adobe buildings are common in the Southwest and brick colonial-style structures are prevalent in the Northeast.

Various types of buildings provide space for services and housing for residents. The buildings range from high-rise apartment buildings and single family homes to administrative and maintenance

CHARACTERISTICS of TYPES of FSRC GROUNDS	
Grounds	Common Attributes
High rise	• mid-rise or high-rise buildings(s) • little or no grassy area • underground parking and/or parking lots • opens to street or parking lot
Small campus	• apartment building(s) with parking lot(s) • cottages with small yards (resembles suburban residential neighborhood) • garages, carports, and/or on-street parking • limited outdoor activities
Large campus	• all of the attributes of the small campus FSRC plus: • many acres • outdoor activities • walking & bicycle trails • areas of natural terrain • body of water • natural buffer between FSRC & adjoining properties

Figure 4-1

complexes. Some have many separate buildings and others have one huge structure.

INDEPENDENT LIVING AREAS (IL)

The physical features of an FSRC can create the atmosphere of a country club community. Residents live in their own apartments, cottages, or single family homes and socialize in the community center.

IL: Common Areas

The larger the community, the more common areas there will be. Usually an apartment building houses the dining room, activities rooms, health care, and administrative offices on the lower floors.

Some will have a separate community center; others will scatter the common areas throughout the property or the building.

IL: Common Areas: Community Center

When visiting FSRCs, keep in mind that the community center will be part of your home. What do you want your home to look like?

Common areas of independent living.

Clean buildings with fresh paint and doors that open effortlessly reflect the management's attitude toward the quality of life. Nicely decorated, up-to-date interiors are necessary elements for achieving a pleasant environment. This building or central area of an apartment building usually houses all of the activities and the dining room.

The decor sets the tone for personal interactions. Warmth and coziness are often hallmarks of the casual decor. On the other hand, an elegant, sophisticated decor usually creates a more formal atmosphere in which many are comfortable. Plants not only improve air quality, but warm a room up. Even silk plants make it a more pleasant place to be.

The living room of the community center is where residents will be drawn together if it has convenient, comfortable seating in lobbies, lounges, and sitting rooms. Check for furniture that is clean and not worn and arranged in conversation groupings that encourage sharing. People who are not so agile prefer chairs that are easy to get in and out of. A fireplace can warm the body as well as the soul.

Photo by Tim Schoon © 2004. Courtesy of SFCS, Inc.

Independent living dining room with salad bar.

The dining room is usually centrally located. Most of the time, it is large enough to seat all of the residents at once. A few communities are required to have staggered sittings (for example, 5:00 p.m. and 6:00 p.m.) because the dining room is too small to seat everyone at the same time. Sometimes it is one large room that encourages table-hopping; other dining rooms are separated into cozy areas of four to six tables by half walls or room dividers. Many communities have more than one dining room, usually one formal and one or more informal. Residents may choose which one they will dine in.

Food service varies from community to community; sometimes more than one kind of service is available within an FSRC. Many have formal, seated dining with a wait staff. Buffets are very popular, particularly for a salad bar. A few communities offer meals cafeteria style. Some combine various types of service in the same dining room for different meals or in different dining rooms on the same property. The style of service can vary with the meal, as well.

Tray service is usually available to the ill for no extra fee. More progressive communities are offering take-out meals to residents of independent living.

Independent living activity area off hall.

The **activities rooms** should be as varied as the activities themselves. Virtually every FSRC has an all-purpose room that serves many functions. Open areas and glass walls or large windows that separate the activities rooms, lounges, and other common areas from the halls create a bustling air that welcomes everyone and keeps them interacting.

Of course, all of the common areas should be accessible to wheelchairs, including the public restrooms. Electric doors would make this task easier for residents who need help.

The staff are the people you will see every day. This includes everyone from the cleaning crew to management. It is imperative that they are not just polite, but warm and friendly. Grouches should not be welcome. One FSRC we visited lists a naturally cheery disposition as a requirement of employment.

The cleanliness of the common areas is a clue as to how well kept the whole community is. One must wonder how well kept the kitchen and skilled nursing (SN) are when the face the FSRC puts on for the public is dirty and worn. Common areas must be well kept with spotless, well-supplied public restrooms.

IL: Common Areas: Connecting Areas Between Buildings

Communities that have more than one large apartment building ideally need to have the option of covered and/or enclosed walkways. It is a bonus if they are climate-controlled. Even where the climate is mild, scorching heat, high humidity, and whipping wind are uncomfortable, drastic changes from air conditioned interiors. Having to go outside to get from building to building might make it difficult or even prevent a less agile resident from going to dinner in inhospitable weather. Missing meals is not, as we all know, the way to optimum health.

Windows would make these walkways more pleasant. One community thoughtfully frosted the panes of glass nearest the building so apartment residents could have more privacy. Handrails and electric doors are a necessity, not a nicety.

IL: Common Areas: Common Areas of Apartment Buildings

The halls in all buildings should have handrailings and seating by the elevators and doors. They are useful for waiting for friends to go to dinner and for spontaneously socializing with one's immediate neighbors. Ideally, the residents should have a place to sit along long halls. In some states the fire code prohibits furniture in the halls. Perhaps convenient alcoves for sitting areas are an alternative.

The Tennessee Association of Homes and Services for the Aging successfully lobbied its legislature for a change in this law. Maybe others will follow suit. This simple convenience allows the residents to stay independent longer.

There are too many FSRCs where the halls are dismal. If you live in an apartment, the hall is the street where you live. An indoor version of a tree-lined street with attractive, well-kept houses and lawns makes the neighborhood cheerful. To achieve this appeal in halls, they need to be brightly, but indirectly, lit and architecturally interesting. Alcoves, shelves, or curio cabinets beside the apartment doors encourage the residents to decorate them in their own styles.

Plants are always appreciated in the halls. Natural light from windows is a much welcomed plus.

Just like the walkways between the buildings, the halls need to be climate controlled. The older we get, the less able our bodies are to adapt to changes in temperature. Living in air conditioning and walking through sweltering hot walkways for any length of time can be quite uncomfortable and distressing. It is a tremendous convenience for residents to have public restrooms on long halls.

Gathering rooms on each floor make projects and entertaining easier for residents. A seamstress, for example, could easily cut out a garment on the long tables. A resident who is a member of a group outside the community could entertain the members in a gathering room when it is his or her turn to be host or hostess.

For communities that don't have washers and dryers in every home, laundry rooms that have attached activities rooms with game rooms and/or satellite libraries are merely good sense. There would be fewer complaints about having to leave one's apartment to do laundry when the residents have a comfortable, interesting place to pass the time while laundry is being done.

Photo by L. Brancati, Courtesy of FCS, Inc.

Independent living, single-family house.

IL: Common Areas: Parking

Parking facilities vary from community to community. Single family homes might have garages, carports, or off-street parking.

Otherwise, there will be open parking or assigned parking on a lot. Sometimes there are covered spaces, but rarely for all. The more urban the surrounding local area, the more likely there will be underground parking. Residents are sometimes given just one assigned space. A second car might have to be parked away from the building in a less convenient place.

A few communities charge residents who have cars a sizeable road usage and parking fee that is added to the entrance fee; it can be as much as $5000, sometimes more. Everyone benefits from goods and services that travel over the community's roads. It is more common just to charge for covered or garage parking, but not for parking on an open lot or for using the roads.

IL: Living Accommodations

Independent living homes come in many of the sizes and shapes that one finds outside the FSRC. There are single family homes, townhomes, garden or atrium apartments, and single-story cluster homes (duplexes, triplexes, quadraplexes, and others). These types of housing are often referred to as cottages or villas (hereinafter cottages). The apartment buildings are low rise, mid-rise, and high rise. Many campuses have a combination of building types.

Independent living duplex.

An atrium apartment building is essentially one with outdoor halls instead of indoor halls. Each home has windows on two opposing

Atrium apartments.

walls instead of the usual one wall. The center, where the hall would be between the apartments, is open to the sky.

IL: Living Accommodations: Emergency Call System

While it might seem a given that all homes, including independent living, have emergency call systems, this is not necessarily the case. Homes without them are rare; those that do have several types of systems. The most common is a pull chain or button that is accessible from the bedroom and the bathroom. Some have thoughtfully devised a call system that can be reached from sitting and standing height and also from the floor, thinking that someone who needs help might have fallen. Advanced systems have a portable device that the residents can wear around their necks while in their homes. State-of-the-art systems can track residents anywhere on campus when they wear a very small lapel pin.

IL: Living Accommodations: Sizes of Homes

Cottages and apartments come in all sizes. As a rule, studio apartments are in the apartment building. They usually start at about 400 square feet. The newer ones are larger.

Photo by Tim Schoon © 2004. Courtesy of SFCS, Inc.

Independent living apartment with balcony.

One bedroom homes might be in the form of cottages or apartments in an apartment building. The older, unrenovated apartments often start at 700-800 square feet and go up from there. Newer homes offer 1½, 2, or 2½ baths. Some have dens as well.

The two bedroom homes are usually 1000 square feet or more. The number of bathrooms varies. Dens are also available. Again, the newer apartments are larger. They come with as many as 2000 square feet and 2500 or more in corner apartments, single family homes, and penthouses.

Three bedrooms are becoming more widespread. Experts in senior housing at the American Association of Homes and Services for the Aging (AAHSA, page 194) predict that more of the larger homes will be built to accommodate the wishes of the Baby Boomers.

If these sizes seem small to you, read the section on downsizing on page 152. Looking at the community's common areas as part of your home might help you.

IL: Living Accommodations: Storage Units

Storage can be a problem in some communities; however, many offer additional enclosures. Some floor plans allow for space that is designated storage only. This is particularly true in newer buildings.

Many apartment buildings provide 4' x 4' x 8' locked storage units on the same floor as residents' apartments, although some are smaller. Entry into these areas is usually through a locked door from the hall. Sometimes the individual spaces are in the basement instead of on each floor.

Storage units are most commonly constructed with chicken wire and 2x4s. Each area locks with a padlock. Some upscale communities will make these units entirely from plywood and give them real doors with deadbolt locks.

Occasionally, residents are offered the use of an open basement space. Extra storage for cottages is usually located somewhere in the home or off the patio, carport, or garage. If not, a separate building might house storage units for several nearby cottages.

IL: Living Accommodations: Elder Friendly

You would think that all areas of FSRCs are elder friendly, but many of the independent living homes are not—even in the new communities.

Many FSRCs are willing to widen doorways and make other adjustments for wheelchairs in independent living. Some might have structural limitations that keep them from doing so, while others still might be hindered by local, state, and/or federal laws. The marketing representative can expand on this point if it concerns you.

When an apartment or single family home is elder friendly, it has wide doorways; low light switches; and door levers, not knobs. In the kitchen there should be pullout shelves in lower cabinets, lazy susans in corner cabinets, and levers for faucet handles at the sink.

Bathrooms should have walk-in showers with a seat or two, a raised toilet, a sink that a wheelchair can get under, grab bars, and levers for faucet handles at the sink and in the bathtub.

Raised toilets, ideally, should be available for those who need them. Otherwise, standard-height toilets are better. A resident told us that after living in the FSRC for seven years and using only the raised toilet, she could no longer lower herself to a standard-height

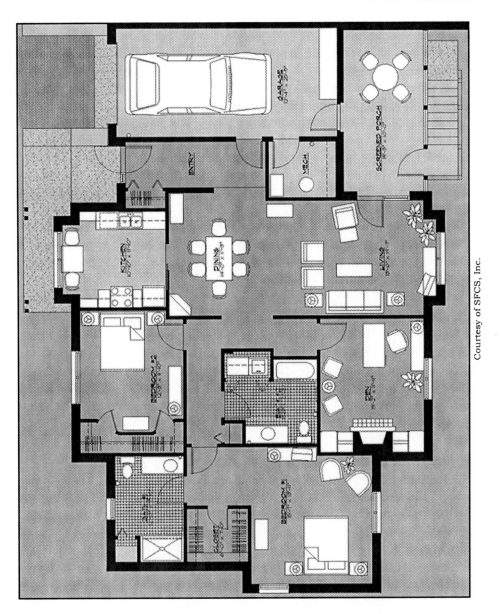

Courtesy of SFCS, Inc.

Floor plan of 2300 square-foot duplex in independent living.

toilet. She had no other impairments of mobility. Using a crutch now, before you need it, might unnecessarily limit your abilities at some point in the future.

IL: Living Accommodations: Kitchens

A few of the oldest communities have no kitchen areas in independent living homes. A handful have kitchenettes with only a refrigerator and a microwave oven. Progressive FSRCs are rapidly renovating for future residents who want full-sized kitchens.

For the most part, independent living kitchens include all large appliances. In some states, the refrigerator is not part of the package. These are usually the states that do not require homeowners to sell their houses with a refrigerator in them. If residents must buy their own refrigerators, the FSRC might or might not maintain them.

Most have garbage disposals, usually as a health aid. Not all communities provide dishwashers and ice makers. As a rule, the newer the community or the more recent the renovations, the more modern and complete the kitchen is.

IL: Living Accommodations: Bathrooms

Bathrooms do not always have both a bathtub and a separate shower. When there are two full baths, there is usually a bathtub (with a shower) in one and a shower only in the other. If the apartment has only one bath, walk-in showers are critical for residents whose range of motion and balance might become impaired.

IL: Living Accommodations: Laundry Areas

As communities renovate, it is more common to find washer and dryer hookups in each residence. Sometimes the spaces accommodate full-sized or apartment-sized stackable washers and dryers. Space for side-by-side appliances does exist in some communities.

Most commonly, the apartments come with washers and dryers that belong to the FSRC and it maintains them. If the residents have to supply their own, sometimes the community will repair them; sometimes it will not.

Often, the laundry facilities are in a room down the hall in apartment buildings or in centrally located freestanding buildings amid cottages. While this might seem like a huge inconvenience, the laundry room is a good place to meet people and make friends, especially if there is an activities room attached to the laundry room.

IL: Living Accommodations: Outdoor Access

Outdoor access from the homes varies. Some communities offer no balconies or patios; others have balconies or patios with every apartment, even studios; yet others have some homes with them and some homes without them. Garden and atrium apartments open to the outside at the front door and the back door.

IL: Living Accommodations: Refurbishment On Moving In

It seems that almost all of the FSRCs will at least clean the carpet and paint before you move in. Most will also routinely replace the carpet and some will also replace the appliances. A few will replace the kitchen cabinets after each resident moves out.

Once you are ready to move in, the FSRC might offer you some help. You will bring your own furniture and may decorate as you wish. Many communities employ interior designers who will assist you in selecting which furniture to take with you to the FSRC, in decorating your apartment/cottage, and in recommending modifications to the home. Most have move-in teams who will help you on moving day. Some communities will charge extra for this service, while others do not.

Most endowment communities will do minor things at no extra charge; for instance, they might add extra shelves in closets, hang pictures or mirrors, and replace light fixtures. Some communities will move walls and build additions as zoning and building codes allow. The more extensive the renovations, the more likely the new resident will be charged a one-time fee to have them done.

Many communities offer enclosures of patios and balconies. If you select a home that already has this area enclosed, the entrance fee might not be higher than other homes without the enclosure, because the previous resident paid for the improvements. If you elect to glass in the patio or balcony, you will most probably be charged for the construction costs. In either case, the monthly fees will probably reflect the increased costs of upkeep, including housekeeping.

In equity communities (see page 121), new residents take possession of their homes as is. The condition the previous residents left the home in is what they get. Lease communities vary widely as to what they will do to renovate homes between residents.

ASSISTED LIVING AREAS (AL)

When a resident cannot perform one to three of the Activities of Daily Living (page 24), the resident, his or her family, his or her doctor, and the health care staff of the FSRC will discuss a move to the assisted living (AL) area. It is a slow process that is usually considered over a long period of time. The resident's input in the decision is essential.

In assisted living, the residents can consistently get the quality care they need to continue living a more independent life than if they stayed in independent living. Even when residents move to assisted living they should be welcome to continue socializing in the independent living community center if they are able.

AL: Common Areas

Assisted living areas should look very much like the independent living portions of the community, only on a smaller scale. The common areas have their own dining rooms, activities rooms, and lounge areas with a TV; sometimes it is a big-screened TV.

Warm and friendly decor makes this home a pleasant place to be. Comfortable seating is a plus for residents who are not so agile as they once were. Plants, birds, and fish bring a relaxing cheer to any area.

As in the apartment building, the halls should be wide and have railings and seating, where fire codes allow. Good lighting is absolutely necessary.

The permanent transition from independent living (IL) to assisted living (AL) or skilled nursing (SN) and from assisted living to skilled nursing (SN) can be unsettling. If these areas can look more like independent living, the move will be emotionally easier.

AL: Common Areas: Cleanliness

The whole community must, of course, not have any visible dirt. All areas should be well maintained. A coat of fresh paint shows signs of attention to maintaining the buildings, as do carpet and upholstery that are not worn. The public restrooms must be impeccably clean and well-supplied. What is **most important** is that these areas should be completely **odor free**. Temporary, localized odors may be excused.

Assisted living dining room.

AL: Living Accommodations

The assisted living area is often housed in a separate wing off the community center. Sometimes it is in a separate building; sometimes near the center of the property and other times across campus. The closer it is to the independent living residents, the easier it is for spouses and friends to visit.

AL: Living Accommodations: Emergency Call System

All assisted living homes should have an emergency call system. The button is usually accessible from the bed and the bathroom. Most likely, residents can speak with someone at the nurse's station through an intercom.

AL: Living Accommodations: Sizes of Homes

Often assisted living homes are studio apartments, but it is ideal if they are one or two bedroom apartments. Those that have single hospital-like rooms are confining and often dreary. This model seems to be declining.

One popular style of assisted living homes consists of more common areas with bedrooms off homelike living rooms and family rooms. Some communities offer the same floor plans in assisted living as they do in independent living. This way, the transition to assisted living can be made more smoothly.

For the most part, residents may decorate their assisted living homes as they wish. Nearly all are unfurnished.

The trend appears to allow couples to stay together when one spouse needs assisted living. Couples who want to should be given the opportunity to do so. Sometimes, changes in styles of homes need to be made in order to accommodate two residents.

AL: Living Accommodations: Storage Units

Storage in assisted living homes varies from community to community. As a rule, however, no extra storage space is provided down the hall. It is questionable whether the basement is available to residents.

AL: Living Accommodations: Elder Friendly

Virtually all assisted living areas are elder friendly. Look for wide doorways, low switches, levers for door handles, and so on.

AL: Living Accommodations: Kitchens

Assisted living apartments might or might not have kitchens. Few are full sized; others are complete, but very small. Still others might have a tea kitchen (sink, microwave oven, and refrigerator). Many of the new and newly renovated do have kitchen facilities.

AL: Living Accommodations: Bathrooms

Apartments mean private bathrooms. Rarely will residents who live in rooms have to share a bath with their next-door neighbor. This is much less common in newly built or newly renovated communities.

AL: Living Accommodations: Laundry Areas

All laundry should be done for the residents. There is often a community laundry room down the hall for residents who want to wash a few of their delicate items. Hopefully, it is not coin operated. This should be in place in fee-for-service communities, in particular, for residents who are able to do their own laundry and do not want to pay for the service.

Occasionally, you might run across an assisted living area that has washers and dryers inside the apartments. As the trend progresses toward moving couples into assisted living apartments, we might see more of this.

AL: Living Accommodations: Outdoor Access

It is imperative that residents of assisted living have easy access to an outdoor area that they may visit at will. Many communities have beautiful gardens filled with flowers and trees. Well-landscaped areas can be appealing the year round, even in cold weather. Benches and other places to sit under awnings, trees, and other shelters provide an outdoor getaway and an opportunity for fresh air.

SKILLED NURSING AREAS

Skilled nursing (SN) renders an essential service. This care in FSRCs should be top notch because prospective residents, visitors, and the residents in independent living are constantly observing their performance as they call on spouses and friends.

SN: Common Areas

Every skilled nursing wing has an activities room. There is always a TV and some even have one big-screened TV. In addition, many have a living room, a separate dining room, and a patio with a garden. All the halls have handrails and are wide and well lit.

While it is difficult to make skilled nursing look warm and homey, the decor in the common areas can certainly go a long way to impart a homelike feel. Upholstered furniture is not only pleasant to sit on; it also improves the eye appeal. Plants, fish, and birds are comforting and bring life and interest.

Health care area's patio.

SN: Common Areas: Cleanliness

It is absolutely imperative that the skilled nursing area is clean. The first sign of this is that there is **no odor** on first walking in and **no odor** as you continue to walk through. If there is an odor, it might be temporary; it should be isolated to one area and not be pervasive.

The public restrooms must be spotless and well-supplied. Check for fresh-looking paint and clean upholstery that is not worn. If there is carpet in the activities room, it should not be drab looking, dirty, and/or stained either.

SN: Living Accommodations

Like assisted living, the skilled nursing area is usually a wing off the community center or in a nearby building. The closer it is to independent living, the easier it is for spouses and friends to visit.

SN: Living Accommodations: Emergency Call System

All skilled nursing homes come with an emergency call system. The residents can reach the button from their beds. Usually an intercom connects residents with the nurse's station.

SN: Living Accommodations: Sizes of Homes

Residents of skilled nursing typically live in semiprivate hospital-type rooms, although the trend is toward more private ones. Most FSRCs encourage residents to bring some of their own furniture. They are usually welcome to decorate their rooms to their own tastes.

SN: Living Accommodations: Storage Units

As a rule, storage for permanent residents of skilled nursing is confined only to the space they have in their own rooms. Many do have generous closet space, particularly if the building has been renovated lately or is new.

SN: Living Accommodations: Elder Friendly

All skilled nursing areas are elder friendly. Look for levers instead of knobs, low light switches, and other such features.

SN: Living Accommodations: Kitchens

Residents do not have kitchens in skilled nursing. Many have a refrigerator and cabinet stocked with snacks that are easily accessible to residents.

SN: Living Accommodations: Bathrooms

Many residents in skilled nursing, even in private rooms, share a half bath with either a roommate or a next-door neighbor. Some have their own half baths. Bathing facilities are in a separate room down the hall. Newer skilled nursing areas are building full baths for each room or pair of private rooms.

SN: Living Accommodations: Laundry Areas

Personal and flat linen laundry service is provided by the staff. Washers and dryers for the use of residents are not found here.

SN: Living Accommodations: Outdoor Access

A peaceful garden is soothing to many. Easy access to a sunny spot with attractive landscaping calms the soul; benches in the shade are welcome in the hot weather. Those in the sun and sheltered from the wind make the garden enjoyable in the fringe seasons.

ALZHEIMER'S/DEMENTIA AREAS

The above comments about the common areas of assisted living (AL) and skilled nursing (SN) are pertinent to the discussion of the memory support area also. Their common areas are, in particular, more homey than the rest of the community.

The halls in an architecturally progressive dementia area might be circular; this means that residents who are confused cannot get lost. Locked curio cabinets outside each door, filled with treasured mementos of a lifetime, aid residents in identifying their own homes.

Alzheimer's/dementia living and dining rooms.

Residents who suffer with dementia usually have private, homelike rooms if they just need personal care (assisted living). These communities will have separate areas for those who need medical care (skilled nursing); these rooms are hospital-like. Other communities intermingle all dementia residents in hospital-like rooms.

The garden for Alzheimer's/dementia residents is different from the other gardens. Because memory support residents tend to walk aimlessly, they need a garden with a circular path that will always bring them back to the door going inside. Growing simple plants in their own small garden plots can be quite therapeutic.

※※

Full service retirement communities (FSRC) are like snowflakes. When you have seen one FSRC, you have seen *one* FSRC. They have similar characteristics, yet each is different. *There is no perfect FSRC, and no* **one** *FSRC is for everyone.* As Tina Turner said in song, "You'd better shop around!"

※※

This chapter has given you an idea of what the grounds and buildings of FSRCs could look like. Chapter 5 discusses the possible amenities and services that you might find at a full service retirement community.

5

AMENITIES AND SERVICES

Don't simply retire from something,
have something to retire to.

—Harry Emerson Fosdick
American Clergyman, 1878-1969

The amenities and services that full service retirement communities (FSRCs), also known as continuing care retirement communities (CCRCs), offer are two of the most wonderful characteristics about them. For years we worked both inside and outside our homes to improve our standards of living. For most of us, that level of effort will be reduced when we move to an FSRC and our lifestyles will be improved. Which services and how many are provided depend on the type and size of the community and how posh it is.

AMENITIES

Amenities are offered by most communities. Some larger FSRCs can resemble a small village. Retail and service businesses, such as

POSSIBLE AMENITIES	
Special Features	**Activities**
Your home: • emergency call system • storage • carport/garage • washer/dryer • patio/balcony • fireplace • dishwasher • ice maker • pullout shelves • Internet access ***Common areas:*** • activity room(s) • community center • chapel • fireplace • private dining room • guest rooms • auditorium/ theater • extra storage	• library • music library • video library • art studio • crafts/sewing room • woodworking shop • lapidary studio • stained glass studio • TV/radio studio • card room • billiards room • garden plots • greenhouse • Internet access
Commercial	**Fitness**
• barber shop • beauty shop • convenience store • shoe repair • dry cleaning • bank • post office • café • cocktail lounge • pharmacy	• golf course(s) • tennis courts • swimming pool, indoor/outdoor • fitness equipment • water sports • whirlpool • sauna/steam rooms

Figure 5-1

a bank, barber/beauty shop, convenience store, shoe repair, and dry cleaners, might actually operate within the complex. Indoor amenities could encompass a wide range of interests; for example, a card room, billiards room, greenhouse, fitness center, swimming pool, bowling alley, woodworking shop, chapel, library, crafts room, music room, and theater. Outdoor amenities might include lawn bowling, croquet court, putting green, a three-hole golf course, tennis courts, and swimming pool. Figure 5-1 summarizes the amenities you might find in FSRCs.

Special Features

All community centers, apartments, and cottages have basic features; however, there are many that do not offer extras. The price and size of an FSRC usually determine which special features might be offered and how much space is devoted to them.

Community Center

Larger communities need a lot of square footage in the community center to accommodate the activities of up to two thousand people. They might have a theater (in addition to an all-purpose room) with a real stage and/or a large room with a hardwood floor that serves as a ballroom. Smaller communities will probably have a portable dance floor if their population dances. Some living rooms have a big-screened TV.

Housing

Whether or not there is outdoor access from the homes varies widely. Carports and garages are not the norm. Newer communities and those that are renovating will add extras, such as ice makers, dishwashers, and microwave ovens. Some builders opted for the lower-priced, noisy, and inflexible, freestanding heating/cooling systems that are like those in some hotel and motel rooms.

In a few communities (mostly newer ones) you will find Internet access in each home. When you do, most commonly, it is a hookup for another phone line. Rarely will you find high-speed Internet access. Fireplaces are also quite rare; and when you do find them, they are usually not wood-burning.

Hobbies

The more people there are in residence, the more likely the community will provide specialized rooms for a wider variety of hobbies. Smaller and more inexpensive communities will tend to use rooms for a multitude of purposes. For instance, the billiards table might be in the back of the all-purpose room or the library might be in a corner of the lobby. Sometimes painting, ceramics, crafts, and sewing are combined in rooms with stained glass. In large and/or expensive communities these hobbies could have separate rooms for each.

Some hobbies, by their natures, cannot be shared with others. Woodworking, for example, is a dusty and noisy endeavor that always has its own room. A few FSRCs have TV studios for their closed-circuit television channels. The humidity and warmth of a greenhouse make it unlikely that another activity would share that space with the gardeners.

Many communities provide individual plots for gardeners to grow their own flowers and/or vegetables. As a rule, the staff turns over the ground in the spring for the residents.

Libraries are sometimes in a multi-function room, which houses related interests. The computer club might consist of one computer in a corner of the library or it could have a whole room with a dozen or more computers. Records, cassette tapes, CDs, and DVDs of current and past music frequently occupy one small section of the library. A few communities have a music room for listening with many bookcases filled with recorded music and a wide variety of equipment on which to play it. The same holds true for video tapes and DVDs of movies.

Usually the residents themselves determine how extensively some endeavors should be entered into. For example, readers love libraries, but some libraries have only books donated by residents, while others will not accept books that are old and/or worn. Some libraries subscribe to magazines and daily newspapers. The American Association of Book Publishers has programs for new books on loan that some communities may participate in and others get rotating books from the county bookmobile.

COMMERCIAL AMENITIES

A great many communities lease space to some commercial businesses on their properties. This is a tremendous convenience for all.

Beauty/Barber Shop

A beauty/barber shop is in every FSRC. It is invariably located in or near the assisted living (AL) and/or skilled nursing (SN) portions of the community. Larger communities will also have these shops in independent living (IL), as well. Payment methods vary.

Bank

Another common commercial entity is a bank. The services and the hours the bank provides might be limited, but very often the bank is a full service one. Rarely will there be ATMs and safety deposit boxes on site. Occasionally, there is no bank, but a representative comes in once or twice a week.

Shops

A convenience store, gift shop, and/or thrift shop are often in the community center. Many are staffed and/or run completely by residents. Sometimes they are commercially owned and operated.

Café

The café is becoming more popular, especially in new communities. Sometimes it is an extension of the food service department and other times the space is commercially leased to a local restaurant. Usually it serves breakfast and lunch only, but an informal dinner could be offered there as well.

Payment for food varies in method from community to community. If only one meal per day is included in the FSRC's monthly fee, then eating a second meal there is usually pay as you go. Some communities use a smart card, much like a credit card. Purchases are electronically recorded and added to the resident's bill each month.

Gift shop.

The smart card can also record each resident's visits to the café or the dining room. It, therefore, can serve as an alert as to whether residents are in need of attention.

Pharmacy

Residents undoubtedly appreciate a full service pharmacy that is on the premises; they are usually found only in very large communities. Sometimes a local pharmacy will deliver to individual residents. Some FSRCs will provide a prescription refill service for no charge or a nominal fee.

Alcohol Service

A cocktail lounge, leased by a commercial entity, could be on site. There are various ways to run it and accept payment. Sometimes a community will have a liquor license and sell beer, wine, and/or liquor themselves. Other communities allow residents to store their own bottles behind the bar with the community providing the setups. Yet others serve alcohol, particularly wine, as part of the meals and do not charge extra for it. Some FSRCs serve no alcoholic beverages at all. Policies are driven by state and local laws, the management, and/or residents.

Café.

Other Services

A dry cleaning and/or shoe repair service will, once in a while, be among the other business establishments that are on site. The U.S. Post Office sometimes has a satellite branch in the community. Packages can be left for UPS and FedEx pick up at some FSRCs.

SPORTS

Sports in FSRCs are fairly new. As FSRCs compete with age restricted communities that make golf, tennis, and other active sports available, they are expanding their selections of activities. With the influx of younger retirees and the increased popularity of physical activity, more communities are offering indoor activities and outdoor ones, as well. A few waterfront communities have marinas to house the residents' boats. The chef might cook their catches of the day.

Residents who are interested in health and exercise are becoming more common today than in the twentieth century. Consequently, the health club has moved into progressive FSRCs. New retirees are looking for sophisticated fitness rooms and indoor swimming pools with whirlpools and sauna or steam rooms. Active residents participate in aerobics and yoga classes, using mats. A TV and VCR are often available to entertain and teach those who are exercising. A water fountain or cooler is essential for residents who are really working out.

Indoor pool.

SERVICES

FSRCs provide a myriad of services—all designed to keep the residents functioning as independently as long as possible. The convenience services are available to residents at all levels, as is some sort of care. See Figure 5-2.

CONVENIENCE SERVICES

Virtually every community offers all of its independent living residents the services of a housekeeper, laundress, chauffeur, cook, dishwasher, gardener, handyman, and security guard. Some FSRCs also provide the services of a receptionist, concierge, wait staff, entertainment director, trainer, personal shopper, chaplain, interior designer, and contractor.

Fitness room.

The convenience services that almost all communities offer are exterior maintenance and some kind of activities, often with an activities director. Almost always there is a bus that will take residents to and from medical appointments and shopping centers. Some run on schedules; others run continuously. Very often transportation for hire is available.

Additional services are added by other FSRCs. These might include interior maintenance, one to three meals daily, housekeeping, and laundry of bed and bath linens.

CARE

A continuing care retirement community (full service retirement community) is a senior living residence that, by definition of the American Association of Homes and Services for the Aging (AAHSA, page 194), provides three levels of care under one umbrella in an independent living (IL) section, an assisted living portion (AL), and a skilled nursing part (SN). See Figure 5-3. Progression through life's stages is meant to be as stress free as possible. The full service retirement community is designed to allow its residents to stay in their homes for as long as possible (or age in place, as the industry calls it), a wish of many seniors.

POSSIBLE SERVICES of FSRCs		
Convenience	**Personal Care**	**Health/Medical Care**
• 1-3 meals daily • special diets • private dining • meals to go • laundry of flat linens • personal laundry • housekeeping • exterior maintenance • interior maintenance • bus transportation • catering • activities directors • professional entertainment on site • planned outings • personal shopper • concierge service • religious services • utilities • local phone service • cable TV • security • residents' association • Internet access • plus many others	*aid with physical tasks:* • getting in/out of bed or chairs • using the bathroom • bathing • dressing • eating • getting around inside the house *aid with cognitive tasks* • cleaning the house • planning & shopping for groceries & other household items • cooking meals • using the phone • making & keeping appointments • taking medications as prescribed • balancing the checkbook • getting around outside of the house	• exercise program w/ trainer • emergency call system • nurse's office • doctors' offices • pharmacy • tray service for the ill • blood pressure checks • cholesterol tests • routine physicals • dental care • podiatry care • physical therapy • occupational therapy • recreational therapy • speech therapy • psychological therapy • psychiatric therapy • cardiac rehabilitation • weight management • wellness programs • health education programs • short-term nursing care • long-term nursing care • respite care • adult day care

Figure 5-2

LEVELS of CARE of an FSRC	
Level of Living	**Services Provided**
Independent living (IL)	• activities • convenience services • meals • transportation • security • maintenance, usually
Assisted living (AL)	• all of the above items plus: • personal care • three meals daily • personal laundry service
Skilled nursing (SN)	• all of the above items plus: • medical care

Figure 5-3

The FSRC becomes the residents' homes when they are still independent. As they age and need more care, help is available to them on prearranged terms in familiar surroundings by people they already know.

The levels of care really go beyond just the three that the industry generally thinks of with a continuing care retirement community. The whole idea of going to such a community is to have a seamless ride through life with as few traumatic moves as possible. The more levels of care that are offered, the smoother the ride will be and the less likely that residents will have to move to an outside facility.

Although FSRCs advertise themselves as having continuous care, we have observed that a comprehensive FSRC really has five levels of care. They are: 1) independent living, 2) assisted living, 3) separate assisted living for Alzheimer's/dementia residents, 4) skilled nursing, and 5) separate skilled nursing for Alzheimer's/dementia residents.

While it is optimal that a community has five levels of care, a minimum of four is really essential. See Figure 5-4. In our opinion, every FSRC must offer at least independent living (IL), assisted living (AL), skilled nursing (SN), and Alzheimer's/dementia care (A/D). This way residents will need to leave the community only for hospital (acute) care and, perhaps, temporary subacute care, which some FSRCs offer.

Health Care

All the things we do—or should do—for ourselves to preserve and improve our health come under the topic of health care. We all know that we should eat a healthy, well-balanced diet and skip no meals. Exercise is very important in keeping our bodies finely tuned. Regular medical and dental checkups not only help prolong life, but preserve its quality, as well. FSRCs make it easier to do these things for ourselves.

LEVELS of CARE for the COMPREHENSIVE FSRC			
Essential		**Superior**	
1	Independent living (IL)	1	Independent living
2	Assisted living (AL)	2	Assisted living
3	Skilled nursing (SN)	3	Skilled nursing
4	Alzheimer's/dementia (A/D)	4	Assisted living for Alzheimer's/dementia
		5	Skilled nursing for Alzheimer's/dementia

Figure 5-4

An FSRC without a wellness program is not gearing up for the coming Baby Boomers, most of whom value this feature. This program is more than physical exercise and healthy menu choices. A comprehensive program includes health education classes, support groups, constructive activities, and a wellness center, among others.

Independent Living

Life in an FSRC's independent living portion gives its residents freedom—freedom from home repairs, freedom from cleaning, freedom from yard work, and freedom from cooking, if desired. Residents have time to indulge their passions and enjoy family, friends, and life overall.

Otherwise, the major difference between living in an FSRC and in one's own home of many years is the community's worry-free lifestyle. Residents enjoy the safety net of having personal and medical care standing by, if and when it is needed.

The daily check is at the heart of the services that residents in independent living benefit from. Without it, communities could unknowingly allow a resident's health to fail. Almost all FSRCs have some method for checking to see that residents are up and about each day. The more unobtrusive the approach, the better it is.

In some communities, security personnel flip a lever on each front door in the middle of the night. When the door is opened, the lever falls to another position. As the security personnel make their daily rounds, they phone residents whose lever's position indicates that the door has not been opened.

Some communities have noninvasive electronic systems, such as motion detectors in the bathroom, while others ask residents to check in by phone, either with another resident or an employee. The latter system leaves room for human error, which makes it more likely that the system could be compromised.

FSRCs that keep an eye on whether or not residents are showing up for meals can come to the aid of a faltering resident much more quickly and effectively than communities that do not. Eating regular meals keeps one's strength up. Diseases, such as pneumonia, which commonly strikes seniors, can, more likely, be nipped in the bud.

Some FSRCs allow residents the right to opt out of the daily check should they so desire; however, doing so might compromise a resident's health. Communities that allow this option need to be extra aware of the residents' well being.

Personal Care

Once residents begin to have difficulty with one or two of the Activities of Daily Living (page 24), personal care is needed. A caregiver would help residents with, say, bathing and dressing.

Home Health Care

Home health care services provide for an aide to come into independent living and deliver personal care to residents. This enables them to prolong the length of time they spend in independent living. It positively affects their mental states and, in fee-for-service communities (page 140), might save money.

While home health care (HHC) is not absolutely necessary for an FSRC to be comprehensive, it is an added feature that many people like. Residents of fee-for-service and life care communities (page 136) alike pay extra for this care. Long-term care insurance might cover these services.

Assisted Living

People who require personal care need help eating, bathing, dressing, using the toilet, moving from bed to a chair, and mobility. These are physical impairments. Some communities also assist residents who need help with the Instrumental Activities of Daily Living. These are the cognitive skills one needs in running a household, such as balancing a checkbook, fixing meals, doing light housework, making phone calls, taking medications correctly, and getting to and from shopping and doctors' offices. (See the list of impairments in Figure 5-2.)

Medical Care

When residents need help with three or more of the Activities of Daily Living, communities will most likely ask them to consider moving from assisted living (AL) to skilled nursing (SN). Also when residents need medical care for temporary acute illnesses or chronic diseases, this portion of the FSRC can be of help. Those who suffer with dementia might eventually need medical care, as well.

Skilled Nursing

Differing degrees of medical care are provided by FSRCs. Here residents receive medical and nursing care around the clock. Care following hospital stays is usually temporary. More comprehensive skilled nursing wings also administer subacute care for those who need intensive medical care for a short time (page 104). Rehabilitative therapies are also available. Skilled nursing areas provide permanent residency when necessary.

Alzheimer's/Dementia

Residents who suffer from Alzheimer's or a similar dementia that sometimes afflicts the aging might, at some point, need special care. Sufferers might be otherwise healthy, while some could have additional debilitating diseases. Treating these residents requires special considerations.

A community that does not provide all of the essential levels (independent living [IL], assisted living [AL], skilled nursing [SN], and Alzheimer's/dementia [A/D]) could put residents in the uncomfortable position of having to leave their communities in the future to seek housing and care elsewhere. They might have to incur extra costs, in addition to leaving friends, perhaps a spouse, and familiar surroundings behind.

※※

There are many advantages to a full service retirement community. While no community is perfect, the pros outweigh the cons for a rapidly growing number of seniors. See Figure 2-5 for the pros and cons of an FSRC.

※※

This chapter has given you an idea of what services and amenities you might find in FSRCs. The next chapter continues the discussion of services by describing in more detail the health, personal, and medical care that FSRCs render.

6

HEALTH, PERSONAL, AND MEDICAL CARE

*Health and cheerfulness
mutually beget each other.*

—Joseph Addison
English Poet, 1672-1719

One of the main reasons people move into a full service retirement community (FSRC), also known as a continuing care retirement community (CCRC), is for the care that they give—health (independent living), personal (assisted living), and medical (skilled nursing). Other compelling reasons include the socialization, the centralized services, and the activities, among others.

The FSRC, as a concept, is designed to make the transitions that lie ahead—whatever they might be and however unlikely—as smooth as possible. The good news is that, statistically, fewer residents in FSRCs enter skilled nursing on a permanent basis than do people who stay in their homes. This lifestyle keeps residents healthier longer.

A large family of communities conducted a very small study to determine how many skilled nursing beds they needed to build in one of their communities. It showed that only one in fourteen of its residents needed skilled nursing care on a **permanent** basis, as opposed to one in four of the general population (according to AARP). These statistics, although gathered from a small sample, reflect positively on the theory that worry-free retirement living with socialization, good nutrition, quality activities, and opportunities for exercise keep residents healthier longer.

It's very tempting for a community to put the greater portion of its money in independent living, where new residents are attracted. On the other hand, communities with a larger number of residents in assisted living (AL) and skilled nursing (SN) than in independent living might have a greater emphasis on care and might be turning into a two-level community. Check to be sure that residents in all three sections receive the care and services that they need and that all levels have the same look and feel.

HEALTH CARE

Independent living focuses on catering to its residents in order to improve and enhance their welfare. Some FSRCs leave residents to their own devices in independent living, expecting them to provide most of their own entertainment and attention to their physical, mental, emotional, spiritual, social, and vocational well being. Others almost take responsibility for these things. Human nature often leads us to take the easiest path, rather than the best one. If the community makes it easy and fun for us to take better care of ourselves, most of us will. An added bonus of FSRC living is the opportunity for a more fulfilling life with many activities and friends to enjoy them with.

PHYSICAL HEALTH

"Use it or lose it" applies to the body as well as the mind. Statistically, most of us don't exercise as much as we should. FSRCs make it easier to get up and just do it, because you will have someone to do it with.

Health Education

Education is a vital part of a wellness program. Nutrition classes will help residents learn to control diabetes, cholesterol, triglycerides, and calories. Other classes will inform them of the latest in medical research, diet, wellness checkups, and dental care.

Emergency Services

Emergency calls are almost always answered by someone with some sort of medical training. In some states, the registered nurses (RNs) in skilled nursing are not allowed, by law, to leave their posts for an emergency elsewhere. In their stead, security personnel who are emergency medical technicians (EMTs) could provide a timely response in case of crisis.

Many communities would prefer that the residents contact security, the wellness center, or the nurse in skilled nursing instead of calling 911. This enables a calm person to direct an ambulance to the ailing resident. Security will then meet the medical personnel on arrival. When distraught persons give directions to a stranger on how to find them in a community of several hundred, the scene for a disaster might be set.

Wellness Center

Good health is promoted through a wellness center in independent living. Services provided by a doctor, nurse practitioner, or registered nurse will be essential to residents. There you can expect to get your blood pressure monitored, your blood sugar tested, your cholesterol and other blood values checked, and dressings on wounds changed. A nurse practitioner will be able to write prescriptions for infections and routine medications for chronic conditions, among other things. Some of these services might be included in the monthly fee, while others might be available for an extra charge. This varies greatly from community to community.

Check the hours, as well. A few wellness centers are open twenty-four hours a day, seven days a week (24/7). Others might have very limited hours. Sometimes a clinic doctor can take walk-ins, but most likely, only appointments.

A few wellness centers are sponsored by local hospitals. Many FSRCs provide office space for doctors to practice part time or full time in the community. These doctors are very often geriatricians (specialists for the aging); sometimes they are dentists, podiatrists, cardiologists, internists, and ophthalmologists.

Much has been written about the attitude of some physicians toward the elderly. Often they think that aging means having to put up with disease and disability. Therefore, seniors, arguably, get the least respect and the worst care than do any other age group in our society. Osteoporosis is not part of the natural aging process, nor are high blood pressure or glaucoma. Physicians who practice at FSRCs should not share these archaic and prejudicial views.

Therapeutic Services

Many FSRCs also provide the services of many kinds of therapists. They include rehabilitation, therapeutic massage, and physical, occupational, speech, recreational, and psychological therapies. Payment for them is made through the residents' medical insurance.

Diet

We all need nutritious meals and healthy habits to maintain our bodies in a state of wellness. The food we eat—or don't eat—is, arguably, the single most important thing that we do for—or to—ourselves. Eating healthily is, of course, easier when the choices are healthy. Residents who need special diets for medical reasons should be able to get them in their own homes—their FSRCs.

Menu Choices

Aside from special diets, you will want to have a wide variety of foods with many choices offered at each meal. Each FSRC has a rotating menu; usually the meals repeat every four to eight weeks. Many FSRCs provide a continental breakfast. While that is an enjoyable service, a breakfast with protein (meat, poultry, fish, eggs, cheese, or soy) would be far healthier.

For the main meal of the day, some have a choice of two entrées with whatever sides the kitchen is serving that day. Others offer, and ideally so, a beef, chicken, fish, **and** vegetarian entrée every day with more options of side dishes. Still, others have broader selections. For example, the right side of the menu might list two to four choices of today's entrées and several side dishes. The left side of the menu would be the same every day and usually include more familiar foods, such as roast beef, chicken, and/or baked fish with several choices of steamed vegetables.

Healthy Foods

Menus with many daily selections offer a wide variety of foods. We all need assorted foods for our diverse digestive systems. Hopefully, the foods will be healthy. While it is inevitable that some comfort foods will be served, look for menus that focus on healthy selections. See Figure 6-1 for a summary of a healthy diet.

Healthy foods mean high fiber, lots of vitamins and minerals, adequate amounts of unsaturated oils, low to moderate cholesterol content, low to moderate saturated fats, and low salt and sugar content. Heavy sauces and gravies add extra calories, few nutrients, and unneeded saturated fat. The fried entrées should be kept to a minimum.

The side dishes should, ideally, include choices of complex carbohydrates, starchy, and non-starchy vegetables. Look for plenty of healthy complex carbohydrates, such as legumes (beans), whole grains, winter squash, and sweet potatoes. Starchy vegetables, such as potatoes, corn, lima beans, green peas, white pastas, and white breads, should be eaten in small amounts. Broccoli, spinach, summer squash, green beans, carrots, and bell peppers are examples of non-starchy vegetables that should be eaten in abundance.

A self-served salad bar with a variety of fresh fruits and vegetables is essential. Dark leaf lettuces, raw spinach, and other leafy greens are more healthy choices than iceberg lettuce. Look for low calorie raw vegetables, such as celery; onions; carrots; radishes; cauliflower; green, red, yellow, and orange bell peppers; and broccoli.

HEALTHY DIET			
Protein	Fats	Carbohydrates	
	Unsaturated	Complex	Salad Bar Items
• meats • poultry • fish • eggs • cheese • soy	• olive oil • canola oil • avocados • nuts • seeds • olives	• legumes (beans) • whole grains (oats, wheat, brown rice) • winter squash • sweet potatoes	• green leafy vegetables (spinach, kale, dark green lettuces) • broccoli • bell peppers (red, orange, yellow, green) • summer squash • carrots • green beans • onions • radishes • cauliflower • fresh fruits

Figure 6-1

Avocados, nuts, seeds, and olives will deliver essential fatty acids. Canola and olive oils in salad dressings are also good sources of these necessary nutrients. Whole grains, nuts, and seeds in breads, cereals, and salads add fiber, vitamins, minerals, and other nutrients. Dishes with mayonnaise (potato salad, macaroni salad, and cole slaw) should be eaten sparingly, as mayonnaise contains saturated fat.

Meal Plans

Most FSRCs include one meal per person per day in the monthly fee. More progressive communities offer a meal plan of 15-30 meals per person per month in the monthly fee. Uneaten meals almost always carry over to the next week, but not usually to the next month.

Other communities offer a meal allowance. When residents eat in the dining room, the cost of the food is charged against the meal plan. The prices are on the menu, just as in a restaurant. In most communities, any extra money left on the monthly allowance cannot be carried over to the next month.

Food Costs

Competent managers keep track of the costs of everything in the community. Food is tracked by the **raw-food-per-plate cost**; it drives the decisions on what can be offered on the menu and how often. The difference of 25¢ or 30¢ can mean the difference between having steak and shrimp once in a while or not having it at all. Adding another $1.50 or so per plate allows steak and shrimp to be offered daily.

A comparison of this figure against the menu offerings at several FSRCs will be quite revealing. The chief executive officer (CEO) probably knows the raw-food-per-plate cost off the top of his head. Sometimes this figure will be quoted as a raw-food cost per **person** per **day**; sometimes it includes the continental breakfast, and other times it is the sum of the noon and evening meals. Studying the cost per **plate** per **person** (per **meal**) allows you to compare apples with apples.

Extra Meals

The expense of adding extra meals should be affordable to residents. Their health depends on it, which ultimately affects the FSRC's coffers. Virtually all FSRCs charge extra for adding the other two meals daily. The amount of that extra charge varies widely from community to community. Regardless of how expensive or inexpensive the community is, some charge what one might pay in a moderately priced to an expensive restaurant to add one extra meal. Other FSRCs charge less than the price of a meal at a fast food restaurant or approximately the cost of the raw food per **plate** plus about 15-20%.

Making additional meals available at the lowest possible cost furthers the FSRC's mission of aiding residents in achieving optimal health. Making these meals affordable is not a lost source of income to the community, but, arguably, a reduction in long-term healthcare expenses, particularly in a life care community (page 136).

Exercise

The risk of falls among seniors is high. Much of the risk lies in lack of balance, flexibility, and strength of core muscles. Most communities offer *Tai Chi* or other similar balance classes. Yoga stretches muscles and tendons, improving the range of motion. Pilates exercises strengthen core muscles that control posture. They all reduce the risk of falling.

Aerobic activities, such as dance classes and walking and hiking groups, aid residents in maintaining a healthy weight and exercising the heart and lungs. Weight-bearing exercise helps prevent osteoporosis. When walking measured routes, benches along halls and trails make it easier to participate.

A fitness room with strength training equipment is essential. Using the machines correctly requires the supervision of a trainer. Air pressure, rather than lead weights, for resistance is more senior friendly.

Water aerobics is kind to joints and muscles. A whirlpool soothes the body after exercise and promotes muscle relaxation and good blood circulation.

The Grounds

Our environment can subtly undermine or improve our physical condition. Some environments might limit our exercising outside. A nearby park allows residents to walk on natural terrain, instead of concrete.

Hilly terrain helps to stretch both tendons and muscles. That flexibility aids in maintaining a wider range of motion of our feet and ankles, in building strength in our leg muscles, and in improving our balance.

We have proprioceptor nerves that automatically and unconsciously correct our balance when we step on rough terrain. Walking on paved or indoor surfaces all the time causes many of these nerves to atrophy or die. This is another use-it-or-lose-it situation. We need to continue to walk on uneven surfaces in order to keep these nerves in prime condition and greatly reduce the risk of falling. Walking on sand, gravel, and small surface tree roots helps keep these nerves healthy. In checking out FSRCs, look for nearby trails with natural terrain that are accessible and safe.

Some FSRCs boast of all covered or indoor walkways as a means of getting around the campus. When the weather is bad, this is, of course, wonderful. However, our bodies need exposure each day to the sun and fresh air. The sun is our natural source of vitamin D, which is essential in the utilization of calcium in building bones, among other things. Fresh air is loaded with negative ions that relax us and boost our spirits.

MENTAL HEALTH

Keeping mentally alert will help everyone feel younger. There are many functions that the mind can do; so, there are many ways to keep it sharp.

Creative Activities

Creative endeavors exercise the mind and feed the soul. Whether you make music or art or just enjoy them, everyone benefits at least some from creativity. By trying your hand at the arts, you might find that you are the next Grandma Moses! If you are shy about trying to create music or art yourself, enjoy the efforts of others by attending music and art appreciation events. Almost everyone loves the movies.

Each time we learn something new we grow more brain synapses and, thus, contribute to our increased mental acuity. Retirement years do not have to be all about deterioration.

Stop to smell the flowers. Better yet, try your hand at growing the flowers or learning how to arrange them. Look for activities centering around ceramics, sewing, stitching, and crafts. Woodworking and stained glass are creative hobbies.

The list is endless. Figure out what appeals to you and look for it in an FSRC. Keep in mind that you should have the option of starting your own activity.

Intellectual Activities

Use it or lose it applies to our intellect as well as to our bodies. Our brains are capable of all sorts of functions. Among them are mathematical calculations, strategy, analysis, recall, and control of the body. From what we have read, playing bridge requires using more of these functions than any other single activity. But there are other ways to keep our brains alert. FSRCs make many of them available.

Classes in a myriad of subjects can be taught in the community's classrooms by resident volunteers, visiting professors, and hired lecturers. Discussion groups can toss about topics, such as health care, current events, politics, ethical issues, philosophical theories, books, and so on. Libraries help prepare you for classes and these discussion groups, in addition to broadening your horizons. Investment clubs can even teach you how to make money in the stock market.

Using computers employs many different skills and creates new ones. Make greeting cards or write a best-selling novel. Open the door to the whole world through the Internet. Learn to e-mail photos to family and friends. Develop an informed opinion on legal regulation of the Internet.

EMOTIONAL HEALTH

Part of wellness is emotional health. Being able to understand and express our feelings in a socially acceptable manner is at the center of our emotional well being.

Many residents of FSRCs form support groups, which become an outlet for difficult thoughts. Some are self-guided; some are run by professionals. A few of the topics that they cover are grief, weight control, smoking, and alcohol consumption.

Residents in independent living (IL) quickly form friendships that actually become emotional support groups. This is most true for women.

SPIRITUAL HEALTH

It is through spiritual activities that we find meaning and purpose to our lives. Our spirits are fed from many sources. Creative endeavors, as mentioned above, are just one. Others include a positive outlook on life, uplifting surroundings, and religion.

A sour attitude is hard to maintain when you are greeted every day by a naturally cheery staff and positive residents. Find evidence of this in your visits to FSRCs by listening for spirited chatter and laughter in the dining room and in the common areas. Also, look for well-attended activities.

Religion

Religion feeds the souls of many, whether it is through organized institutions or not. Even if you do not participate, you might find that being surrounded by those who do will bring more loving, caring people into your life. A full time chaplain will minister to the residents in many ways, not just during on-site church or vespers services. Bible studies bring peace and support to many.

SOCIAL HEALTH

Of those who choose to stay in their own homes, as discussed in Chapter 1, loneliness and depression can be serious problems among seniors. Once they become unable to drive, they depend on others and simply do not get out enough. When their friends also become housebound, social interaction slows or even stops. The elderly sometimes become prisoners in their own houses.

FSRCs are designed to encourage friendships. The welcoming committee usually greets each new resident. The communities often publish short biographies and photos of new residents in their newsletters or post them on bulletin boards.

Town meetings get the residents together to discuss issues of common interest. When the residents run activities, through the activities director, there is a cohesiveness and comradery to the resident body that we have not seen in FSRCs where only the activities director runs things or there is no activities director.

Informal gatherings are made easier when there are sitting areas throughout, both indoors and outdoors. When a host or hostess seats residents in the dining room, a policy to have no assigned seats and to fill each table encourages new friendships. Some communities set up a large table where residents who wish to meet others may sit.

VOCATIONAL HEALTH

We all need a sense that we have made a contribution of our knowledge, skills, and abilities to society in general and, perhaps more important, to our local area. Before retirement, this satisfaction was gained through careers, jobs, caring for a family, and volunteer work.

Opportunities for volunteer work abound both within the community and in the local area. Willing hands are needed at the Red Cross, hospitals, and other medical institutions. Consultants in business fields are sought by the Small Business Development Center (sponsored by the Small Business Administration) and the Chamber of Commerce.

Part time jobs might be had in the local area. Adjunct faculty and tutors are welcomed by students.

Fund raising for the FSRC's benevolence fund is often achieved through a bazaar that sells the handicrafts of residents. Skilled nursing always needs people to read to residents or run errands for them. Those who play an instrument are always urged to entertain all.

Living in an FSRC brings many opportunities to fill one's life with meaningful activity. It will give you the time and energy to do the things that you really want to do.

PERSONAL CARE

Once residents can no longer perform a minimum number of the daily tasks of caring for themselves (Activities of Daily Living, page 24), personal care is available. Here, the community assumes the responsibility for that care in addition to the health care the resident has received in independent living.

HOME HEALTH CARE

Residents who need help with the Activities of Daily Living need personal care. How many of these activities they need help with is relevant to the decision to move from one level of living to another. When they need help with just one or two of the Activities of Daily Living, home health care (HHC) might be an option.

HHC: Services

Home health caregivers go to the residents' homes in independent living (IL) and provide needed assistance. Residents pay an extra fee for these services.

Home health care is not available at all communities. Many administrators have had unfavorable experiences in trying to convince residents to move into assisted living, once home health care is in place. The residents become attached to this care in their independent living homes.

While none of us wants to admit that we are less capable than we once were and no one looks forward to moving into assisted living (AL) or skilled nursing (SN), it is a reality for some. These two sections of the community are designed to serve residents better than home health care. Receiving the care one needs in the most advantageous setting improves the quality of life.

From a business standpoint, keeping people in independent living beyond their abilities to care for themselves reduces the turnover of these homes and, thus, slows the influx of new money that is needed to maintain the FSRC. In addition, the marketing department has a harder time selling the independent portion of the community as a place for active, vibrant, and youthful seniors.

When home health care is offered, there are three ways to do it. 1) The community might contract with a home health care agency that will, for a fee, deliver services to residents in their homes. 2) The residents might contract the care on their own. 3) Some FSRCs provide the service themselves. There are pros and cons to all three models of home health care. See Figure 6-2.

In your evaluation of FSRCs, remember there are two sides to home health care: the resident's and the community's. A community that does not offer home health care is not necessarily shortchanging the residents.

HHC: Activities

Residents receiving home health care should be able to participate in activities in the independent living community center. Only their abilities should limit them.

HOME HEALTH CARE		
Provider	**Pros**	**Cons**
Home health agency	• interviewed by FSRC • prices negotiated by FSRC • liability of having caregivers in residents' homes assumed by FSRC, possibly • quality ensured by FSRC, possibly • bonded caregivers • attendance of caregiver assured • varying range of services • skilled care more likely, which is paid by Medicare	• agency chosen by FSRC • percentage to FSRC • services & fees controlled too much by FSRC • skilled care more expensive • reduced turnover of IL homes • IL could turn into AL
Individual privately retained by resident	• broad choice of agency/caregiver • terms more negotiable, maybe beating the price of FSRC • more control to resident • varying range of services	• difficulty in hiring & supervising staff when resident is ill • varying quality of services • poor attendance of caregiver • caregivers not bonded or insured • caregivers who quit without notice • reduced turnover of IL homes • IL could turn into AL
FSRC's employees	• known provider • substitution easier for caregiver who doesn't show up • screened employees • insured caregivers • more flexible scheduling minimum hours	• expensive because employees receive better benefits, as a rule • narrower range of services • skilled services less likely • Medicare reimbursements unlikely unless skilled care • reduced turnover of IL homes • IL could turn into AL

Figure 6-2

HHC: Meals

Tray service should be available for residents who are not able to go to the independent living dining room. Sometimes an extra fee is charged for this service. Knowing how many residents receive tray service on a *regular basis* will give you a clue as to whether the community might be turning into an assisted living/skilled nursing facility.

ASSISTED LIVING

Assisted living (AL) is the area of the community where residents can get the help they need taking care of themselves in the Activities of Daily Living (Figure 6-3). A permanent move to assisted living should be as seamless as possible, with very little trauma to the resident. Assisted living homes that look like independent living would accomplish this goal more easily.

PERSONAL CARE	
Activities of Daily Living (Physical Impairments)	Instrumental Activities of Daily Living (Cognitive Impairments)
• getting in/out of bed & chairs • using the toilet (continence) • bathing • dressing • eating • getting around inside the house	• housekeeping • shopping • meal planning & preparation • using the phone • making & keeping appointments • taking medications as prescribed • balancing a checkbook • getting around outside the house

Figure 6-3

AL: Services

Delivery of personal care is probably the single most important service provided in assisted living, as defined in Figure 6-3. By law, the staff can offer no medical care, although they may dispense medications.

Flat linen laundry is done for residents. Personal laundry service is most often provided, although, some communities offer residents the facilities to wash their own clothes if they wish. Housekeeping, maintenance, and all of the other services provided in independent living are available in assisted living.

As you tour, observe the treatment the residents are receiving from the staff. Watch the interactions among the employees. It is essential that you see attentive, friendly, cheerful people giving kind, compassionate care.

AL: Activities

Life should continue much like it did before the transition to assisted living. **If residents are able,** they should be allowed to get on the bus and go shopping, play bridge in the community center, or soak in the hot tub. In no way should a community restrict the activities of assisted living residents, just because they are in assisted living. What residents do each day should be restricted only by each person's limitations and not by blanket rules for the convenience of the staff or management.

Nola's medical condition made it difficult for her to cook, dress herself, and take her medications, but once she had help with these activities, she was raring to go! She played cards with the girls, took the community's bus to the mall for shopping and the movies, and generally led life as she did before she moved into assisted living.

For residents who are not so mobile as Nola, the activities within the community should still be available to those in assisted living. The calendar should be full of a variety of imaginative activities.

On your tour, look for good attendance at the events. Check for activity in the common areas.

Please note that many FSRCs are so successful in keeping residents in independent living for such a long time that, by the time they get to assisted living, they really are not able to continue many, if any, of their activities in independent living.

AL: Meals

IF the residents are capable of feeding themselves neatly and interacting with decorum, they should be allowed to continue eating in the independent living dining room with their spouses and/or friends, **IF** they so choose. Some assisted living residents need only the type of help that does not affect their abilities to interact with independent living residents. For these residents, being confined with those more frail could be demoralizing.

Virtually all assisted living areas serve three meals daily in a dining room. Tray service is available, also. The meals served in assisted living should be from the same menus as in independent living. They should be hot and not taste rewarmed and dried out. Placing assisted living close to the kitchen helps with this. Often, there will be a finishing kitchen in assisted living. The food is sent in large insulated containers from the main kitchen and served onto plates in the finishing kitchen. Presentation is important. The plates should look as appetizing here as in independent living. The dining room should look cozy, warm, and inviting.

Many residents who are able want to cook, if they have kitchens. No matter what kind of kitchen the assisted living homes are equipped with, the management and nursing staff often will adapt the surroundings to suit the skills and needs of the resident. For instance, Ruth had a stroke; handling sharp knives and hot things were difficult and, therefore, dangerous for her. The stove and the microwave oven were disconnected. With her consent, sharp knives and the coffee pot were removed from her assisted living home.

In another instance, when Lou needed help with medications, dressing, and cooking, he moved into assisted living. Yet he is able to take the community's bus and go to the grocery store. Even though his FSRC provides three meals daily, he likes to enjoy a bowl of puffed rice for breakfast in his pajamas. His favorite sandwich, salami and provolone on pumpernickel bread, is not on the FSRC's menu. Having the freedom to shop for groceries and the kitchen space to fix these simple meals makes him feel more independent.

MEDICAL CARE

Should residents need medical care, skilled nursing (SN) is standing by. It also provides health care and personal care. Those afflicted with Alzheimer's/dementia (A/D), especially in its later stages, can get the help they need at many, but not all, FSRCs.

SKILLED NURSING

Nursing facilities are the second most regulated industry in this country, behind nuclear energy. The good people running them work hard to comply with all of the regulations from the federal, state, and local governments; yet, some do better than others. As you tour, look for sparks of life in the residents here as in other areas of the community. The question section of this book will help you with this (page 231).

SN: Services

Registered nurses (RNs) and a staff of nurses' aides provide the medical care residents need. Sometimes the law limits what kinds of medical care can be given outside a hospital. The equipment and the FSRC's budget also dictate how extensive the care can be.

Skilled nursing provides medical care on both a short- and long-term basis. It is usually divided into two levels: skilled nursing and intermediate care. As a rough rule of thumb, residents needing skilled care are usually bedridden; residents receiving intermediate care are commonly more mobile.

Some skilled nursing areas provide a higher, third level of medical care, called subacute care. It is designed to treat medical conditions that are expected to improve. This temporary care is more hospital-like than traditional nursing homes. Subacute care generally involves a medical team of doctors, nurses, and therapists and is often administered following surgery or some other hospital stay.

Doctors often hold office hours in the skilled nursing area. Communities that offer more extensive services will house rehabilitation equipment and offer many therapeutic treatments for residents. The cost for this treatment is charged to the residents' medical insurance companies.

SN: Statistics

The level of care that is given is reflected by a statistic called the nursing hours per patient per day (NHPPD). Keeping track by this method is federally mandated, but each state sets the minimum number of hours a community must meet. Hopefully, FSRCs are at least meeting, if not exceeding, this level. The CEO should know or be able to get from his staff the state requirement and his own compliance figures.

This number is not just an indication of how good the care is; it also tells how sick most of the residents are. Skilled nursing can give excellent care with fewer staff if they do not have a high number of acutely ill residents.

The ratio of staff to residents tells the story of how much care is given. This is an older style of keeping track, but many communities still use it. The number of nurse managers, registered nurses (RNs), and licensed practical nurses (LPNs) can make a difference in the quality of medical care.

Many states have laws that dictate the minimum number of residents per staff in skilled nursing. The CEO will know what the state requirement is and what numbers his community strives for. Many FSRCs do much better than the state minimum.

The number that really affects the quality of life day in and day out is the number of residents per certified nursing assistant (CNA). With a ratio of 8:1 on the day shift, residents will get more attention than with a ratio of 20:1. Numbers do not tell the whole story; how debilitated the residents are also affects how the attention is divided.

During your tour of the skilled nursing portion of the FSRCs, you can observe much. Look for cheerful staff members who treat the residents and co-workers kindly.

SN: Activities

How busy and active residents can be should be defined only by their capabilities and not house rules. An activities director should keep the calendar full of interesting things to do. Look for imaginative pursuits, as well as the much-loved bingo and card games. An exercise program is also important. Check for good participation levels, as well.

SN: Meals

IF the residents are capable of eating in a sociably acceptable manner, they should be welcome in the independent living dining room, **IF** they so choose. As in assisted living, this is highly dependent upon the residents' conditions.

The dining room itself is a nicer place to be when its decor is warm and cozy and not like an institution. The menu should be the same in skilled nursing as it is in independent living. While there might be other qualifying variables, we observed that skilled nursing residents who were served the same menu as independent living residents were noticeably more alert than others.

Menus should not consist of doughnuts for breakfast, hot dogs and potato chips for lunch, and fried fish sticks and French fries for dinner, as we saw in one FSRC's skilled nursing section. Omitted from that menu were sufficient protein, fruits, and vegetables. Naturally, special diets are available for residents who need them, as they should be throughout the community.

The food should be hot and not rewarmed or dried out. Each meal should look as pleasing and inviting as it does in the independent living dining room.

Hopefully, skilled nursing is close to the kitchen. A finishing kitchen will aid in achieving the goal of fresh meals. It is here that you can see if plates are being served from large insulated containers. Some communities will have a separate kitchen for assisted living and skilled nursing.

ALZHEIMER'S/DEMENTIA

Not all communities have the capabilities to care for residents with Alzheimer's/dementia (A/D). For those that do offer this level of care, it is comforting to know that help is nearby. Some residents with dementia often live with their spouses during the early stages of the disease. Eventually, there comes a time when these residents need more care.

A/D: Services

As dementia progresses, patients forget how to do things. Those in the middle stages of Alzheimer's/dementia need more care than an elderly spouse can give; they need assisted living. In the later stages, medical care is likely to be required. This situation is further complicated by other diseases.

Because wandering is a common symptom of dementia, these residents must be contained for their own safety. It is not fair to others who live in assisted living to be locked into their own homes; a separate wing should be reserved for those with dementia.

Residents in the later stages of dementia will need an environment where they can express themselves freely and still get medical care. Other residents of skilled nursing should not be subjected to the intrusive behavior and noise that sometimes accompanies dementia.

The community should ideally have separate wings for dementia residents who need assisted living (AL) and for those who need skilled nursing (SN). Others mingle all of the memory support residents together.

A/D: Activities

Activities for dementia residents are different from those other residents find entertaining. Exercises and games are used to keep memories fresh about common items in the house, history, the weather, sports, and jobs, for example.

A/D: Meals

When there is a separate residential area for Alzheimer's/dementia residents, they have their own dining room. The menu should be the same as in the independent living dining room, barring medical conditions that make eating these foods difficult.

❧❧❧

This chapter has given you an overview of the care that a full service retirement community delivers to its residents. The next chapter will discuss legal forms of occupancy, their ramifications, and costs involved in living in a full service retirement community.

7

OCCUPANCY OPTIONS
AND FEES

Mere parsimony is not economy. . . .
Expense, and great expense,
may be an essential part of true economy.

—Edmund Burke
British Statesman, 1729-1797

Virtually every full service retirement community (FSRC), also known as a continuing care retirement community (CCRC), has an up-front fee to get in. Then, after moving in, all communities charge a monthly fee. All have some entrance requirements such as age and health. With the exception of rentals, an entry fee buys your housing for the rest of your life.

There are three legal forms of occupancy. The endowment community is by far the most common. Lease communities are the second most common. A new form, the equity community, is just beginning to gain popularity.

In endowment communities, the entrance fee buys the right to live in a home and a bonus, its perpetual upkeep. In equity communities, you buy either a home or a lifelong contract, which allows you to live there. In lease (rental) communities, residents do not buy a lifetime contract up front. Instead they sign a lease (a contract) for varying time spans and pay rent monthly.

The entry fee in lease communities—if there is one—is usually less than $15,000. Their monthly fees are the highest of all of the occupancy options.

The entrance fees for endowment FSRCs start at well under $50,000 and go up to a million or more dollars, with most falling between $100,000 and $300,000. The range of purchase prices for equity communities starts higher than endowment.

The monthly fees are in a much narrower range. Of course, the more services that are offered, the higher the monthly costs. The price of providing similar services seems to be fairly close from community to community, but another variable could be location, namely, oceanfront, lakeside, resort areas, exclusive neighborhoods, and so on. Higher overhead raises fees at all levels.

Nearly all endowment communities charge a second person entry fee of roughly 10%. Virtually all equity communities do not add a second person fee to the entry fee. All FSRCs add an additional amount to the monthly fee for the second person.

OCCUPANCY OPTIONS

Basically, residents "buy into," buy outright, or rent their homes. The occupancy programs fall into three groups respectively: endowment, equity, and lease. See Figure 7-1. The subcategories of these options are listed in Figure 7-2. They are discussed in more detail below. These different occupancy forms carry varying types of property interests or no property interests at all.

OCCUPANCY OPTIONS		
Type	**Pros**	**Cons**
Endowment ("buy ins")	• mutual commitment between management & residents • benevolence fund possible • possible refundable entry fee • financial security	• high entry fee • may not finance entry fee • decision sometimes irrevocable • covenants
Equity (buy outright)	• resalable • gain equity • tax benefits • may finance entry fee • may invest monies that would have been spent for entrance fee in endowment community	• high purchase price • deed conditions, covenants, & restrictions (CC&Rs) • benevolence fund unlikely • limited resale options • high transfer fees • problems typical of condo/homeowners' association • might share majority of appreciation with management and/or lender
Lease (rentals)	• no or low entry fee • easy to withdraw from community	• lack of commitment by both parties • no benevolence fund • limited control by residents over management

Figure 7-1

ENDOWMENT COMMUNITIES

Endowment (EN) communities are by far the most common form of FSRCs. More often than not, they are true *continuing care* retirement communities (CCRCs), in that they offer three or more levels of care, and are almost always nonprofit. See page 29.

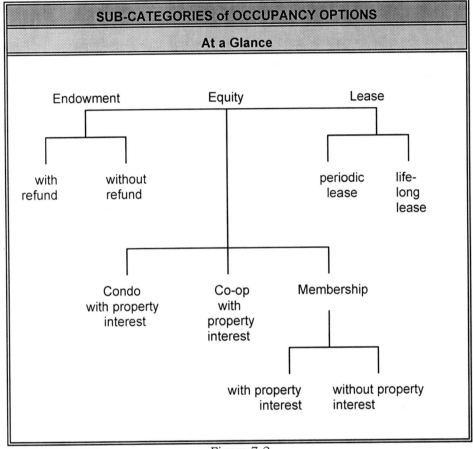

Figure 7-2

EN: Occupancy

Residents are buying a contract that allows them to live in the community for the rest of their lives. They have a right to use all of the common areas. No interest in real property accompanies this transaction.

EN: Waiting Lists

For those communities whose occupancy levels are high or for individuals who want to apply well before they are ready to move in, waiting lists are usually available. Many communities offer two lists.

Both require the signing of a contract that is exclusively for the waiting lists.

The first list requires, roughly, a 1% deposit. It is usually $1000 to $3000 per home, not per person. Rarely will the deposit be charged per person when two people will share a home. This payment will seldom, if ever, lock in the price, protecting it from future raises.

Once you are ready to move in, you may place your name on the ready list (the second list). This might protect you from price increases—maybe not.

When the residence of your choice becomes available and your name is at the top of that list, you will be asked to pay another deposit, most commonly 10%. You will be expected to move in within ninety days or so once you are offered a home. It is during this period that you will usually be asked to take the physical, sign the rest of the paperwork, and pay the rest of the entrance fee.

Other communities have only one waiting list or one list per type of floor plan. Once your name is at the top of the list, you may accept or refuse the offer. Many decline because, for whatever reason, they are not ready to move. Some communities will allow their names to stay at the top of the list, no matter how many times they turn it down. Others, after one to three refusals, will put their names at the bottom of the list. This inflexibility is an indication for concern and you should look further for other inequitable policies in that community. Some FSRCs will allow prospective residents to request when to start calling them, thus allowing their names to stay at the top of the list until they are ready to move in.

The deposits are usually refundable if the prospective resident cancels the contract. However, many FSRCs retain a processing or application fee. An exception might be made if the resident cancels due to illness or some other serious situation. If the community cancels the waiting list contract, virtually all communities refund all of your money. See Figure 7-3. The applicant might or might not receive the interest on the deposit. If you move in, all deposits and sometimes the accrued interest will be applied to your entrance fee.

EN: Fees

All endowment communities require a large sum up front and a monthly fee. These fees vary widely. The degree of luxury, location,

REFUND of DEPOSITS BEFORE MOVING IN	
At a Glance	
Cancellation by the potential resident	• 96 to 100% refund, mostly depending on policy & state law • sometimes with interest • if new construction, financial penalties on cancellation likely • refund might be delayed until the next depositor places his deposit
Cancellation by the community	• usually 100% refund • sometimes with interest

Figure 7-3

size of the homes, and the number of services provided usually affect the price the most. Choice locations, such as oceanfront, might also drive the price up. Homes with a view, higher floors, or private lots within a community might have a premium added to their entry fees.

Entrance fees and monthly fees for life care (LC) communities are higher than for the fee-for-service (FFS) communities. See the discussion about monthly fees beginning on page 136. In an endowment community, the entrance fee is tantamount to paying rent in advance, although it is technically neither rent nor a house payment and could, perhaps, be refundable. (See below.)

EN: Fees: Non-Refundable Entrance Fee

The non-refundable fee is the traditional payment plan of the endowment community; it requires one fixed entrance fee that is payable up front. Just because it is the oldest or seemingly inflexible does not mean that it is not a suitable arrangement for you. It is the cheapest way into an endowment community. It might or might not be the cheapest in the long run. Your age, health, and finances all play important roles in coming to a decision. Your financial planner can advise you.

EN: Fees: Variable Entrance Fees

Now that FSRCs have become more competitive, they provide more payment options. The variable entry fee offers the choice of lower

113

entrance fees with higher monthly payments or higher entrance fees with lower monthly payments.

VARIABLE ENTRANCE FEE For the Same Home			
FSRC	Plan	Entrance Fee	Monthly Fee
A	1	$121,000	$2100
	2	$148,000	$1800
B	1	$100,000	$3000
	2	$180,000	$2100

Figure 7-4

For instance, choice #1 might offer an entrance fee of $121,000 with a monthly payment of $2100; choice #2 might have a $148,000 entry fee with an $1800 monthly payment for the same home. Your financial planner can advise you as to which would be most advantageous to you. See Figure 7-4.

EN: Fees: Rescission Period

Almost all FSRCs offer a honeymoon period after moving in. During this time, called a rescission period, residents can get all (or almost all) of their money back if they want to move out right way. Most communities keep a small administrative fee (about 4%). The length of this period is sometimes regulated by the states and varies from one week to one year, with thirty days being common.

EN: Fees: Refund on Declining Balance

Most policies allow for the non-refundable entry fees to be returned according to a sliding scale. Residents can get their money back on the declining balance (the norm) for a short period of time. As an example, let's say the fee declines at a rate of 2% per month. Should the residents leave after ten months, they would be entitled to a refund of 80% of the entry fee. The community would keep 2% per month for every month residents lived there or 20%. If the community is one that keeps a 4% administrative fee, residents would recoup 76% in all.

Had the residents used any of the personal or medical care services, some communities could withhold enough money to cover those costs as well. When residents move out of either life care or fee-for-service communities, the FSRC could charge them the difference between what they paid for the medical services and the market rate.

EN: Fees: Refund Plans

The refund plan was created to make endowment communities more competitive and to appeal to the segment of the population that balks at the non-refundable fee. Its purpose is to allow residents to preserve their estates for loved ones.

Communities have formulated a wide variety of refund plans. At first blush, having some or all of the entrance fee refundable takes the sting out of sticker shock. Only reading the fine print carefully will tell you the whole story.

Some communities offer one or more partial refund plans, while a few will give a "full" refund (less a 4-10% administrative fee—really a 90-96% refund) at anytime. Refund plans have a higher entry fee. Once in a while, the monthly fee will also be higher with a refund plan. Figure 7-5 gives you a quick glance at how much more the refunds are likely to cost. Figure 7-6 shows the most common types of refunds, and Figure 7-7 gives examples of the same plans in dollar figures.

Both the partially and fully refundable entry fee plans refer, as a rule, to the first person entry fee only. The second person entry fees are usually not eligible for partial or full refunds. They are most commonly subject to the same kind of return of monies as the non-refundable entry fees, which is ordinarily 2% per month on the declining balance.

A refundable entrance fee means that residents could, in some cases, leave the community at any time, if they wish. **Some refunds are payable only to the residents' estates and NOT on moving out.**

Refund plans might not necessarily be the good deal that they appear to be on the surface. Many factors must be considered, such as your age, health condition, and personal financial situation.

If you were to live in an endowment FSRC for, say, twenty years, you or your estate might not receive the actual amount of the refund you anticipated when all things are considered. Evaluate taxes on imputed interest (page 119) along with the loss of deductibility of fees, higher entry fee, inflation, and lost investment growth. In some cases, it might be cheaper over time to pay a lesser, non-refundable entrance fee. The younger you are at move in, the less of a deal the refund plan might be for you. Also, and sometimes most important, the details of the refund alone could drive your decision. An accountant or financial planner can help you weigh the alternatives.

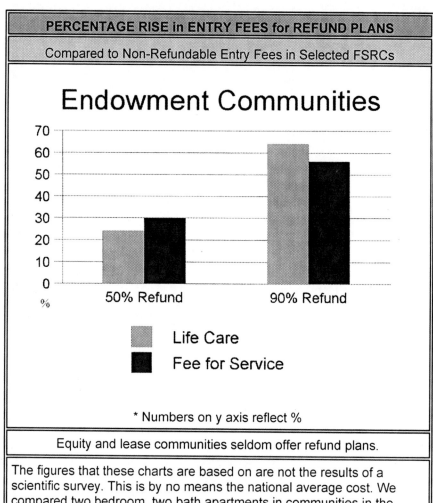

Figure 7-5

Refundable fees are not likely to be found in for-profit communities. Such a payment constitutes income to the community in the year in which it was received. This could have large income tax consequences for them.

If equity communities do refund all or part of certain monies, the payment is most often called a deposit, but entrance fees (called purchase prices in equity communities) are not refundable.

COMMON REFUNDS PLANS of ENTRANCE FEES			
Endowment Communities Only			
During rescission period	• 96-100% • usually 30 days, sometimes several months to a year		
Non-refundable plan	• on the declining balance • less admin. fee	1% per mo. (best) or 2% per mo. (good) or 4% for first 5 mos., then 2% per mo. or faster (poor)	• refund might be delayed until home is sold • some refunds available on moving out; others payable only to resident's estate • on move out, possible deduction at market rate for health care services utilized
Partially refundable plan	• 30%-85%	• subject to declining balance refund up to the point of the refund • refund might be delayed until home is resold • increased entry fee • some refunds available on moving out; others payable only to resident's estate • shorter rescission period, relative to · amount of refund • possible deduction at market rate on move out for health care services utilized	
"Fully" refundable plan	• 100% with no admin. fee (rare) • 90-96%		

Figure 7-6

EXAMPLES of REFUND PLANS Endowment Communities Only					
$150,000 Entrance Fee At a Glance					
During rescission period	100%, but sometimes 4% admin. fee	$144,000 to $150,000			
Non-refundable plan		after 6 mos.	after 12 mos.	after 48 mos.	after 100 mos.
	less 1% per mo. & 4% admin. fee	$135,000	$126,000	$72,000	0 (after 96 mos.)
	less 2% per mo. & 4% admin. fee	126,000	108,000	0	0
	less 4% per mo. for first 5 mo., then 2% per mo. & 4% admin. fee	111,000	93,000	0 (after 43 mos.)	0
Partially refundable plan	50% refundable fee, declining at 1% per mo.	141,000	132,000	78,000	75,000 (after 50 mos.)
	85% refundable fee, declining at 1% per mo.	141,000	132,000	127,500 (after 15 mos.)	127,500
"Fully" refundable plan	90% refundable fee, declining at 1% per mo.	141,000	135,000 (after 10 mos.)	135,000	135,000
	96% refundable fee, declining at 1% per mo.	144,000 (after 4 mos.)	144,000	144,000	144,000

Figure 7-7

Lease communities have no refundable entry fees. However, what you pay up front might be called a deposit and could, under certain circumstances, be refunded.

EN: Taxes

Residents of FSRCs face different tax situations from those of owners of real property. Those who live in endowment communities are in unique positions.

EN: Taxes: Tax Deductions

One of the perks of owning your own home is the fact that the mortgage is almost always tax deductible. A tax break might not be lost. The IRS rules are different for life care communities than they are for fee-for-service communities (page 140). Whether the entrance fee is refundable also affects taxes.

Built into the life care monthly fees for independent living are charges for prepaid long-term care insurance premiums. These portions of the payments might be deductible as prepaid medical expenses once you exceed the required percentage of nondeductible medical costs on your federal income tax return. For example, if the community is life care (page 136) and the entrance fee is not refundable, that entrance fee might be partially deductible from your federal tax return as a prepaid medical expense in the year you enter the community. The same could be true for a percentage of the monthly fees.

In fee-for-service communities, a portion of the monthly fees might also be deductible as medical expenses for those who live in the assisted living (AL) or skilled nursing (SN) sections of the community. There is no deduction for prepaid medical expenses in a fee-for-service FSRC.

Refer your accountant or tax attorney to IRS Revenue Rulings 76-185, 75-302, 76-106, and 76-481. A number of Private Letter Rulings have also addressed this subject.

EN: Taxes: Imputed Interest

For communities that offer a refundable entrance fee, there might be taxes to pay on imputed interest. It works this way: The IRS could consider the entry fee that you have paid to the community to be a loan. Usually the entrance fee earns no interest for the resident. The IRS then figures that you could have invested the money somewhere else—somewhere where the money would have drawn interest at the market rate. That interest would have then been taxable to you as income. Now the IRS thinks that it has lost taxes and it might come after you for the taxes on the income that you voluntarily denied yourself.

Not all refundable entrance fees are subject to taxes on imputed interest. The residents can be subjected to these taxes if their FSRC meets several of the enumerated criteria in the law. There might be an exemption for the first so many dollars of the entrance fee. The IRS resets the interest rate and an exemption level every year. Historically, the exemption level has risen every year. At its current level, moderately priced communities are almost free of imputed taxes.

There are other considerations as well. The marketing representative should have a tax letter that will tell you more about the situation for that community. Section 7872 of the Internal Revenue Code will be helpful to your accountant.

EN: Taxes: Capital Gains

When we sell our houses, some of us must pay capital gains taxes on the appreciation of our present primary residence if the amount of the gain exceeds a certain limit. The occupancy option you select could cause your deferment of capital gains taxes to disappear. Your accountant can advise you on this subject.

EN: Taxes: Real Estate

Residents of endowment and lease communities are not liable for real estate taxes. A portion of the residents' monthly fees, however, includes a prorated share of the community's real estate taxes.

EN: Taxes: Homestead Exemptions

In some states, legislatures have granted some owners of real property homestead exemptions from real property taxes. Holders of real estate titles who meet certain requirements could qualify. Some of these state legislatures have extended this tax deduction to residents of certain full service retirement communities (FSRCs). The marketing representative and your accountant should have more details on this.

EN: Services

In life care communities, as a rule, all of the services are included in the monthly fee except those of doctors and therapists. Fee-for-service communities (page 136) vary as to how many services are included in the monthly rate. For instance, some might show movies and serve popcorn for free, while others will charge a small fee. Some fee-for-service communities will charge for interior maintenance, to ride the bus, and to use party rooms, a storage bin, fitness equipment, and parking spaces. Others only charge extra for the use of assisted living and skilled nursing services.

EN: Management

A board of directors usually comprises citizen volunteers from the local area, many of whom are professionals in the fields of banking, investments, health care, business management, and others. Its members make the major decisions, while administration controls the day-to-day functions of the community. As a rule, the residents have some say in how things are run. Some FSRCs even have residents on the board of directors. A residents' association (or council) advises the board of directors.

EQUITY COMMUNITIES

In equity (EQ) communities, residents purchase a resalable interest in the community. Most commonly, it is a real property interest. When people own this interest, they own the legal right or title to property, which is land and whatever is erected and grown on it. With ownership of any kind of property comes the right to any benefits that accumulate during the ownership period—in particular, the appreciation of its market value (equity).

Ownership also carries the burdens of paying taxes and complying with any laws that govern the property. With land and buildings, this usually means the owner must pay real estate taxes and abide by the laws controlling the owner's use of the land. Tax deductions of certain expenses related to the land (*e.g.*, taxes) might be deductible from the owner's personal income tax obligation. Should the value of the property depreciate, the owner would bear the loss.

The equity communities are the least common of the occupancy options for FSRCs; however, they might experience growth in the coming years because Baby Boomers, as a group, value ownership of their homes.

The options for occupancy in equity communities are the familiar **condominium**, the less common **cooperative**, and relatively unknown **membership** (similar to country clubs or health spas). Figure 7-8 summarizes them. The purchase prices of equity communities are usually the most expensive of all of the occupancy options.

TYPES of EQUITY COMMUNITIES		
Type	**Legal Characteristics**	
Condominium	Residents own separate parts of the whole (their homes) and jointly own parts of the undivided whole (common areas). Residents own property interests. Their homes may be resold.	
Cooperative	A corporation owns the land and buildings. Residents own shares of the corporation that leases the homes and the rights to use the common areas to the shareholders (the residents) of the corporation . Residents own an equity (ownership) interest in a corporation that owns a property interest, yet residents are considered to own a property interest. The shares may be resold.	
Membership	without property interest	Residents own salable memberships that may be resold. Residents lease living spaces and the rights to use the common areas. They own no property interest or equity (ownership) interest.
	with property interest	Residents own their own homes fee simple. They have non-salable memberships in the community, similar to a country club, and the right to use the community center.

Figure 7-8

On resale in a good economy, the resident will recoup his purchase price plus any equity. Deducted from that will be fees (discussed below). The resident may finance his purchase price, leaving the principle invested in growth vehicles. A financial planner or CPA can help you figure out if this model will pay off for you.

Equity communities have been mostly age restricted housing and resort retirement communities without health care—until recently. The full service model is growing rapidly. Communities that are also called **master-planned communities**, **active retirement communities**, and **independent retirement communities**, among others, are usually not FSRCs. However, some are adding health care to their community's services.

Many equity communities are not true FSRCs, but might bill themselves as such. On the other hand, a community that might advertise itself and stress that it is an independent living community could very well offer assisted living (AL) and skilled nursing (SN).

When communities are planned, developers choose the occupancy option(s). Sometimes, the state law is the driving force. For example, one state's law requires less of a financial reserve for membership communities than it does for others. It would be useful to know if this will significantly affect the financial stability of the community in the future. An attorney and/or CPA can serve as a guide as to how this will affect you.

EQ: Condominium Communities

The legal ownership model of the condominium is essentially the same as in non-age-restricted housing. The condominium is the most popular legal form of the equity communities. Many of the features of the endowment community, including services, are offered in the condominium community.

EQ: Condo: Occupancy

In the condo community residents own their homes fee simple. (A fee simple ownership means that the owner retains all the rights to the property and has not relinquished mineral, air, or other rights.) With that fee simple property interest comes an ownership of an undivided portion of the common areas. Residents actually own an interest that can appreciate or depreciate and can be resold.

We often associate the term condominium with apartments, but it is actually a term that describes only the form of legal ownership. It has nothing to do with the shape of the building. A condominium can also be a townhome, a duplex, a single family home, and so on.

As a rule, condos have deed conditions, covenants, and restrictions (CC&Rs) that control, for instance, the outside color of the residents' drapes and whether children and/or pets can live there. In a retirement community, the overall character of the community can be lost without CC&Rs. **When the developer retains some interests, the condominium community as a whole is more likely to succeed as the original concept of a retirement community that offers continuing care.** An attorney can advise you further on this topic.

A few equity communities might qualify as nonprofit entities. Most of them are for-profit corporations.

EQ: Condo: Fees

The building of the project is usually financed with short-term construction loans and residents buy their homes outright. The community, itself, has no mortgage. Because residents actually own part of the real estate, they may mortgage their homes, but must use lenders who specialize in these types of properties. Therefore, should one or more of the owners (residents) default on the loan on his or her home, the whole project will not go bankrupt because the community, as a whole, has no debt.

Each month residents pay a house payment (if they financed the purchase price) and condo fees. The condo association fees include prorated shares of maintenance costs, insurance, taxes, and all other expenses. Failure to pay the house payment on the part of the resident would result in an action against the resident, not against the community. Residents also pay separate fees for services and health care.

EQ: Condo: Resales

Condo communities allow resales by the resident, but the buyers must meet certain conditions, such as age, health (usually in life care [page 136] only), and financial qualifications. Typically, the association does not guarantee to buy the home if it does not sell quickly.

The residents' interests in the condo may be resold for market prices. Of course, should the market price decrease, the residents bear the loss, just as in owning any house fee simple. On the other hand, if the market appreciates, the price will be higher than the original purchase price and the owners will reap the benefit. **Usually, the transaction is handled by the administration of the community and it may charge 10-20% of the original purchase price as a transfer fee from the seller for its services. The community may also retain *up to* 75% of the appreciation from a rise in fair market value (equity).**

EQ: Condo: Taxes

With the purchase price (entry fee) of homes in condo communities come the tax benefits and burdens of home ownership. Residents are obligated to pay property taxes, just as they did in their own homes. They also pay a prorated share of the community's real estate taxes, but these payments should be tax deductible.

The possibility of a tax deduction for prepaid medical expenses and entry and monthly fees (page 119), as in endowment communities, is not usually available to independent living residents of equity communities, even in life care. But those who live in assisted living (AL) and skilled nursing (SN) should enjoy a deduction for medical expenses.

Capital gains taxes from the sale of a primary residence over a certain amount are deferred. The one exception is for residents who enter the community directly into assisted living or skilled nursing. Residents receiving health care may deduct certain fees as medical expenses. Be sure to check with an accountant for specific and up-to-date information relevant to your taxes.

EQ: Condo: Services

The services are sold as a separate package that is almost always a required purchase. Services usually include meals, housekeeping, and transportation, among others. Maintenance of the interior of each home is usually the resident's responsibility.

Health care is sold as another separate package. Communities can offer personal and medical care as life care, modified fee for service, or fee for service (page 136). Some communities might offer a choice of health care packages.

EQ: Condo: Management

All residents belong to the condo association. Normally, a condo is run by a board of directors formed from among the residents. The board manages the community for the association and its actions are tightly controlled by law.

When residents manage an FSRC, conflicts of interest might arise, especially when making decisions to solve problems. These decisions could have a financial or personal impact on the board members and/or fellow residents or give board members too much personal information about their neighbors.

When residents govern, disputes between the board members and the other residents can pit neighbor against neighbor. In an endowment community, the board does not consist of all residents. Any dispute between residents and the board seems to create an us-versus-them attitude, instead of resident versus resident.

Condo associations often hire independent management corporations to manage the day-to-day operations of the community. Some FSRCs find that having management teams who are not owners is preferable.

EQ: Cooperative Communities

The cooperative is another legal form for retirement communities. The services and amenities provided resemble endowment, lease, and other forms of equity communities.

EQ: Co-op: Occupancy

In a co-op community, a corporation owns the land and buildings, as a rule. The co-op residents own a transferable share in the corporation that owns the whole property. Residents then lease their homes and the right to use the common areas from the corporation. Residents are considered to own a real property interest. The document that they sign is called a proprietary lease. It can be renewable monthly or annually, or it might be a lifetime lease.

EQ: Co-op: Fees

An entrance fee purchases shares of stock. Some communities allow this fee to be borrowed. A specialized lender is required.

If residents borrowed the purchase price, they make payments on that loan. They also pay co-op or occupancy fees, which are prorated shares of all expenses. This includes a portion of the mortgage payments and yearly property taxes. They also pay separate fees for services and health care.

A co-op is financed with a long-term mortgage, on which it makes monthly payments. Should one or more of the residents fail to make their payments, the co-op association must absorb the loss temporarily. Eventually fees will go up to recoup any permanent losses. Should the community not enjoy full occupancy, its financial stability might become jeopardized. The note on the long-term mortgage will still be due. Without monthly fees coming in, the community must come up with the money on its own. Assessing residents the shortfall is a common method of raising needed funds.

EQ: Co-op: Resales

Resales are allowed but are restricted to buyers who qualify for age, finances, and maybe health (for life care [page 136] plans). Communities, as a rule, do not guarantee to buy the shares back from the resident. **The community usually handles the sale of the resident's shares and charges a transfer fee of typically 10-20% of the original purchase price. It might also claim a portion of the appreciation earned. This share could be as high as 75%.**

EQ: Co-op: Taxes

Residents might be able to deduct from their income taxes their prorated shares of property taxes and interest paid on the community's mortgage. There are some co-op communities where this tax deduction is not available to residents.

Capital gains taxes may be deferred because residents own a property interest. Once residents sell their co-op shares to move into assisted living (AL) or skilled nursing (SN), the previously deferred capital gains taxes will probably come due. The sales agent should have a written statement on the status of all of the community's tax deductions. Also, it never hurts to check with a knowledgeable CPA.

The tax deduction for prepaid medical expenses is not available to residents of the independent living portion of co-op communities.

EQ: Co-op: Services

Co-op communities also offer varying numbers of services, such as housekeeping, transportation, activities, and meals. Sometimes these packages are a required purchase. However, for their own tax reasons, they must offer them to the residents in a separate package and sell them for a separate fee. The community, as a rule, does not maintain the interiors of the homes.

Health care is usually sold separately, as well. Life care (LC), modified fee for service (MFFS), and true fee for service (FFS) are available. See page 136 for the discussion of these terms.

EQ: Co-op: Management

The co-op is controlled by a resident board of directors. While its management's actions are regulated by law, the board has some flexibility.

As in the condo, a management by residents can pit neighbor against neighbor on hot issues. It also gives board members (residents) more private information about health and/or financial matters than some residents would like their next-door neighbors to know. The board of directors may hire a management corporation to take care of daily affairs.

EQ: Membership Communities

Membership communities are found infrequently. They come with and without a real property interest. The membership may be resold. These offer many of the same services as the endowment communities. Some endowment communities call their entrance fees "membership fees," but they cannot be resold.

EQ: Membership: Occupancy

With a property interest: In this type of membership community, a resident buys a home fee simple at market value. A certain portion of the purchase price, either a set percentage or a fixed amount, must buy a non-transferable membership in the community. This price could be 10-15% or around $15,000 to $30,000. When the house is resold, the non-refundable membership fee is paid again to the community on behalf of the new resident.

Without a property interest: New residents join the community as they would a country club or a health spa. They are buying an intangible personal property interest in a membership that can be resold by the residents at market value. Essentially this is a license to live there and use all common areas.

EQ: Membership: Fees

With a property interest: Owners pay a monthly mortgage payment if the purchase price is financed, a membership fee (similar to residents' association fees), and a homeowners' association fee. The membership fee, in all probability, will include a prorated share of the community's debt and its real estate taxes. The homeowners' association fees pay for the upkeep of common areas around the homes. Residents will also pay service and health care fees.

Without a property interest: An initial entrance or membership fee is paid up front. It may be financed. Residents pay a monthly membership fee. A portion of real estate taxes and payment on the community's debt is most likely rolled into this fee. Service and health care fees are extra.

EQ: Membership: Resales

With a property interest: Owners of fee simple houses may sell them to qualified buyers (as defined by the community) at the going rate. Just as in selling anything else at fair market value, the owner assumes the risk of any depreciation. The transaction is usually handled by an outside real estate agent, who is paid a commission, just as in selling any house. A portion of the sales price is taken by the residents' association as a membership fee, as mentioned above. There might be a transfer fee for its sale.

Without a property interest: The membership can be resold on leaving the independent living home. This transaction is usually handled by the community's staff. The residents bear the risk of a depreciation in the market value of their memberships. Buyers must qualify for age, financial status, and, possibly, health condition. **Residents will then pay transfer fees of 10-20%. All of the equity might go to the resident, but, more likely, it must be split with the community and, possibly, the lender.** (Sometimes the lender will offer the buyer a lower interest rate on a shared-

129

appreciation mortgage in exchange for a percentage of the equity when the house is sold.)

EQ: Membership: Taxes

With a property interest: Owners owe real estate property taxes and are entitled to the tax deductions that accompany that burden. Taxes on capital gains from the sale of a primary residence may be deferred until the house is sold because the resident still owns a property interest. When the resident moves into assisted living (AL) or skilled nursing (SN) on a permanent basis and the house is sold, capital gains taxes usually come due.

The tax deduction for prepaid medical expenses is not available to independent living residents of equity communities. More than likely, the residents' association fee includes a prorated share of the community's debt and real estate tax payments.

Without a property interest: Capital gains taxes from the sale of a primary residence cannot be deferred because the resident owns no real property interest. The community's property taxes are shared among its members, but the liability is ultimately the FSRC's, not each resident's. These taxes could be rolled into the monthly membership fee. They are not tax deductible because the residents own no real estate interest. The entry fee is not eligible for a tax deduction for prepaid medical expenses, nor is the monthly fee paid by independent living residents. Always check with a tax advisor for the latest in tax laws and how they affect you.

EQ: Membership: Services

With a property interest: The standard essential services and health care are usually sold as separate packages. Residents, as a rule, maintain the interior of their own homes.

Without a property interest: As in other equity communities, the services and health care are split into separate packages. The community might or might not maintain the interior of the homes.

EQ: Membership: Management

With a property interest: Residents belong to the homeowners' association, just as they might in a subdivision anywhere. They also belong to a residents' association of the FSRC that advises the community's board of directors, staffed by citizens of the local area.

Without a property interest: Membership communities are the least legally controlled of the equity communities. A board of directors comprises nonresidents. Residents belong to a residents' association, as in the communities with a property interest.

Figure 7-9 provides a summary of the details of equity communities. Note that many equity communities do not have the three levels of care that allow its residents to move seamlessly through them; they are not continuing care retirement communities (CCRCs). However, the discussions about FSRCs will still apply to the levels of living that they do have.

LEASE (RENTALS)

Lease (LE) communities are growing in popularity. While they form an occupancy category of their own, sometimes a rental program exists within an equity or endowment community. Renters in an equity community usually sublet from the resident, not rent from the community as in endowment FSRCs. A few communities are subsidized by the state and federal governments and nonprofit organizations.

Many lease (rental) communities are not really FSRCs; they are merely FSRC look-alikes. They do not always have both assisted living (AL) and skilled nursing (SN) areas.

LE: Occupancy

Rental community leases can be month to month, renewable yearly, or leased for the resident's lifetime. **If the contract is RENEWABLE at the end of A YEAR and ONLY at the DISCRETION of the LANDLORD, the community might not be subject to the laws that govern continuing care retirement communities.** Many of these laws were passed to protect residents. An attorney can advise you as to the ramifications of waiving these rights. This is especially important if you intend to live in a rental community on a long-term basis.

LE: Fees

As a rule, rentals require no up-front fee. In some states, a relatively small entry fee (less than $15,000) is charged in addition to monthly fees. Inquire as to whether this fee is refundable and under what circumstances. Very likely new residents will be asked to pay a security deposit just like renting any apartment. After that, monthly rent is due.

LE: Resales

Residents in lease communities do not own a property interest. Therefore, they do not have the right to resell their homes.

COMPARISON of CHARACTERISTICS Equity Communities				
	Condo	Co-op	Membership	
			w/ real property interest	w/o real property interest
Occupancy	• fee simple • own interest in real property	• own salable share in corp. that owns prop. interest • considered ownership of property interest	• fee simple ownership • own property interest • non-salable membership	• salable membership • own intangible personal property • own no property interest
Payments due monthly	• monthly house pmt (if purchase price financed) • condo assoc. dues • service fee • health care fee	• monthly "house" pmt (if purchase price financed) • occupancy fee • service fee • health care fee	• monthly house pmt. (if purchase price financed) • resident assoc. fee • homeowners' assoc dues • service fee • health care fee	• monthly "house" payment (if purchase price financed) • membership fee • service fee • health care fee
Separate packages	• services • health care	• services • health care	• services • health care	• services • health care

COMPARISON of CHARACTERISTICS Equity Communities *(continued)*			
	Condo	Co-op	Membership	
			w/ real property interest	w/o real property interest
Management	• resident board of directors • strictly controlled by law • inflexible	• resident board of directors • controlled by law • more flexible than condos, less than memberships	• non-resident board of directors • homeowners' association • FSRC's residents' association • most flexible of equity communities	• non-resident board of directors • controlled by law • somewhat flexible
Resales	• transfer fee charged • appreciation split • qualified buyers only	• transfer fee charged • appreciation split • qualified buyers only	• transfer fee charged • real estate commission due • possible split of appreciation • qualified buyers only	• transfer fee charged • appreciation split • qualified buyers only
Taxes	• real estate tax deduction • capital gains tax on sale of home deferred until residents move to AL & SN	• real estate tax deduction • capital gains tax on sale of home deferred until residents move to AL & SN	• real estate tax deduction • capital gains tax on sale of home deferred until residents move to AL & SN	• no deduction for payment of real estate taxes • capital gains tax on sale of home *not* deferred

Figure 7-9

LE: Taxes

If you are selling your primary residence and moving into a lease community, you might have to pay capital gains taxes on the proceeds from the sale of that house. The rental community will pass on its real estate and other taxes to residents on a prorated basis and include them in the monthly fee. These real estate taxes are not tax deductible to residents because they do not own a property interest. Residents of rental communities are not likely to be eligible for a tax deduction for prepaid medical expenses, as some endowment communities are. Check with your tax advisor for the latest information.

LE: Services

Services are sometimes included in the monthly fee and other times are provided in packages and the resident is charged separately for them. Among the services might be meals, interior and exterior maintenance, housekeeping, and transportation. As in equity and endowment communities, a variety of programs for the payment of health care exists. Occasionally, these packages are required.

Many rentals are offering long-term care insurance as a benefit of residency. Some include the premium in the monthly fee and others charge separately for it.

LE: Management

Residents of rentals could have the least amount of input to management of the three forms of occupancy; however, residents do usually have some say through a residents' association, which advises management. Without the payment of a large up-front fee, residents do not have as much invested in the community as residents of endowment and equity communities do. This could, perhaps, produce a lack of commitment on the part of residents and, in turn, could result in reduced commitment by the management to its residents. This situation makes for a controlling management. Scrutiny is necessary to see if management leads with compassion.

HYBRID OCCUPANCY OPTIONS

Of course, there are hybrid plans in retirement communities. These are the FSRCs that combine a mixture of payment and care plans. There are as many as the human mind can conceive. It is important, once again, that you carefully question the structure of

	SUMMARY of OCCUPANCY OPTIONS						
	Endowment		Equity Communities				Lease
	Refundable Entry Fee	Non-refundable Entry Fee	Condo	Co-op	Membership		Rentals
					w/ interest in real property	w/out interest in real property	
Entry fee or purchase price	high	moderate	highest	highest	highest	higher	none or lowest
Finance entry fee	no	no	yes	yes	yes	yes	no
Entry fee tax deductible	no	perhaps partially	no	no	no	no	no
Property interest	no	no	yes	yes	yes	no	no
Ownership of common areas & land	no	no	yes, undivided portion	no	no	no	no
Management control	most flexible	most flexible	very high	high	lowest	moderately high	highest
Capital gains tax on sale of home deferred	no	no	yes, except AL & SN	yes, except AL & SN	yes, except AL & SN	no	no
Tax benefits & burdens of home ownership	no	no	yes	maybe	yes	no	no
Tax on imputed interest	maybe on refundable deposit	N/A	N/A	N/A	N/A	N/A	N/A
Resales	no	no	yes	yes	yes	yes	N/A
Resales regulated	N/A	N/A	yes	yes	yes	yes	N/A
Equity/loss to resident	no	no	yes	yes	yes	yes	N/A
Transfer/ admin. fees	4-10%	N/A	10-20% of original price	10-20% of original price	10% plus real estate commission	10-20% of original price	N/A
Appreciation to community	all	all	0-75%	0-75%	0	0-75% & possible portion to lender	N/A

Figure 7-10

135

each community and not trust the label that the community has given itself. See the question list beginning in Chapter 12.

A few communities offer prospective residents an opportunity for either an endowment or an equity occupancy. Some endowment or equity facilities have rental programs available.

⋙⋘

An attorney can sort out the different occupancy options and help you choose which is best for your situation. The above discussion of taxes for each of the occupancy options is vastly simplified; the subject is more complex. A CPA can give you the latest federal tax information; it changes yearly. He or she can also assess your state tax liability for your situation in the community of your choice. A comparison of the occupancy options appears in Figure 7-10.

MONTHLY FEE PLANS

All types of occupancy (endowment, equity, and lease) offer essentially three main monthly fee structures (Plans A-C: life care, modified fee for service, and fee for service, respectively). Plan X (very rare) exists only in endowment communities. See Figure 7-11.

FEE PLANS			
Type of Plan	Endowment	Equity	Lease
A: Life care	✔	✔	✔
B: Modified fee for service	✔	✔	✔
C: Fee for service	✔	✔	✔
X: Assign all assets (rare)	✔		

Figure 7-11

PLAN A: LIFE CARE

Life care (LC), also called the extensive plan, has a two-pronged definition, according to the American Association of Homes and

Services for the Aging (AAHSA, page 194). One is the guarantee to take care of their residents for the rest of their lives and the other is the Plan A all-inclusive monthly fee structure (explained below).

Virtually all life care communities guarantee to take care of their residents for life. A benevolence fund aids the FSRC in this assurance. If they do not have one, it is questionable as to how real their guarantee is. See the discussion on benevolence funds on page 155.

An all-inclusive monthly fee is required for the resident's tenure in the community. Although the fee is "fixed," it is raised each year, according to the cost projections for the coming budget year. Almost all available services, except home health care (HHC), doctors' fees, therapies, prescription drugs, and medical supplies, may be included in the monthly fee.

Equity communities, in particular, might describe life care differently. We have used the most common definition of life care (that of endowment communities) throughout this book.

Some communities use the term "life care" to mean that they have a guarantee, but they do not have an all-inclusive-fee plan as do true life care communities. They are really fee-for-service communities with a lifetime guarantee. Careful scrutiny will reveal the true nature of their fee structure and how they plan to back that guarantee.

Pros of Life Care

Life care protects your assets from the costs of a prolonged illness that requires assisted living (AL), skilled nursing (SN), and/or Alzheimer's/dementia (A/D) care. When residents move from independent living to assisted living or skilled nursing, the fee virtually does not increase. This is especially important for couples, as pointed out in the example below.

In life care, when one spouse is in assisted living or skilled nursing and the other is still in independent living, the fee increases to pay only for the extra meals per day and personal laundry of the one in assisted living or skilled nursing— nominal amounts. If that spouse were to move into assisted living or skilled nursing as well, the only increase in the fee would be for the extra meals and personal laundry. So, with both spouses in skilled nursing, the fee is essentially the same as in independent living.

For example, if a couple were living in a life care community, they might pay $2500 per month in independent living, about $800 a month more than in a fee-for-service (FFS) community (see page 140). The extra money covers services that many fee-for-service communities charge separately for. It also pays for what essentially amounts to long-term care insurance premiums (prepaid medical expenses).

Even though the chance of needing permanent extended care is remote, let us say that the husband moves into assisted living, leaving the wife in independent living. The couple's monthly fee would now be $2500 a month (plus a nominal amount for the husband's extra meals and personal laundry). Should the husband move into skilled nursing and the wife move into assisted living, their monthly fee would still be $2500 a month (plus extra meals and laundry for both of them). Residents of skilled nursing also pay for prescription drugs, medical supplies, and special services. These charges usually add up to 20% or more of the monthly fee.

Because independent living residents pay the extra sum each month, they are paying more than they cost the community. Once they move onto different levels of care, they cost the community more than they contribute. Therefore, it is a financial boon to the FSRC to keep residents healthy and in independent living as long as possible. Needless to say, from the resident's viewpoint this is preferable, as well.

When an FSRC guarantees residents a bed in assisted living or skilled nursing and there is none available, the FSRC will be forced to place the resident in a local facility until an opening occurs. In all probability, the community will pay the difference in cost if it is higher than its own service. Those that do not guarantee access to extended care might or might not pay the extra costs.

Cons of Life Care

The entrance fees for life care are higher than fee-for-service communities, as are the monthly fees, because of the long-term care insurance-like premiums. Should residents never use assisted living or skilled nursing, they will have paid for services they never used. Singles and those of considerable resources might not need the asset protection that some couples could. See Figure 7-12 for a summary of the pros and cons of life care.

LIFE CARE (LC)	
Pros	Cons
• security • predictable expenses • probable guaranteed access to AL & SN • virtually no increased fees for couples or singles in AL &/or SN • less risk of outliving one's assets • partial tax deductions of fees possible	• pay in advance for services not needed • increased initial costs • monthly fees higher than comparable FFS

Figure 7-12

PLAN B: MODIFIED FEE FOR SERVICE

Plan B is a modified fee-for-service plan (MFFS), also called the modified plan. It usually includes 15 or more days of care in assisted living and/or skilled nursing per year. Additional health care and some services are pay as you go (fee for service). This fee plan is less expensive than Plan A (life care), but more than Plan C (fee for service).

Pros of Modified Fee for Service

The modified plan has some of the benefits of life care and some of fee for service. The prepaid days of care cover times of temporary need such as the weeks following surgery, when a resident requires care for a short time. Most plans include fifteen to thirty days of prepaid care in assisted living or skilled nursing.

This means that while residents are receiving temporary care, they will not have to pay separate monthly fees for independent living **and** assisted living or skilled nursing at the same time. Since residents most typically utilize the services of assisted living and skilled nursing on a temporary basis, this could result in a considerable savings.

Cons of Modified Fee for Service

Residents might pay for unused medical care. In most communities these prepaid days of care do carry over to the next month, but not to the next year. Once a resident moves to assisted living or skilled nursing permanently, monthly fees, based on *per diem* rates, are higher than in life care. See Figure 7-13.

MODIFIED FEE FOR SERVICE (FFS)	
Pros	**Cons**
• lower initial costs than life care • lower monthly fees than life care • pay for services only as needed • possible guaranteed access to AL & SN • temporary stays in AL & SN prepaid up to a certain amount • AL & SN fees most likely below market rate	• higher initial costs than for fee for service • higher fees than for fee for service • expenses increase greatly as need does • much more expensive for couples than for singles • risk of outliving one's assets • tax deductions of IL fees not probable

Figure 7-13

PLAN C: FEE FOR SERVICE

Strict fee-for-service (FFS) plans are abundant in the marketplace. The entry and monthly fees are lower than in a life care community because the residents are not paying for as many services and prepaid medical expenses. Only if residents want certain services and/or need assisted living or skilled nursing will they pay for them. Rental and equity communities may offer life care, but they seem to be predominantly fee for service.

Pros of Fee for Service

In fee-for-service communities, the residents pay only for the services they use. To a certain extent, they can decide how their money is spent. Their assets can be invested in growth vehicles, thus, building their fortunes, unless they need these monies early on to pay for medical expenses.

For those residents who need assisted living or skilled nursing, the community usually charges them a *per diem* fee that is below-market rate. Long-term care insurance will offset the assisted living (AL) and skilled nursing (SN) expenses.

Cons of Fee for Service

On the other side of the same coin is the argument that many people have enough money to pay the expenses for one spouse in assisted living or skilled nursing for the average stay of three years. However, it is possible that paying for this care over an extended period of time could deplete their funds and, thus, financially impact the lifestyle of the other spouse who could have many years ahead. Should that spouse also need extended care, the couple's resources could be severely affected.

If a husband or a wife were to move permanently into assisted living or skilled nursing in a fee-for-service community (leaving the other spouse behind in independent living), the couple would have to pay extra for those accommodations. The couple's expenses would more than triple. If the other spouse were to need care at the same time, the expenses would go up yet again. Each would be paying as he or she goes along.

For instance, if the couple in the above scenario were living in a fee-for-service community, they might pay $1700 a month for their home in independent living. (The couple in life care paid $2500 a month. Remember that about $800 was for the insurance premium-like feature of life care and for extra services that are not included in the monthly fee in the fee-for-service FSRC.)

Let us say for our example that the husband moves into assisted living. The couple is paying $4500 for him in assisted living and $1300 (now reduced by the amount of the $400 second person fee) for the wife in independent living, or $5800 per month. If the husband were to move into skilled nursing and the wife into assisted living, they would pay $6500 a month for him and $4500 for her. In all, they will be paying $11,000 a month, instead of the $2500 in the life care community. With both in skilled nursing, the bill would be $13,000 a month.

If one of the same couple experienced **temporary** stays in assisted living or skilled nursing, the fees would be considerably higher. The wife would pay $1700 in independent living. (Some communities will adjust the fee to $1300 a month—less the second person fee for the spouse who is temporarily absent.) In addition, they would pay $4500 a month for assisted living or $6500 for skilled nursing. This would make the couple's bill $5800 with one in assisted living or $7800 with one in skilled nursing. It is this scenario that makes modified fee for service an attractive choice.

Long-term care insurance benefits would reduce these amounts according to the terms of the policy. This could make a considerable difference in the out-of-pocket expenses. If the community has a benevolence fund (page 155), singles, as well as couples, would have an extra layer of protection.

Fee-for-service communities do not have the financial incentive to keep residents in independent living, as do life care communities. They might be tempted to push residents through the system too quickly. Turning the independent living homes over faster makes more money in entrance fees.

Quality communities will make fiscal decisions with compassion and still do the right thing: provide residents with as high a quality of life as possible by keeping residents in independent living as long as possible. Their mission or vision statement should speak to their intention to do just that. See Figure 7-14 for a summary of the pros and cons of fee for service.

PLAN X: ASSIGN ASSETS (OUT OF DATE)

Plan X is a dying option and is seldom found anymore. Residents must turn over all of their assets to the community on entrance; subsequently, the community gives the resident a nominal allowance. This is a holdover from the care facilities of a hundred years ago, which were called life care communities. The name has survived, but today's plans are strictly twenty-first-century style.

FEE FOR SERVICE (FFS)	
Pros	Cons
• lowest initial costs • lowest monthly fees • pay for services only as needed • possible guaranteed access to AL & SN • AL & SN fees most likely below market rate	• expenses increase greatly as need does • much more expensive for couples than for singles • risk of outliving one's assets • tax deductions of IL fees not probable • pay monthly fees for both IL & AL or SN during temporary stays in AL or SN

Figure 7-14

A summary of the monthly fee options and their attributes is shown in Figure 7-15.

HYBRID MONTHLY FEE PLANS

Of course, not all communities follow these plans strictly. Many FSRCs, in an effort to be more competitive and please more people, offer variations on these basic models. Since hybrids vary tremendously, reading the fine print is necessary.

Because most Baby Boomers value choice, many FSRCs, particularly the newer ones, are offering several types of monthly fee and entry fee plans in the same community. A community could offer life care and fee for service to the same potential residents. See Figure 7-16 for a list of possible combinations.

An accountant or financial advisor can point out the possible ramifications that the different plans could have on your personal financial situation. A CPA or financial planner might have software that will run several "what if" scenarios for you. The computer can compare costs with and without long-term care insurance and life care (LC) versus fee for service (FFS).

MONTHLY FEE OPTIONS for IL RESIDENTS			
	Plan A Life Care (LC)	Plan B Modified Fee for Service (MFFS)	Plan C Fee for Service (FFS)
AL and/or SN included	yes	partially	no
Predictable expenses	yes	somewhat	no
Possible medical tax deduction	yes	yes	no
Cost monthly for IL	highest	less than life care, more than FFS	lowest
Increased costs for *temporary* stays in AL or SN	no	no, to a point	yes
Significant increase in costs of AL & SN over IL	no	yes	yes
Significant increase in costs for couples w/ one or both in IL & one in AL or SN, *temporarily or permanently*	no	yes	yes

Figure 7-15

HYBRID COMMUNITIES Possible Combinations		
Occupancy Options	Entrance Fees	Monthly Fees
• endowment or lease • equity or lease • endowment or equity • endowment, equity, or lease	• higher entry fee with lower monthly fee • lower entry fee with higher monthly fee • no refund plan • no non-refundable plan • refund plan (any %) or non-refundable plan • no entry fee	• higher monthly fee with lower entry fee • lower monthly fee with higher entry fee • any combination of LC or MFFS or FFS • meals included or not • all services included or all à la carte

Figure 7-16

❈❈❈

This chapter has waded through the complex structures of occupancy options and fees. Chapter 8 will cover entry requirements and the contracts you will be asked to sign.

8

ENTRANCE REQUIREMENTS
AND CONTRACTS

*The single biggest problem in communication
is the illusion that it has taken place.*

—George Bernard Shaw
Irish Playwright, 1856-1950

A ccurate exchange of information is at the heart of any business
deal. Both oral and written communications need to be so clear
that there is no doubt on either side that there is a meeting of
the minds. Marketing representatives or sales/leasing agents and
CEOs *want* each potential resident to have a clear understanding of
the terms of residency. Discussed below are the issues that might
come up in your conversations. Armed with this outline, you should
be able to ascertain the details.

THE ENTRY REQUIREMENTS

Because of the lifetime of quality care and benefits that residents receive, there are entrance requirements. While most full service retirement communities (FSRCs), also referred to as continuing care retirement communities (CCRCs), are nonprofit, they are still businesses and must keep an eye on the bottom line. We certainly want them to be financially secure. These entry requirements are age, health, certain insurance policies, and financial minimums for prospective residents (Figure 8-1).

ENTRANCE REQUIREMENTS
At a Glance

• minimum age
• able to live independently
• financial
   ▸ dollar minimums
      - 1½ - 2 times the entry fee in assets &
      - 1½ - 2 times the monthly fee in retirement
       income or
   ▸ case-by-case basis
• insurance

Figure 8-1

AGE

Minimum age is a common condition for residency in a full service retirement community. Usually it is 62 or 65. Some FSRCs that started as age restricted communities (page 21) without health care still have their minimum age set at 55. Other communities might still have their entry ages set at 65; however, the trend is toward a lower minimum age. Some FSRCs are making case-by-case exceptions to their age requirements. It is possible that a community might have a minimum age for a younger spouse.

As communities gear up for the coming Baby Boomers, many of whom want to retire at a younger age than their parents, the communities might drop their age requirement to 62 or below. Many of the second generation FSRCs (those now being built with the Baby Boomers in mind) lean toward softer, more creative regulations.

Of those FSRCs that allow residency at age 55, the policies on coverage into the health care program vary widely. Usually younger spouses are welcome. There is some concern, however, about whether they are covered under the health care program.

Younger Spouse Policy

The younger spouse policy applies only to couples and then only to those where just one of them meets the minimum age. Although rare, under certain conditions, the younger person could be asked to leave the community.

Let us give you a *worst case* scenario: A couple, aged 62 and 57, moves into a community where the minimum age is 62. The community accepts the one-person fee from and signs a contract with the older person. The FSRC normally charges a second person fee of roughly ten percent of the entrance fee. But in the case of a younger spouse, the community neither accepts the second-person fee nor adds the second person to the contract until the second person reaches the minimum age of 62.

Let's say that the community has a declining refund policy of 2% per month (page 115); so, in 50 months, no part of the entrance fee is refundable. At month 51, the older person dies, leaving the second person, healthy and still younger than the minimum age for eligibility for residence in the community. At that time the younger person could—in theory—be asked to leave. Realize also that should the older person die at month 25, half of the money would be gone.

In a second situation, should the older person move to assisted living (AL) or skilled nursing (SN), leaving the younger (and still under age) person in independent living (IL), the community could ask the younger person to leave.

In another related example, if the younger person were to move to assisted living or skilled nursing before age 62, leaving the older person in independent living, he or she will most likely have to pay market rates, not the reduced rate for residents. When the younger person reaches the minimum age, most fee-for-service communities (page 140) will adjust the assisted living or skilled nursing fee to the reduced resident rate. Life care communities (page 136) might never offer the younger person the reduced rate because he or she was not healthy upon reaching the minimum age.

Any zealous attorney for the community could strongly recommend that the contract terms be carried out to the letter. We have never heard of its happening; but should the community decide to enforce the contract, it could be possible.

Of course, the odds are long, and we like to think that communities would try to work out an equitable solution—or better yet—allow the younger person to stay. Several marketing reps promised us that they would "work with us" should this happen, but any attorney looking out for *our* best interests would recommend that we, as potential residents, not rely on any oral promises. The written contract would win out in court should a dispute be litigated. We just want you to understand the risks—however remote—that this policy presents.

Equitable solutions have been found by almost all of the FSRCs. They simply accept the younger person into the community or charge a one-time fee that is tantamount to paying advance premiums on long-term care insurance for the limited number of years until the younger spouse reaches the minimum entry age. This is usually a small percentage—maybe 5 or 6%—of the second-person entrance fee for each year the younger person is below the minimum entry age. This could be $500-$1200 per year for every year a spouse's age is below the minimum. For example, the one-time fee would be $2500-$6000 for a spouse whose age is five years below the minimum. The younger person is added to the contract at the same time as the older person and is a full-fledged resident, entitled to all the rights of residency.

HEALTH

Health is another qualifying factor. Potential residents are asked to take a physical exam just before moving in. Sometimes, residents will be asked to pass the health assessment when they put their names on the waiting list. These communities are usually existing fee-for-service (FFS) or life care (LC) full service retirement communities that are new or expanding and are still under construction. You do not need to be in perfect health. However, for life care and the independent living section of fee-for-service communities, you must be able to function independently on moving in. The physical exam for entry into a life care community is more stringent than for a fee-for-service community.

Some FSRCs require only that you be independent to add your name to the waiting list. This means that you must not need help with bathing, dressing, eating, or other daily living functions.

In some fee-for-service communities, applicants may qualify when they put their names on the waiting list. Then, if the health of a potential resident fails before moving in, he or she may go directly to assisted living (AL) or skilled nursing (SN). A time restriction might accompany this policy. Other fee-for-service communities will accept new residents directly into assisted living or skilled nursing.

Some communities might exclude applicants who are already afflicted with dementia, Parkinson's, and some pulmonary ailments. There is no problem if residents develop these diseases after admission unless the community has no Alzheimer's/dementia care. In this case residents so stricken will be moved to an outside facility if they need more care than their FSRC is equipped to handle.

Still, other communities might admit people with these or other diseases on a provisional basis. The FSRC might, for example, exclude residents from the health care program for the first two years. A thorough comprehension of restrictions will prevent misunderstandings later.

A few FSRCs add a premium to the price if prospective residents have debilitating diseases that would surely require the residents to need personal and/or medical care from the community on a long-term basis sometime in the future. These afflictions most commonly include, but are not limited to, COPD (Chronic Obstructive Pulmonary Disease), Parkinson's, matastisized cancer, and congestive heart failure. The premium might be an up-front fee and/or a slightly higher fee in assisted living and skilled nursing, even in a life care community (page 136).

INSURANCE

Virtually all communities require that potential residents have certain insurance policies. Medicare and Medicare, Part B, are almost always necessary. Some require other Medicare parts and/or a

Medicare supplement, too. Long-term care insurance is often expected of new residents.

In the past, long-term care insurance was called nursing home insurance. It is really much more than that now. A good policy will cover varying portions of home health care, assisted living, skilled nursing expenses, adult day care, and other senior services.

Although, long-term care insurance protects the assets of policyholders, not all require it. In life care communities and fee for service, alike, home health care is not prepaid. If residents were to keep their long-term care insurance coverage while living in an FSRC, that policy would cover certified (skilled) home health care and custodial care, if those services are benefits of the policy. Residents of life care communities should inquire as to whether the insurance company will pay claims for assisted living and skilled nursing.

Let's take as an example the resident who moves into assisted living on a permanent basis. She may then file a claim to her long term care insurance company, using a statement of costs from the community as proof of monies spent on her behalf. If the insurance company allows this type of claim, they will pay it up to its maximum per day or month. This insurance will provide further protection for her assets.

Some fee-for-service FSRCs self-insure. This means that they will insure residents themselves, asking them to pay an insurance premium to the community, rather than to a commercial insurer. This way applicants who do not qualify for commercial insurance might become insured by the FSRC.

A financial advisor can counsel you in purchasing this asset-protecting insurance. Not only will he or she look at the policy, but at your overall financial picture with and without this coverage.

FINANCIAL

Financial requirements are essential. Most life care communities guarantee that they will take care of you for the rest of your life. Some fee-for-service communities make a similar promise. In exchange for that promise, they ask that you meet certain minimum monetary prerequisites.

The most common rule of thumb is: 1½ - 2 times the entry fee in assets and 1½ - 2 times the monthly fee in retirement income. The communities will consider, on a case-by-case basis, those who have a higher retirement income with lower assets or those with higher assets and lower retirement income.

Many communities use a formula based on a combination of income and assets to financially qualify potential residents, but it is not absolute. In some circumstances, communities will accept residents with marginal finances who have someone cosign for them. Guarantor forms are provided by each community. The decision is made on a case-by-case basis.

Affordability

Don't let sticker shock scare you away; moving into an FSRC is quite feasible. Essentially anyone who can afford the monthly fee can qualify for a rental. It is not so expensive as it seems—all things considered.

Entry into endowment or equity communities is not so difficult for people who have equity in a house and savings. If you consider the equity in your house the source of the entrance fee and the income from your savings, 401(k), pension, and/or Social Security the source for your monthly fee, you should qualify for an FSRC. If your savings are large enough, they could also pay part of the entry fee, which is essentially a prepayment of your house payment or rent and of future services that are not covered by the monthly fee. See Figure 8-2.

Many FSRCs are for middle-income people; others cater to a more luxurious lifestyle. Some communities are partially funded by HUD (Department of Housing and Urban Development) and are an option for those who qualify with a low enough income. Some of them also have a low-cost section for those who do not meet HUD requirements.

Downsizing

How much house do you need in your retirement? Moving into an FSRC is your opportunity to downsize, if you wish. If you do not, you can find large single family homes with four bedrooms, three baths, a family room, and a two car garage.

Costs are influenced by the square footage of your home. Downsizing will save you money. Changing your thinking about how you will utilize the common areas of the community will help tremendously. They will become an extension of your home. For example, the community's guest suite could house your overnight company instead of paying a larger entry fee and higher monthly fee for an extra bedroom.

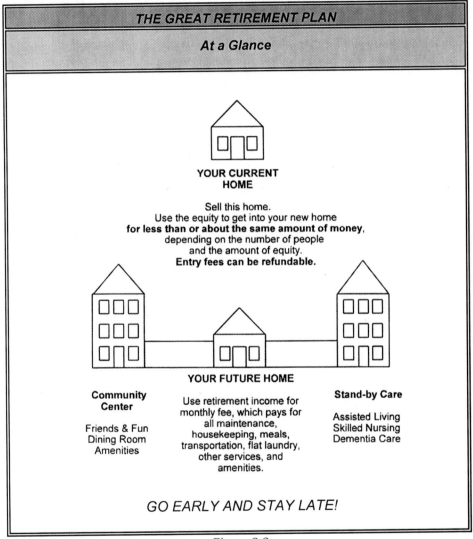

THE GREAT RETIREMENT PLAN

At a Glance

YOUR CURRENT HOME

Sell this home.
Use the equity to get into your new home
for less than or about the same amount of money,
depending on the number of people
and the amount of equity.
Entry fees can be refundable.

YOUR FUTURE HOME

Community Center		Stand-by Care
Friends & Fun Dining Room Amenities	Use retirement income for monthly fee, which pays for all maintenance, housekeeping, meals, transportation, flat laundry, other services, and amenities.	Assisted Living Skilled Nursing Dementia Care

GO EARLY AND STAY LATE!

Figure 8-2

Laurie loves to entertain; she has always had a house with a large dining room for this purpose. Now that she lives in an FSRC, she can

153

hold her parties in the private dining room. When it is her turn to entertain the members of her club, she can invite them to one of the smaller living rooms in the common areas. The community's kitchen will cater these events if she wishes. She no longer needs a large dining room.

Barbara loves quilting and sewing. The arts and crafts room will have large tables with plenty of space for her to work and lots of cabinets to store her projects in progress, as well as her supplies. Now she won't have to pay for an extra room.

Steve is an avid miniature railroader. Because he sponsors a club for others who are interested, the community gives him a room for his large train set to be put up permanently. He no longer needs an extra room in his home for his train hobby.

Cost Comparisons

Costs are more easily understood in figures. The charts in Figure 8-3 compare the entry costs of endowment, equity, and lease communities and the monthly costs of life care versus fee-for-service communities for twenty, fifteen, and ten years. They assume 17.5, 12.5, and 7.5 years in independent living (IL), 15 months in assisted living (AL), and 15 months in skilled nursing (SN). The figures that we used in the examples are for the two floor plans that are growing in popularity: one bedroom with a den or two bedrooms with two baths.

The numbers are not based on a scientific survey. It would be a massive undertaking—if at all possible—to evaluate thousands of communities in different locations with varying services and amenities in different kinds of buildings on different properties in different states with different laws and cost of living levels. In addition, any numbers gathered today will be out of date by the time any book is published. Consequently the numbers are very soft.

What is important are the relationships between the numbers. The current structures of endowment, equity, and lease, as well as life care and fee for service, dictate the pricing. Absent a massive reorganization, the relationships should be reasonably stable at any price.

This figure also gives you an opportunity to compare for-profit communities versus nonprofit ones. The endowment FSRCs are most commonly nonprofit and the equity and lease communities are almost always for profit.

The main conclusions to be drawn from Figure 8-3 are as follows. 1) It's cheaper to go early and stay late. 2) Life care might be cheaper for couples. 3) Personal preference dictates the differences between endowment, equity, and lease communities. 4) Personal values separate nonprofit from for profit.

Figure 8-4 will enable you to see just what the monthly fee includes when compared to how much it costs to run your house. Moving into an FSRC is a real possibility when you look at the big picture. It is not so much money as it sounds like at first blush.

Figure 8-5 shows cost comparisons of communities in a large metropolitan area on the East Coast. It is interesting to see how the occupancy options affect the entrance fee and how life care and fee for service have an impact on monthly costs. Should you wish to compare costs of communities that you are considering, the blank worksheet in Figure 8-6 will help you organize the figures you collect.

The Benevolence Fund

Many communities will guarantee to take care of you for the rest of your life, particularly in life care (LC). A benevolence fund is designed to bail out residents who, due to no fault of their own, run out of money. Communities with refund plans will draw down on the refundable entrance fee before they tap the benevolence fund.

Some state laws require that a life care community have a benevolence fund; others do not, but many communities will have one anyway. Endowment communities almost always have a benevolence fund or some mechanism that serves the same purpose. Equity and rental communities tend not to have this kind of assistance.

Once you do qualify for residency (and assuming that you do not deliberately impoverish yourself), FSRCs with benevolence funds will never ask you to find residence elsewhere because you run out of money. Some of these funds are supported by donations; yet others might be created from the fees everyone pays.

These programs are called by many names and their terms vary, so check carefully. Also, inquire as to their source of money. All nonprofit FSRCs that have a benevolence fund accept tax-deductible

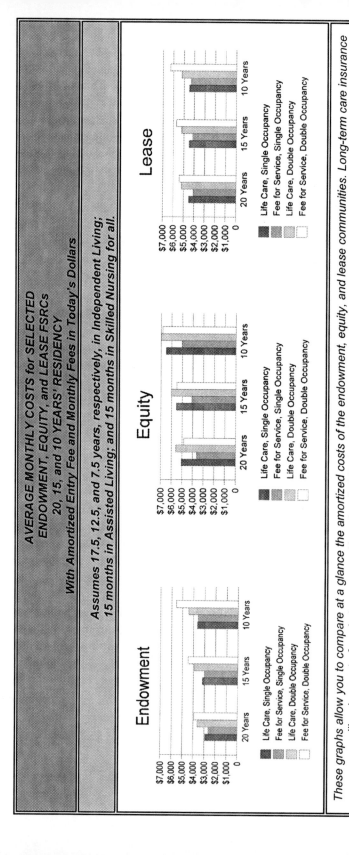

AVERAGE MONTHLY COSTS for SELECTED
ENDOWMENT, EQUITY, and LEASE FSRCs
20, 15, and 10 YEARS' RESIDENCY
With Amortized Entry Fee and Monthly Fees in Today's Dollars

Assumes 17.5, 12.5, and 7.5 years, respectively, in Independent Living;
15 months in Assisted Living; and 15 months in Skilled Nursing for all.

Endowment

$7,000
$6,000
$5,000
$4,000
$3,000
$2,000
$1,000
0

20 Years   15 Years   10 Years

■ Life Care, Single Occupancy
■ Fee for Service, Single Occupancy
□ Life Care, Double Occupancy
□ Fee for Service, Double Occupancy

Equity

$7,000
$6,000
$5,000
$4,000
$3,000
$2,000
$1,000
0

20 Years   15 Years   10 Years

■ Life Care, Single Occupancy
■ Fee for Service, Single Occupancy
□ Life Care, Double Occupancy
□ Fee for Service, Double Occupancy

Lease

$7,000
$6,000
$5,000
$4,000
$3,000
$2,000
$1,000
0

20 Years   15 Years   10 Years

■ Life Care, Single Occupancy
■ Fee for Service, Single Occupancy
□ Life Care, Double Occupancy
□ Fee for Service, Double Occupancy

These graphs allow you to compare at a glance the amortized costs of the endowment, equity, and lease communities. Long-term care insurance will reduce out-of-pocket expenses. Keep in mind that cost is not everything. All forms of FSRCs have their pros and cons.

The figures that these charts are based on are not the results of a scientific survey. This is by no means the national average cost. We compared two bedroom, two bath apartments in communities in the suburbs of large cities across the nation. The FSRCs seemed to have similar attributes, services, grounds, and buildings. They seemed to appeal to groups of similar economic levels. One bedroom with a den will cost less than a two bedroom home. One bedroom will be more inexpensive than these, unless they are in resort areas. Many quality FSRCs dot the country and most will be more inexpensive than these, unless they are in resort areas.

Figure 8-3

YOUR MONTHLY HOUSEHOLD EXPENSES				
Item	My current household expenses	If included in monthly fee, repeat numbers in these columns		
		FSRC #1	FSRC #2	FSRC #3
House payment/rent	$	$	$	$
Utilities (gas, electric, water/sewer, trash)				
Property insurance and real estate taxes				
Homeowners' association dues				
Condo, co-op fees, or membership fees				
Repairs (new roof, furnace, appliances, siding, etc. [last 15 years' expenses ÷ 180 months = avg. cost of repairs per month])				
Maintenance (lawn care, snow removal, carpet, paint, yearly furnace/air conditioner checkups [last 15 years' expenses ÷ 180 months = avg. cost of maintenance/mo.])				
Hired help (cleaning, yard work, etc.)				
Groceries: 40% of your grocery bill, if the FSRC you are considering includes one meal/day; 70%, if two; 90%, if three.)				
Security system (monthly fee)				
Basic cable TV				
Basic phone				
Computer lines				
Flat linen laundry				
Long-term care insurance premium				
Visits to see nurse in clinic				
Transportation, local				
Spa/gym dues				
Country club dues				
Other				
Other				
TOTALS — Add each column.	$	$	$	$
TOTALS — Monthly fee of each FSRC		$	$	$

Figure 8-4

			SAMPLE COST COMPARISONS of OCCUPANCY OPTIONS And LIFE CARE vs. FEE FOR SERVICE From Selected Communities in one East Coast Metropolitan Area 2 bedroom/2 bath apartments, single occupancy							
			Refundable Entry Fee							
FSRC	Non-refundable Entry Fee (NREF)	Independent Living Monthly Fee	% of First Refund Plan	Amount	% Increase over NREF	% of Second Refund Plan	Amount	% Increase over NREF	Assisted Living Monthly Fee	Skilled Nursing Monthly Fee
ENDOWMENT—LIFE CARE										
A	$163,000	$2800	50%	$220,000	35%	100%	$325,000	99%	$2800	$2800
B	158000	2200	N/A						2200	2200
C	268000	2600	50%	367000	37%	90%	428000	60%	2600	2600
ENDOWMENT—FEE for SERVICE										
D	150000	1500	N/A			90%	243000	62%	4300	7000
E	N/A	1700	N/A			100%	255000	N/A	4700	5900
F	85000	1900	N/A			90%	170000	100%	4200	6500
EQUITY—LIFE CARE										
G	350000	2600	N/A						2600	2600
EQUITY—FEE for SERVICE										
H	200000	1800	N/A						4500	6000
I	279000	1700							4800	6600
LEASE—LIFE CARE										
J	0	4500	N/A						4500	4500
LEASE—FEE for SERVICE										
K	9500	3600	N/A						4000	6000
L	0	3400							4000	7200

Figure 8-5

bequests and donations. They might also receive money from entrance fees and fund raisers. For-profit communities need to have a nonprofit subsidiary before they can accept tax-deductible donations. A more stable benevolence fund will have a regular, steady source of income.

| FSRC | Non-refundable Entry Fee (NREF) | Independent Living Monthly Fee | Refundable Entry Fee | | | | | | Assisted Living Monthly Fee | Skilled Nursing Monthly Fee |
			% of First	Amount	% Increase over NREF	% of Second Refund Plan	Amount	% Increase over NREF		
YOUR COMPARISONS										
ENDOWMENT—LIFE CARE										
A										
B										
C										
ENDOWMENT—FEE FOR SERVICE										
D										
E										
F										
EQUITY—LIFE CARE										
G										
H										
EQUITY—FEE FOR SERVICE										
I										
J										
LEASE—LIFE CARE										
K										
L										
LEASE—FEE FOR SERVICE										
M										
N										

Figure 8-6

159

If the community does not have a benevolence fund, it is questionable as to how real their lifetime care guarantee is. Careful questioning will reveal its true nature.

Value for Your Money

So, what does all this money buy for you? Virtually all full service retirement communities (FSRCs) at all price points offer the same basic services. The location and the level of luxury are the major differences.

WHAT SHOULD YOU EXPECT for YOUR MONEY?			
	Low End	Middle Range	High End
Housing	all apartments	apartments & cottages	apartments & single family homes
	small selection of floor plans	some variety of floor plans	many choices of floor plans
	small to adequate	small to large	adequate to spacious
	functional architecture	interesting architecture	sophisticated architecture
Convenience services	special diets accommodated	special diets accommodated	special diets accommodated
	cafeteria-style meals with few choices	buffet-style meals with several choices	served gourmet meals with abundant choices
	scheduled bus or van transportation	scheduled bus & car for hire	scheduled bus & car or limo
	necessary exterior maintenance	adequate exterior maintenance	extensive exterior maintenance
	light housekeeping	light housekeeping with some heavy cleaning	extensive housekeeping
	part time activities director	full time activities director	two or more full time activities directors
	occasional outings	frequent outings	regular weekly outings
	minimal personal services, usually help with making appointments	some personal services	extensive personal services (valet, concierge, dog walking)

WHAT SHOULD YOU EXPECT for YOUR MONEY? *(continued)*		
Low End	**Middle Range**	**High End**
banking services	bank on site	full service bank on site
swimming pool nearby	lap pool	lap pool & swimming pool
golf course in local area	golf course nearby	golf course on site
barber/beauty shops w/ minimal services & hrs.	barber/beauty shops w/ variety of services & hrs.	barber/beauty shops w/ extensive services & hrs.
patios	patios & a few balconies	patios or balconies in every apartment
all-purpose room	all-purpose room with stage	auditorium plus all-purpose room
library	library with magazines & newspapers	library with current books & periodicals
measured walking trail around or within the building	measured walking trail around or within the building or property	measured walking & nature trails with lights & benches
fitness room with minimal equipment	adequately equipped fitness room with water cooler	fitness room w/ state-of-the-art equipment & mats, water cooler, TV, VCR/DVD player, mirrors
quality care	quality care	quality care
semiprivate rooms	choice of private rooms or apartments	apartments
quality care	quality care	quality care
rehabilitation nearby	rehabilitation on site	rehabilitation on staff
semiprivate rooms	choice of semiprivate or private rooms	all private rooms
nurse's office on site	doctor's office on site	many doctors' & dentists' offices on site

The leftmost rotated category labels are: Amenities (first group), Health care, Personal care, Medical care.

Bear in mind that many FSRCs will have a combination of features in all of the ranges. A quick tally of how many features your prospective community has in each column will give you the big picture.

Figure 8-7

On the important things, such as health, personal, and medical care, price does not seem to affect their quality. Rather, it is affected by the same things as in other businesses: leadership. That is why there is no substitute for visiting a community to evaluate it.

The low end communities offer meals; transportation; maintenance; a library; activities rooms; housekeeping; and health, personal, and medical care, just as do the upscale communities. But the more expensive communities do it with style and fringe benefits. For instance, their fitness rooms are more likely to offer state-of-the-art exercise equipment in a mirror-lined room with a TV, DVD player, mats, water cooler, and a full time trainer. The least expensive community should have equipment to do the job without all the frills.

The chart in Figure 8-7 gives our rough assessment of what your money will buy in select communities. There are many exceptions. Sometimes a midrange community will offer delicious, gourmet meals in a dining room, served by a wait staff. The same community's fitness room might consist solely of one stationary bicycle in a basement storage room.

There is not much doubt, however, that only at a high-end FSRC will you find a stretch limo to pick you up at the front door of your single family home and drive you a quarter of a mile to the community center for dinner every night. Sometimes you will find a lower-priced community with a lovely lighted walking path along the bank of a picturesque lake inhabited by water fowl.

The three factors that affect price more than any other are "location, location, and location," just as the real estate agents say. An average community that sits on an oceanfront site can command high fees for fewer services and amenities than can the same community in the middle of nowhere.

Summary of Decisions to Be Made

Accountants would generally tell you to delay payments as long as possible. On the other hand, insurance agents would tell you to protect your assets against future disasters. It's all in one's viewpoint. Yours is based on your financial reserves, personal goals and values, health, and medical history. It is the role of your financial advisor to help you balance seemingly contradictory issues in arriving at a custom decision that is best for you alone.

DECISIONS to BE MADE	
Choose Your Preference in Each Row	
Occupancy	• endowment • equity • lease
Entrance fee	• refund plan & amount • no refund plan
Monthly fee	• life care • modified fee for service • fee for service
Legal ownership structure	• nonprofit • for profit
Insurance	• long-term care insurance (LTC) • no LTC insurance

Figure 8-8

In short, you need to make five choices. The advice of a financial planner could be invaluable in calculating whether you would benefit from 1) an endowment, equity, or lease occupancy options; 2) a life care, modified-fee-for-service, or a fee-for-service monthly fees; 3) a refundable or a non-refundable entrance fee; 4) a nonprofit or for-profit community; and 5) long-term-care insurance. The options are listed in Figure 8-8. It might take several visits to different kinds of FSRCs to help you to see for yourself how the differences show up in everyday life.

The worksheets in Figures 8-9, 8-10, and 8-11 will help you with the numbers. After you perform the simple calculations, you will know approximately how much of an entrance fee and monthly fee you will most likely be able to afford.

RESIDENT CONTRACTS

Once you have selected your future home, there will be contracts to sign. It is wise to have an attorney review everything you sign—before you sign it. Of course, be sure you understand what you are agreeing to in the contracts.

WAITING LIST CONTRACTS

Many communities have two waiting lists. One reserves your place in line. The other, the ready list, tells the community that you are willing to move in within ninety days of your name's coming to the top of the list.

Usually, there are separate contracts for the waiting list and the ready list. They should cover the amount of the deposit, how long it will be held, whether it is refundable, allocation of the interest, and other fees, if any. The contract should also discuss the terms for rejecting offers of a home and for cancelling the contract, both by the resident and the community. Any penalties or extra fees should be listed clearly.

In equity and lease communities, waiting list procedures might be different from endowment communities. This is because homes are actually transferred as real estate purchase and leasing deals. An attorney can help you weed through the fine print.

RESIDENT AGREEMENTS

You might have very little leverage over the content of the contract. Some states regulate what contracts must cover. Virtually all states require that a state agency approve the contract before presenting it to prospective residents. Florida, for example, requires that all residents of a community sign the same contract. No side agreements may be signed.

ASSETS WORKSHEET	
At a Glance	

ASSETS	
Checking accounts	$
Money market accounts	
401 (k) or 403 (b)	
IRA, Keough plan	
Real estate, fair market value	
Stocks, bonds, mutual funds	
Certificates of deposit	
Accounts/notes receivable	
Collectibles & other assets	
Other assets	
Other assets	
TOTAL ASSETS	$

LIABILITIES	
Credit card debt	
Accounts/notes payable	
Real estate mortgages	
Other debts	
Other liabilities	
TOTAL LIABILITIES	$

NET WORTH (Total Assets minus Total Liabilities) (This figure is simply called "Assets" by FSRCs.)	$

Figure 8-9

165

MONTHLY RETIREMENT INCOME WORKSHEET		
At a Glance		
INCOME SOURCES		
Social Security, mine	$	
Spouse's		
Pension, mine		
Spouse's		
401 (k) or 403 (b), mine		
Spouse's		
Keough plan, mine		
Spouse's		
Dividends/interest		
Annuities		
Royalties		
Rental income		
Other		
Other		
Other		
Other		
TOTAL MONTHLY RETIREMENT INCOME	$	

Figure 8-10

Contract Contents

The contracts that residents sign vary according to the type of legal occupancy. Whether the papers you sign are one all-inclusive contract or a series of contracts, they should include explanations of the services offered, admissions, transfers (to other independent living homes, assisted living, skilled nursing or other communities

FSRC AFFORDABILITY WORKSHEET	
At a Glance	

Entrance Fee	My total assets (net worth) $_____ $\div 2.0 =$ $_____(a)$
	My total assets (net worth) $_____ $\div 1.5 =$ $_____(b)$
	I will probably qualify for an entry fee of $_____(a)$ to $_____(b)$.
Monthly Fee	My monthly income $_____ $\div 2.0 =$ $_____(x)$
	My monthly income $_____ $\div 1.5 =$ $_____(y)$
	I will probably qualify for a monthly fee of $_____(x)$ to $_____(y)$.

Should your assets or income be relatively unbalanced, the marketing rep of the communities you visit can tell you what price range you will most likely qualify for.

Figure 8-11

within the family), fees, terminations, rescission period, refunds, resident rights, and owner and manager information. See Figure 8-12.

Endowment Communities

The endowment community is the most common form of occupancy and the contract is probably the least complex. Contracts impart the right to live in the endowment community as part of the agreement. There is usually just one contract to sign for independent living (IL). Some communities might have another contract when residents permanently move into assisted living (AL), skilled nursing (SN), or Alzheimer's/dementia (A/D).

CONTRACT CONTENTS		
Deposits	**Refunds**	**Resident Rights**
• amounts & due dates • interest rates & refund policy on deposits • interest rates & refund policy on preconstruction deposits	• rescission periods • cancellation before occupancy • preconstruction deposits • change in health status	• form associations • participate in decision-making • grievance procedures • independence • dignity
Fees	**Services**	**Transfers**

• entrance fees
  ▸ second person fees
  ▸ younger spouse fees
• monthly fees
• other fees
• caps on increases (*e.g.* consumer price index)
• optional charges
• method for changing fees
• taxes
• policies for residents' outliving funds
• method of notification of changes
	• services included in monthly fees
	• services available for extra fees
	• method of notification of changes
		• entrance fee changes on transfer from one style home to another
		• guaranteed bed in AL/ or SN
		• policy if AL or SN bed unavailable & who pays if fee is higher
		• assessment method for transferring resident from IL to AL or SN, temporarily or permanently
		• change in fees
		• from FSRC to FSRC, within family
		• marriage or divorce

CONTRACT CONTENTS *(continued)*		
Admissions	**Credits**	**Terminations**

• entry policies
  ▸ minimum age
    - younger spouse
  ▸ minimum health
    requirements
  ▸ pre-existing
    conditions
    - extra fees
• coverage of second
  person in health care
• health or long-term care
  & other insurance
  requirements
	• adjustments in
	  monthly fee for
	  absences from
	  community
	• policy for credits for
	  missed meals
		• rescission periods
		• termination by
		  residents
		• terminations by mgt.
		• no termination of
		  residents w/o cause
		• inability to pay
		• conditions for holding
		  bed in AL or SN during
		  hospital stays

Owner and Sponsor	**Homes**	**Other**

• name & contact info of
  each
• liability of each
	• description w/
	  location
	• amenities
	• renovations
		•
		
		•

Endowment Communities	**Equity Communities**	**Lease Communities**

• declining balance
  refund of entrance fees
• refundable entry fees
  ▸ refund amortization
    schedule, if needed
  ▸ time & conditions for
    refund
	• ownership
	  description
	• resale regulations
	• allocation of equity
	• details of service &
	  health care packages
	• transfer fees
	• taxes
		• length of lease
		• terms for renewal
		• option of landlord or
		  resident to renew
		• details of service &
		  health care packages
		• security deposit

Figure 8-12

Contracts should state whether entry fees are refundable and under what circumstances. A refund amortization schedule that explains when and how much money will be refunded should be attached to the contract. Times and conditions for the refund should be clearly explained. In fee-for-service communities, the contract should discuss extra fees, as well. An itemized list of services and their costs should be included.

Equity Communities

Separate contracts for the independent living home and services are required in equity communities. Another contract might be required for assisted living, skilled nursing, and/or Alzheimer's/dementia.

Since the home is purchased, the contract for the residence, in all probability, complies with recommendations and regulations for standard real estate transactions from the local Board of Realtors. It will enumerate taxes, commissions, and other fees that must be paid and to whom. It also should bear an explicit legal description of the property being purchased.

The details of resale regulations should be precisely identified. Who gets the equity? How much? Is a transfer fee charged? How much?

Particulars of the service package need to be itemized, listing specific information about each service and its cost. These usually include meals, housekeeping, transportation, and so on.

The health care package must be described distinctly, specifying whether the coverage is life care, modified fee for service, or fee for service. Check especially for exclusions in the coverage, particularly certain health conditions.

Lease Communities

One contract for the lease and another for the services are common in lease communities. As in equity communities, health care coverage might also be yet another contract. It might be required of all residents.

Lease community contracts specify the length of residency. It should also include the terms for renewal of the lease. (See the *caveat* on page 131.)

As in the equity contracts, the particulars about the service and health care packages must be all inclusive and intelligible. The fine print usually has the exclusions listed in it.

❋❋

Before signing the contract(s), it would be wise to double check the issues in Figure 8-12 against the contract. **It does not matter what the marketing representative or sales/leasing agent, the CEO, other staff, or residents tell you; NOTHING IS BINDING UNLESS IT IS IN THE CONTRACT. Get everything in writing.**

It is absolutely necessary that an attorney review all agreements. Sometimes they are long, seemingly contradictory, and often written in legalese, but an attorney can guide you through them. The Resident's Association/Council and/or the CEO might be able to recommend local attorneys who are familiar with the contracts of full service retirement communities.

NEGOTIATED RISK AGREEMENTS

Some communities are asking residents to sign a negotiated risk agreement. In essence, this agreement makes a deal with the resident that if the community will allow the resident to indulge in risky behavior without nagging him or her about it, the resident will refrain from suing the community for negligence for not protecting the resident from him- or herself.

For example, Mary has fallen several times lately. She always wears high heels, which, of course, make her less stable on her feet. The administration has pointed out that she should wear flat shoes; she refuses. Should she fall and seriously injure herself, she or, more likely, her family might try to sue the community for not protecting her from this hazard. If a negotiated risk agreement were in place, she would have signed her right to sue away.

Some communities have similar clauses built into their resident agreements; others might have a separate document. Before signing anything, check with your attorney.

❋❋

This chapter has helped you to see how you can afford and qualify for a full service retirement community and what contracts you will have to sign. Chapter 9 will cover how things are run at FSRCs.

9

OWNERSHIP, SPONSORSHIP, AND MANAGEMENT

Business, more than any other occupation,
is a continual dealing with the future;
it is a continual calculation,
an instinctive exercise in foresight.

—Henry R. Luce
Cofounder, *Time* Magazine, 1898-1967

The overwhelming majority of people employed in full service retirement communities (FSRCs), also known as continuing care retirement communities (CCRCs), are warm, kind, caring people who work hard at making a conscientious effort to provide the best environment possible for their residents. For the most part, you will find that the care given is excellent and the management is skillful. Sometimes these two necessary ingredients for a successful FSRC are not found in the same community. Rarely, neither will be present in a community.

That is why you, the consumer, must do your homework. Always ask who the owner, sponsor, and management are. Sometimes they are all the same; other times they are not. Often the owners, sponsors, and/or management will be large corporations that operate other FSRCs. While the names might have little or no meaning now, they will become increasingly more familiar as you read their information packets.

Ownership

Full service retirement communities are almost always owned by large corporations or charitable foundations. A few belong to individuals.

Philosophy

Usually the owner sets the tone of the community by steering it toward a philosophy of management. By determining goals, defining issues, and selecting methods to achieve these goals, the owner sets the direction for the community. This is reflected in the community's mission and vision statements.

All FSRCs exist primarily to serve their residents. However, some also offer philanthropic support to the local area. Often communities sponsor senior activities or host the meetings of the local commission on aging. The community might offer the needlepoint guild a place to meet or participate in charity fund raisers and other such purposeful endeavors. Being a good neighbor is part of its philosophy of management.

Look for plaques and awards in the lobbies and offices of the FSRC for signs of support of the local area. Communities that are good neighbors are, perhaps, looked upon more kindly by legislators, city councilmen, county supervisors, and citizens of the local area.

NONPROFIT VERSUS FOR PROFIT

One of the meaningful differences in legal ownership structures usually falls along the for-profit and not-for-profit (same as nonprofit) lines. Some FSRCs are for profit; however, the overwhelming majority are nonprofit. The for-profit communities are increasing at a relatively rapid rate. Each has its pros and cons. See Figures 9-1 and 9-2.

NONPROFIT	
Pros	**Cons**
• decisions made with their hearts (compassionate) • nontaxable • able to accept tax-deductible donations &, thus, generate donations • benevolence fund more likely • long history of care for the elderly • more money & resources spent on resident care	• decisions made with their hearts (might favor compassion over sound business judgment) • less experience with customer service • less experience with offering amenities

Figure 9-1

FOR PROFIT	
Pros	**Cons**
• decisions made with their heads (sound business judgment) • usually have long history in the hospitality industry • experience with amenities • birthplace of customer service • more sound financially, perhaps	• decisions made with their heads (might favor the bottom line over compassion) • portion of each dollar received goes to taxes & profit • unable to accept tax-deductible donations unless they own a nonprofit subsidiary (important for benevolence fund) • benevolence fund unlikely

Figure 9-2

These pros and cons are not absolute. There are exceptions to everything; these comments are intended to serve only as a guide. Just be aware of the downsides and look for leaders who are *both* highly skilled and compassionate business administrators.

Decision Making

In communities whose roots are in charitable activities, compassion often wins when making decisions that affect quality of care. These vital decisions cannot be made only with the heart, for that policy will eventually bankrupt an FSRC. Communities that spring from a business background, rather than a charitable one, are sometimes guilty of making fiscal decisions strictly with the head; compassion must also be included in the formula. Quality management will not lose sight of this.

Administrators walk a fine line. Without a stable fiscal foundation, there cannot be quality care over decades—it costs money. Full service retirement communities (FSRCs) are not charities and do not have never-ending sources of money; they are businesses that provide humanitarian services—nonprofit and for-profit communities, alike. Not only must the current financial picture be sharp, the long-range lens must be in focus, as well.

Spending Money

For-profit and nonprofit communities seem to spend their money differently. For-profit FSRCs seem to expend larger sums on marketing than do nonprofits.

During good times, for-profit FSRCs appear to invest in the latest bells and whistles. Residents enjoy the newest in technology, decor, and entertainment, and so on, long before many others.

Nonprofit communities, as a group, are more conservative in spending their money. They are slower in investing in the latest in technology and entertainment. Their wait-and-see attitude sometimes buys them the luxury of benefitting from improvements in products.

Hopefully, regular refurbishing is a budgeted item in every community. If not, the community could become rundown in longer spans between surges of profit. This could adversely affect the number of new residents. Once the community declines, the next surge of profit might never happen.

FAMILIES OF COMMUNITIES

Many corporations own several communities, called families. These families often have the same policies, styles, and, sometimes, the same architecture. Those who own many communities are, arguably, more experienced at operating them than those who own fewer.

Most of the time, if you buy into one FSRC in state A and want to move to another community in the same family in state B, you are welcome to do so. As a rule, little or no additional entry fee will be charged. However, this is not always true. Check before relying on this information.

SPONSORSHIP

The sponsor of a full service retirement community (FSRC) is usually a religious, municipal, or fraternal organization. Sometimes it owns the community and sometimes not. Its main role is to set the vision and mission of the community or family of communities. This is particularly true of religious organizations. Some hospitals are reaching out to sponsor FSRCs, as well.

Residents do not usually have to belong to the religious sponsor's group in order to live in its community. However, when cities or counties fund communities with taxes, residency in the municipality is necessary in order to live in the community. Fraternal organizations, as a rule, open their doors only to their members.

Sponsors vary widely as to how much liability they will assume in community operations. The contract should spell this out explicitly.

MANAGEMENT

Running an FSRC is an immensely complex undertaking. The direction that the management takes reflects the values, purpose, and mission of the owners and sponsors.

Management is responsible for running several businesses within one. They include, but are not limited to, food service, health care, transportation, entertainment, and property management. Some FSRCs are managed better than others.

APPROACH TO MANAGEMENT

Owners try to hire an individual or a team of managers that will support their philosophy. Chief executive officers (CEOs) should be able to tell you just what their communities' approach to business is.

Philosophy of Management

The chief executive officer should be able to discuss his or her philosophy of management with you. You should learn what the primary focus of the FSRC is, what its goals are, and how management plans to achieve them.

This information is very important. It will affect many areas of the community.

Styles of Management

All managers or teams of managers have an understanding of what it means to be a good manager and how that concept should be realized. They have their own styles of managing, which are based on who the CEO is, as an individual. Sometimes managers will use different approaches with different personalities among the employees and the residents. Other times, the style used depends upon the tasks and not the people.

Of the three major styles of management, autocratic, participative, and *laissez-faire*, one usually comes naturally for each manager. They primarily differ by how much power or authority the supervisor assumes. The autocratic manager makes the decisions and

177

announces to all the path to follow. The participative manager requests input from employees and, maybe, residents and then makes a decision. Middle management will most likely have some leeway in carrying out a plan. The *laissez-faire* manager essentially gives all employees a free hand, with little or no guidance. Policies then, can become inconsistent from department to department. See Figure 9-3.

STYLES of MANAGEMENT	
Type	Description
Autocratic	makes own decisions, expects all to follow
Participative	requests input & wants help from all in decision making & implementation of new plan or policy
Laissez-faire	decisions by employees; little guidance from the CEO

Figure 9-3

Eden Alternative

Nursing homes have been the birthplace of a new style of management. The Eden Alternative essentially empowers the employees to make decisions as to how their jobs will be done.

For instance, certified nursing assistants (CNAs) are the people who deliver most of the custodial care to residents in nursing homes. Under the Eden Alternative, the supervisors would explain to teams of CNAs what needs to be done and then check to be sure that it is done. The nursing assistants would set their own work schedules within certain parameters and decide who does which tasks and when. What the CNAs' supervisor might not do is decide that Kristin gets Thursdays off and Heather works the east wing, rather than the north wing.

Supporters of this concept believe that, if given the chance, workers will take the initiative and have more pride in a job well done. For example, Mrs. Jones has a difficult time with her weekly physical therapy treatment. She is more comfortable with Kristin and does better when Kristin is with her. In order for things to run smoothly, Kristin needs to change days off. In theory, Kristin will accept this change more readily if she and her co-workers are in charge of arranging their own schedules than if a supervisor has to order her to change days off. Kristin will supposedly understand that making the change will serve a greater good.

One of the most commonly used aspects of the Eden Alternative is the placing of pets and plants in skilled nursing (SN). Studies show that fish, birds, cats, dogs, and other pets improve the quality of life for residents. Pets are also effective tools in the Alzheimer's/dementia (A/D) area. Plants soften the sterile look of skilled nursing and make the community feel more like home.

When the Eden Alternative is carried over into independent living, employees would be able to fix little wrongs without having to ask the supervisor every time. For example, if a wait-staff member were to spill gravy on a resident, an empowered employee would be able to tell a resident that the manager will pay for the dry cleaning bill without having to run to the supervisor at the time of every spill.

This approach is still new and controversial, but many FSRCs have instituted the pet and plant portion of the policy. There are several interesting books on the topic if you would like more information on this style of management.

DIRECTION OF THE FSRC

If the management governs well, every decision it makes will be a step toward supporting its mission and vision statements. Accordingly, these statements should tell you where the money is being spent. They might or might not endorse your values.

In some communities, an ethics committee steers management along a moral path. Ideally the members include residents, board members, administrators, and managerial staff.

BOARD OF DIRECTORS

Virtually all endowment FSRCs are governed by volunteer community leaders who comprise a board of directors or a board of trustees. The boards of equity communities are usually made up of residents. Their jobs are to make sure that the community is financially sound. They are also responsible for assuring that systems for providing quality care for residents are in place and functioning well. It oversees the mechanism that ensures that the corporation is in compliance with local, state, and federal laws and regulations.

PLANNING

Long-range planning is essential to the long-term success of an FSRC. Many types of plans must be in place to ensure a successful venture far into the future.

Strategic Plan

At the heart of these programs is the strategic plan that looks down the road several years. Its purpose is to look for potholes ahead in their paths and to fix them before they become so big that they wash out the roads or to find alternate routes around them. The ideal strategic plan is integrated with every other plan: financial, health care, risk management, emergency preparedness, and maintenance, among others.

Risk Management

Managing an FSRC is fraught with risk on every front. Every community should have a formal, written risk management plan. Emphasis on risk management plans is relatively recent and not all communities have one.

As a corporation, the FSRC must comply with volumes of legal regulations. Health care, building and equipment maintenance, and employment issues, among others, create liability. The risk management plan should be fully integrated with the strategic plan, as should all the other plans a successful community has.

In this litigious society, FSRCs must protect themselves in a number of ways. The obvious solution is insurance, but it cannot be the only answer. Insurance rates have skyrocketed in recent years, placing even more importance on the prevention of potential problems. Many issues can be dealt with effectively by education and training—starting with the board of directors and working all the way down the organizational chart to the dishwasher.

A safety plan can prevent accidents. A regular schedule for maintenance and repair of buildings, grounds, and vehicles is another area for preventive actions. Giving quality care to residents helps to deter lawsuits. These programs could result in reduced insurance premiums.

Generation Gap

The generation gap poses, arguably, one of the biggest planning challenges that the industry has ever faced. The difference between generations was born in the twentieth century. Never before in the history of mankind have the times changed so fast that human beings couldn't change with them.

The twentieth century started with many people living in homes without electricity, running water, indoor bathrooms, and refrigerators. People walked, rode a horse, or paddled a boat to get around; the average person never traveled more than twenty miles from home in a lifetime. The century ended with microwave ovens, cellular phones, and Internet access in most homes. Two or more cars are parked in front of nearly every family's house. Air flight to faraway lands is common and astronauts, a politician, and a billionaire have taken journeys into outer space.

As each successive generation came along, its members adapted to the times of their youths. The next generation rejected its parents' values and beliefs because that value system was not compatible with the current times.

FSRCs have the very difficult task of pleasing four generations:

- G.I. Generation, the oldest of the current residents,
- Silent Generation, the youngest of the current residents,
- Baby Boomers, the next residents, and
- Generation X, the current employees.

The Baby Boomers

What must an FSRC do to attract the coming wave of Baby Boomers who turn 62 in 2008? They have different values and different expectations of an FSRC than does the current generation of residents.

The G.I. Generation and the Silent Generation members are not the users of exercise and fitness equipment that the Baby Boomers are. So, FSRCs are being forced by the marketplace (if they wish to be competitive) to add fully equipped fitness rooms and indoor swimming pools.

Baby Boomers also expect a whole host of other amenities. According to demographic studies, they, as a group, want a café, specialized activities rooms, and larger homes. All of these things cost a great deal of money. They will not happen without long-range planning.

Even if you are reading this for an older relative, the preparations for the Baby Boomers are still important to you. Your loved one will want to live in a viable community. FSRCs that do not become competitive in attracting the Baby Boomers have a much higher chance of losing new residents to those that do plan for the future. Without new residents, communities will experience a less than bright future.

Employment Issues

Employment issues are becoming critical. The current shortages in nursing and administration are not expected to ease in the coming years. FSRCs must make their communities attractive places to work; otherwise, the quality employees will go elsewhere.

Communities should already have in place a benefits package that will entice high caliber employees to join their teams. Creative perks might include a day care center for employees' children and, perhaps, the children of the local area. (This also provides an opportunity for the retirees to interact, on a volunteer basis, with the children.)

Every business needs good employees to remain competitive. Tomorrow's residents want to be able to see twenty or more years down the road, assured that the quality that exists in today's community will be there tomorrow.

FINANCES

Everything in business is ultimately about money. FSRCs are no different. Decisions are driven by the bottom line.

Is the FSRC that you are looking at ready for this next generation of retirees and employees? Can it afford to make the changes to keep up with the expectations of new residents and new employees? Its financial plan should take these changes into effect and will if it is integrated into the strategic plan.

Value

There are two important requirements that a successful FSRC must satisfy. Quality of care is one and the other is financial stability. Our society is quick to judge quality by the cost of an item. That value system does not always work in FSRCs.

Relatively inexpensive FSRCs do provide top quality care. What they are most likely missing are the elegant surroundings, upgraded services, opulent amenities, and a choice location. For potential residents whose budgets do not allow for a more expensive FSRC or who do not want to pay for these features, there are excellent communities available. Additionally, lease communities attract residents who are unwilling or unable to pay a large entrance fee, but who can afford the monthly fee.

On the other hand, some very expensive communities might not offer many amenities; they are essentially selling "location, location, and location" (*e.g.*, oceanfront property). They also virtually always offer quality care. Some FSRCs are like country club communities and many others are more modest. All too often the more modest ones will charge nearly the same monthly fees and, sometimes, entrance fees, as do the more luxurious communities. "You'd better shop around." (Tina Turner)

Cutting Costs

Good management always looks for ways to cut costs without cutting quality. The residents are a path to this goal. They come with a wide range of skills, and there are always many willing hands.

Decorations for holidays can be made with great enthusiasm and talent by the arts and crafts group. The garden club will want to maintain some of the community's flower beds. Woodworkers can, and often do, contribute by doing minor maintenance chores for residents and by building all sorts of projects, from shelving to furniture.

Virtually all communities will raise the monthly fee each year. The increase will be higher than the cost of living because it is based directly on the community's projected expenses. Medical costs are rising faster than the cost of living.

Some communities even out the raises by a fair-share allocation plan. This means that the increases in fees that residents experience will be based on the square footage of their homes, just as the entry and monthly fees are.

Management has to walk a fine line between giving in to the requests of residents and keeping the communities up to date. It is hired to see the big picture. Not only must it please and care for today's residents, but it must attract tomorrow's residents, as well. Full service retirement communities must also find and keep high caliber employees while operating the FSRC within a budget and retaining the level of quality as a whole. Sometimes the essential, but expensive, decisions are unpopular with the residents, but, once in place, they are virtually always pleased with the changes.

While no one wants to pay for increased costs, it is necessary to spend money to keep the community evolving with the times. It is vital that FSRCs attract new residents who bring new funds. Today's residents who fight the increases in monthly fees force management, if it gives in, to gradually cut back on services and the raw-food-per-plate costs (page 93), among others. Increasing monthly fees protects the residents' initial investments in their communities.

Cutting services, rather than raising monthly fees, diminishes the overall quality of the community. As a result the entry fee will remain low, as competitors raise theirs. New residents with income levels that would qualify for the competitors will not consider a community of lesser quality. Thus, begins the downward spiral.

Progressive FSRCs are always looking for ways to increase income without raising monthly fees. The residents and staff appreciate convenience stores, coffee shops, and cafés and the community might enjoy a share of the profits.

Opportunities for short-term rentals include winter visitors (snowbirds) and summer visitors who are fleeing oppressively hot summers. Others are rehabilitation or respite care (care of frail elderly while their caregivers take a short break or a vacation). Elderly residents of the local area need services, such as adult day care, delivery of meals, and visiting nurses.

FINANCIAL SOUNDNESS

Of course, you would not buy into a community that is having financial troubles now—but you won't know if you don't look into it.

An accountant can study the financial statements that each community must give you.

Certified Public Accountants (CPAs) use ratio analysis to evaluate the figures. Each industry has a range of values that is considered optimum for each of these ratios. The Commission on Accreditation of Rehabilitation Facilities/Continuing Care Accreditation Commission (CARF/CCAC) has prepared a superb publication that will tell your accountant what values are suitable for the CCRC industry. He or she will be better informed to evaluate the soundness of an FSRC/CCRC. The publication is entitled *Financial Ratios and Trend Analysis of the CARF/CCAC Accredited Organizations* and can be purchased for a reasonable fee from CARF/CCAC. See Appendix A.

Each nonprofit community (501[c][3] corporation) is required to file a form 990 with the IRS. This is public information and reports the community's income and expenditures. You can get a copy by making a formal request to the IRS.

Standard & Poor's rates the bonds issued by FSRCs. The communities need very strong credit and must comply with their benchmarks for FSRCs. Your attorney, CPA, or financial advisor can help you investigate.

STAFFING

Every business faces problems in attracting and retaining skilled employees. The health care industry is no different; in fact, its problems are worse than some other industries. The current nationwide shortage of registered nurses is not expected to end soon. Administrators are also scarce.

If you are going to live in an FSRC for a couple of decades, it is very important to you that skilled people will want to work there. What are FSRCs doing to combat this problem? Forward-moving communities are aggressively recruiting and constantly selecting good people.

Employee morale is a vital part of an FSRC. When employees feel that they are a part of the family, they take pride in what they do. This creates a happy place for people to work and live. Look for signs of good team spirit.

Secure employees make valuable contributions to any organization. Empowering employees to make a difference in doing their jobs encourages them to continue working there. Workplace training enables employees to advance and eventually lead. Competitive wage and benefit packages will help with retention.

Ratio of Total Staff to Residents

Ask about the ratio of total staff to residents. The exact numbers are not necessary, but even a very rough estimate is often telling. Of course, part time versus full time employees and in-house versus outsourced labor all affect the accuracy of the numbers, but a very informal survey tells us that most communities seem to have one staff member for every two residents (1:2). Even a ratio of **one** staff member to 1½ to 2½ residents (1:1.5-2.5) does not seem to be far out of the norm. The real red flag appears to be when the figure is badly skewed.

When the number of staff is equal (1:1) to or greater than the number of residents (*e.g.*, 2:1), we wonder if management might be providing an inordinate number of services. On the other hand, perhaps the population is so frail that it needs that much care. We visited an FSRC that had almost two staff members to every resident. Later we discovered it was in transition from an FSRC to an assisted living/skilled nursing facility only. Of course, there is the rare case of management's squandering the residents' money. If the number of staff approaches one staff to three or four residents (1:3-4), we must wonder how poorly services are being provided, if they are at all.

These conclusions are far from a scientific survey. They are not even based on any formal studies. Nevertheless, we found the answers very telling. Asking the staff/resident-ratio question led us to discover information that we had previously been unable to uncover. See Figure 9-4.

MARKETING/SALES

Superior marketing is crucial to the future of the FSRC. This is where the personality of the community is put forth to the public. It

STAFF-to-RESIDENT RATIO Not a Scientific Survey!		
Number of Staff	**Number of Residents**	**Possible Conclusions**
1+	1	extraordinary number of services provided, frail population, or, perhaps, poor management
1	1.5 to 2.5	about average
1	3+	too few services being provided, perhaps

Figure 9-4

is through the community's publications and representatives that you will learn the most about the community.

Look for what FSRCs do not tell you. For instance, if a toll-free phone number is not offered in its printed materials, you might wonder how aggressively they are seeking future residents from out of the region. Is there a guest suite available for use by the marketing department? If so, are they charging prospective residents for a night's stay? The more difficult and expensive they make it for distant shoppers to visit, the fewer they will attract.

A diverse population is necessary to the vitality of the community. Envision two octogenarians swapping tales. One man lived in the desert all of his life. If the other had lived in the Yukon, Manhattan, or Greece, you could picture the spark their conversation would have. Now imagine that the desert dweller's companion was also from the desert.

Terminology

The marketing department is where the sales take place and the money changes hands. The term "marketing" is used in endowment communities and personnel are marketing representatives. Equity communities hire real estate brokers and agents to occupy their sales offices. Leasing agents work out of rental or leasing offices in rental communities. We are using the most common term, "marketing representative," as a catchall phrase for real estate, sales, leasing, and rental agents. See Figure 9-5 for a summary of terminology.

Watch for misnomers. Marketing materials might tell readers that they are "buying" a home, when they are, in fact, buying only the right to live there. Apartments are mistakenly called "condos" when the resident owns no property interest, as in the legal definition of condominium. Some endowment communities will incorrectly label its entry fee as a membership fee.

When marketing reps call their communities "continuing care," they are often referring to the payment plan, which is really fee for service or modified fee for service (Plans B or C). Conversely, when most other reps use the term "life care," they mean the all-inclusive payment plan of the extended contract or Plan A. Some fee-for-service marketing reps call their communities "life care," referring only to the lifetime guarantee of care.

SUMMARY of TERMINOLOGY					
Type of Community	Name of Office	Title of Rep.	Monthly Payments	Entry Fees	Name of Legal Document
Endowment	marketing	marketing rep.	monthly fee	entrance fee	resident agreement
Equity — condo	sales	real estate or sales agent	condo, health care, & service fees	purchase price	varies
Equity — co-op			occupancy, health care, & service fees	purchase price	varies
Equity — membership			membership, health care, & service fees	membership fee	varies
Lease	leasing or rental	Leasing or rental agent	rent, health care, & service fee	entry fee or deposit	lease

Figure 9-5

RESIDENT LIFE AND WELLNESS

Management is responsible for running the programs, services, and amenities that enhance the residents' tenures in the community. Residents can expect treatment with a level of respect that preserves their dignity and independence and a physical environment that will be safe and attractive.

Every FSRC has its own personality and focus. Its differences spring from the approach that the owner, sponsor, and management take to their relative positions and how much money there is available to run the budget.

Focus of the Community

Many communities tend to cater to residents in independent living while caring expertly and warmly for those who need assisted living, skilled nursing, and Alzheimer's/dementia care. These communities will do whatever they can to keep residents in independent living as long as possible.

Long halls will have seating for residents who need to rest and handrails for those requiring a little assistance. Exercising will be made easier by having fitness rooms, indoor measured walking routes, nature trails, and/or paved walking and biking paths with lots of shady places to sit along the way.

Home health care (HHC) is permitted at some FSRCs and at not others. Having it or not having it is neither right nor wrong; it is merely a different approach to managing the health care program (page 84).

Each part is interdependent upon the others, but skilled nursing (SN) is the heart of a closely knit community. It enjoys the support of the whole community that a freestanding nursing home does not experience.

It is fairly common knowledge that the nursing home resident who has family visit every day gets consistently good care, but not everyone enjoys daily family visits. Residents of a quality FSRC's skilled nursing area almost invariably get top notch care because the residents are under the watchful eye of current residents, visitors, and potential residents. Assisted living and Alzheimer's/dementia (A/D) residents also enjoy quality care for the same reasons.

Care plans for each resident should address the decision-making process to ensure that the residents get the personal and medical care they need for as fulfilling a life as possible. Administrators and staff should be sensitive to the fact that they work in the residents' homes—not that the residents live at their workplaces. Life is an emotional experience and the soul needs to be handled with care.

COSMETICS OF THE PROPERTY

While it might seem to some that having pretty surroundings is a frivolous item on an FSRC's agenda, it is actually very important. A beautiful campus is one of the factors that makes the community a contender for new residents. These resources buy capital improvements (below) and medical care. New people also contribute to refreshing the mood in the community.

Signs that management cares about keeping the community up are well-maintained grounds, buildings, roads, and parking lots. Attractive landscaping and flowers throughout add to the morale of the residents and staff. Cohesive color schemes are pleasing to the eye. The architecture is more attractive when it is interesting and follows a common theme.

The interior should also reflect the same high standards. Decor that is warm, inviting, and up to date pleases everyone. Clean public areas are nicer to live in, not to mention healthier.

Some experts are of the opinion that it is only the care that matters and that keeping up with the Joneses doesn't count. In an assisted living or nursing home facility, where the average stay is three years, that is probably correct if the care is really top notch.

However, in an FSRC, the thinking has to be a little different. The average stay is about fifteen years and will probably rise. In order for an FSRC to be competitive in the marketplace, it must, at the very least, keep up with the times. Ideally, it should be preparing for the next generation and its different values before new retirees arrive.

You want to be assured that the community that you choose will not become a dreary, rundown place and drop below optimum quality of care during your term of residence. When a community is not up to date, it will not attract new residents. They bring in entrance fees that are the source of funds for capital improvements (high-cost long-lasting construction, repairs, and/or purchases), medical care, and other long-range financial needs and commitments.

POLICIES

Much, but not all, of the residents' life and happiness centers around the approach of management to rules, policies, and procedures. These organizations are run for the benefit of the residents. Some FSRCs lose sight of this, and some policies do not enhance the quality of life for its residents.

Problem Solving

Management is called upon to solve many problems. For the most part they do a great job. Once in a while, however, something falls between the cracks. For instance, in one community we visited, a number of books were missing from the library so management locked it on evenings and weekends—without thinking that could be prime time for library visiting by the residents.

Situations like this are too common. It is not that we think mean-spirited people are making bad rules. We really believe that, in trying to solve one problem, another is created. Scrutiny of the big picture is sometimes missed by well-meaning—but busy—administrators.

Sometimes management does not look for creative solutions. In one situation, when residents took home too many pieces of fresh fruit from the dining room each day, management took all the fruit away from everyone. Another manager in another community, faced with the same problem, had the wait staff give one piece of fruit to each person after dinner. California law requires that residents have access to one piece of fresh fruit per person per day. Communities in other states offer it as a part of a nutritious diet.

We visited a number of communities whose residents in assisted living are discouraged—or even forbidden—from ever going into the independent living areas. This banning of residents from spouses, friends, and familiar social activities, in effect, shuns them. Too many communities still have these policies. (See the full discussion on page 102.)

Resident-Driven Policies

The policies of retirement communities often reflect the personalities and values of the residents. "No wheelchairs in the dining room" is one policy that is usually set at the request of the residents. This is sometimes driven by the fact that many people want to feel that they have moved into an independent living community. So residents in some communities request that management ban these devices in common areas, especially the independent living dining room.

This policy means that mobility-challenged residents would be forced to move into assisted living homes long before it might otherwise be required. On the other hand, marketing representatives find it hard to sell a community to very independent people when the dining room is a sea of metal devices.

Many communities offer a compromise that seems to be acceptable to most. Residents in wheelchairs and those using walkers are asked to transfer to a chair in the dining room. The staff then removes the wheelchairs and walkers to an adjoining space.

Sometimes management is willing to give the squeaky wheel the grease, rather than consider all sides. Petty rules could be a sign of weak management. Residents in one community we visited must have complained that guests were working on too much of their community jigsaw puzzle, for beside it was a small sign telling all that "Puzzles are for residents only."

Tipping

Tipping the staff could become a problem in FSRCs. In theory, people who tip usually get better service. Virtually all of the communities we visited had a no-tipping policy. In that case, residents may contribute to a fund that all employees will share at Christmastime. This creates an incentive for employees to give everyone equal treatment and to stay in the FSRC's employment.

Pets

The pet policy varies from community to community. Many do not allow them at all. Some permit residents to move in with the pets that they have at the time, but do not want the residents to replace them when they pass away. Others welcome pets, but might have a size or breed restriction.

Some of the newer second generation communities have erected dog runs. They might have cordoned off areas for pets to run freely, without leashes. Strategically located stations provide handy places to deposit pets' waste. Progressive FSRCs might even have a veterinary clinic on site.

Community pets often live in some of the assisted living (AL), skilled nursing (SN), and Alzheimer's/dementia (A/D) areas. Visiting pets provide therapy for residents. (See the discussion about the Eden Alternative on page 178.) One community we visited even had a community dog in independent living (IL).

ASSESSING THE OWNERSHIP, SPONSORSHIP, AND MANAGEMENT

Beware of communities that are finding it difficult to keep up with the times. FSRCs are caught between pleasing the current and future residents. The G.I. Generation and the Silent Generation value sameness and thriftiness. Communities must attract the incoming Baby Boomers who value choice, individuality, and elegance—and are able and willing to pay for it. Managements of older FSRCs are having to spend the dollars of today's thrifty residents to attract tomorrow's residents who live very different lifestyles. They must also provide competitive employment benefits for Generation X employees that seem excessive to their frugal residents.

Addressing the generational challenge is where the newly constructed FSRCs are pulling ahead of many of the existing communities. Only those older communities whose managements have twenty-first-century vision will be able to compete with the second generation FSRCs.

Progressive managers of FSRCs are constantly seeking ways to overcome tomorrow's problems before tomorrow comes. Education, sharing, and cooperation among the leadership of FSRCs nationwide provide the pathways for achieving this goal.

Trade Associations

Trade associations watch out for the best interests of their members. Many lobby Congress for laws that are favorable to the issues that affect the industry. The better associations educate their members at regularly scheduled conferences.

American Association of Homes and Services for the Aging (AAHSA)

Forward-looking nonprofit communities belong to the large and very active American Association of Homes and Services for the Aging and attend its conferences. Its leadership is progressive and innovative and works very hard at encouraging its membership to look ahead.

It is at its twice yearly meetings that FSRC administrators, developers, and lenders meet and exchange ideas. Educational classes on all aspects of the tremendously complicated job of running an FSRC are offered. One of the primary focuses of the national association and its state counterparts is to lobby Congress and state legislatures for changes in laws that will ultimately benefit their residents. In addition, exhibitors also display the latest in products, services, and systems that will aid the communities in staying up to date while servicing the needs of their residents.

American Seniors Housing Association (ASHA)

Progressive for-profit and nonprofit communities belong to the American Senior Housing Association. Though smaller, this association has a similar purpose and many of the same activities as AAHSA. Its members also are operators, builders, and financiers of FSRCs.

Accreditation

Seeking accreditation is a long, expensive process for an FSRC. Being accredited tells the world that communities have passed rigorous tests. This seal of approval aids them in marketing their communities. Some insurance companies lower premiums once communities have become accredited.

There are many excellent FSRCs that do not undergo this process. Communities with high occupancy rates and little competition might not find it is worth the great expense. However, CEOs of FSRCs have shared with us that they were pleasantly surprised at how much the accreditation process improved already great communities.

Competition raises the ante. Many become accredited just because the community across the street does—or to become a better competitor with the non-accredited community a couple of miles away. It is not important why FSRCs choose to become accredited; but what is important is that they do become accredited and, thus, gain the management tools and insight that the process awards them.

Commission on Accreditation of Rehabilitation Facilities/Continuing Care Accreditation Commission (CARF/CCAC)

The Commission on Accreditation of Rehabilitation Facilities (CARF) accredits adult day care, assisted living, medical rehabilitation, and other such facilities, but, heretofore, its accreditation had not usually been sought by FSRCs (CCRCs). While its expertise is beyond reproach, its focus was not directed toward most of what an FSRC/CCRC does.

It is the Continuing Care Accreditation Commission (CCAC) that focuses on accrediting full service retirement communities and sets the standards for excellence in managing FSRCs. CARF and CCAC have just recently merged. Certain reorganizational changes are bound to take place. When inquiring about accreditation, keep in mind that an FSRC's certification may come from CCAC, CARF, CARF/CCAC, or a newly named body.

This new commission closely examines all facets of these communities and awards those who do it well with its seal of approval. This certifying body is particularly strong in its examination of the financial structure of FSRCs. The CCAC also provides formal education and one-on-one guidance in helping communities meet the standards of excellence for FSRCs. A community must have been in business for a minimum number of years and maintained stabilized occupancy of 90% before it can apply for review.

The CCAC standards have been adopted by CARF, as they are specifically tailored for the FSRC/CCRC. It is the only accreditation body that focuses on the aging services continuum. The process focuses on the governance; financial resources and disclosure; and resident life, health, and wellness of an FSRC/CCRC. Figure 9-6 shows more details of these areas. Renewal of a community's accreditation is required every five years.

These criteria are stringent and the review process is long and rigorous. They are constantly being refined by the very competent staff to keep communities current on many fronts with the ever-changing climate of senior care. Look for revised standards in the future.

REQUIREMENTS for CARF/CCAC's STANDARDS of EXCELLENCE (2003) http://www.ccaconline.org		
Governance	Financial Resources & Disclosure	Resident Life, Health, & Wellness
• vision & mission • governing board • risk management • human resources • marketing & promotional materials • agreements & admissions • organizational ethics • information & technology strategy	• current financial position: financial information & disclosure • long-term financial resources • integrated strategic planning	• health & wellness philosophy • health & wellness programs • resident/client services & amenities • care coordination within the continuum • physical environment

Figure 9-6

You might be considering a community that has been accredited by CARF/CCAC. If so, you may rest assured that it has done the hardest part of your homework for you.

Joint Commission on Accreditation of Healthcare Organizations (JCAHO)

The Joint Commission on Accreditation of Healthcare Organizations (JCAHO) is also an accrediting body. Its focus is more on medical and health aspects of various kinds of facilities. Its emphasis is primarily on hospitals, yet its stamp of approval on an FSRC's skilled nursing area is sought by some communities.

Getting the JCAHO endorsement is much more expensive and time consuming than getting CARF/CCAC's accreditation. Since its primary concentration is in a different direction from that of the FSRC/CCRC, not many FSRCs seek its review. However, having the JCAHO certification is a definite plus. Because it is not the standard for FSRCs, communities cannot be faulted for not having JCAHO's accreditation.

Regulation

Certain areas of continuing care retirement communities (CCRCs) are regulated by the federal government. No one federal agency is responsible for regulating FSRCs; however, they must comply with federal laws that apply broadly, *e.g.* Americans with Disabilities Act, Fair Housing, Equal Employment Opportunity laws, and so on.

States vary widely as to which areas and how much control they impose on the communities. Some states regulate CCRCs as insurance agencies; because, in life care (LC) and modified fee for service (MFFS), they provide a form of insurance protection. The departments of consumer affairs, health, and/or aging watch for legal compliance.

State licensing bodies also inspect components of CCRCs, *e.g.* assisted living and skilled nursing, and their findings are public information. Their reports stress numbers of discrepancies. They do not tell the whole story. Ask the CEO the reasons behind any poor reports. Numbers that infer a negative situation might not reflect a negative reality. See Appendix C.

Laws regulate various operations of communities. Those governing consumer affairs require disclosure of information such as finances and contract contents. This is particularly true for FSRCs under construction that have even more regulations to follow.

Communities that are Medicare and Medicaid certified have another large group of regulations to comply with. Appendices B-D list government bodies that can give you more information on this important topic.

New Communities

In decades past, too many FSRCs filed for bankruptcy. Many states retaliated with stringent laws to protect citizens. Now new communities are required to follow a set of strict rules that are designed to protect consumers from the bankruptcies of their FSRCs. Common sense on your part will also help protect your investment.

Finances

We would be leery of a new community being built by a first-time owner with no financial history or management track record. The industry is now old enough that there are many established architecture, accounting, lending, construction, and management firms available for hire. There is no need to go blindly into such a big project without their guidance.

Communities under construction might have different payment policies from established FSRCs. In all likelihood, the first payment will be about 10%. They will probably, and understandably so, charge potential residents a substantial penalty for withdrawing the 10% deposit. These communities are depending on the commitment of certain monies to begin and continue construction. Sometimes depositors will be asked to pay the entry fee in several stages during the construction. This keeps the size of the construction loan and, consequently, interest costs down.

Once deposits are made, they are put into an escrow account. In order to have access to these monies, the developer must meet certain criteria set by law. Once he does, the funds can be transferred to the developer's account. When placing your name on the waiting list of a new community under construction, make your check out to the escrow agent, not the community. This might add a layer of protection for your money in case the project fails.

When moving into a newly constructed community, residents could lose their investments under certain conditions. Be sure subcontractors have been paid according to the contract terms. When they have been, the general contractor will have written releases. This particularly applies to equity communities more than other types. To be absolutely sure, seek the advice of an attorney who is familiar with property law, not just contract law.

Policies

Too many new communities we visited had undefined policies or rules that were not in the mainstream with more established communities. Loni's parents lived in an FSRC for nearly twenty years, when the industry was in transition. As the population of this community aged, new problems were constantly cropping up. The residents often had to push hard to get management to react to their changing needs. Sometimes the arguments were loud and bitter.

By now, equitable policies should be in place and residents should not, in their senior years, have to fight any battles. Management should have learned from the mistakes of other communities and set policies that avoid touchy situations.

❧❦❧

Now that you have a good idea of how FSRCs run, Chapter 10 will give you some indication of how to determine if you will fit in and if you might like living in a full service retirement community.

10

THE PERSONALITIES

*You can tell a lot about a town
from how it treats its visitors.*

—Mary E. Potter

It is important that you learn who the residents are. This is the pool from which you will select your future friends. You'll want to know their characteristics as a group in addition to meeting them individually.

Every community has a different personality. Some are predominantly one profession or one economic level. We visited many full service retirement communities (FSRCs), also known as continuing care retirement communities (CCRCs), whose residents were mainly teachers, farmers, businessmen, or military personnel. Some resident populations were old money while others were low or middle income. As you visit various communities, the character of each group will eventually make itself apparent.

MARKETING REPRESENTATIVE OR SALES/LEASING AGENT

The receptionist and the marketing representative (or sales/leasing agent) are your introduction to the community. Record your first impressions as you make an appointment to visit.

When we traveled several hours away from home, most FSRCs put us up for the night—usually at no charge. Having us stay overnight on a Friday, Saturday, or Sunday night was often problematic. Fridays and Sundays were less difficult than Saturdays. Mostly, we were invited to stay only on Monday through Thursday nights, when the marketing personnel could meet with us.

Most have appointments only during standard business hours. A few are beginning to offer evening and weekend hours. Several communities arranged for volunteer residents to show us around on a Saturday or Sunday afternoon. One resident told us she was not allowed to show us any part of the campus but the community center and was forbidden to answer certain questions. On the other hand, several other communities invited us to come Friday evening and stay the weekend, with free access to the community and its residents. Then we met with the rep on Monday morning.

It is very interesting to note how much the rep will allow you to mingle with the residents. Some marketing reps did not welcome our requests to meet residents. At one community the administration reluctantly decided—and only after much conversation among other staff members—that we could converse with one handpicked couple for dinner only. Another flatly refused. It made us wonder what management was afraid the residents would tell us.

PERSONALITIES OF THE RESIDENTS

Do the residents prefer hamburger or steak? Do they live among country-style oak furniture with braided rugs or among glass and chrome with Rya rugs? Do they bowl or play golf? Do they stay home or do they take trips? Are they educators, business owners, or farmers? Are they primarily Type A or Type B personalities? Are they wine-and-Brie or beer-and-chips people?

Each community will reflect who its residents are. No matter who they are, it is important that you fit in with them if you are going to live there.

STATISTICS

You are looking for a community where you will feel comfortable. Gathering and analyzing statistics can give you a good picture of what the group, as a whole, looks like.

Marital Status

Whether you are a man or a woman, single or married, it could be useful to know how many single men, single women, and couples live in the community. Activities and the overall climate will be different when there is an abundance of one gender over another or singles over marrieds.

Average Age

The average age of the population is one probable indicator of how active the group is likely to be. Sometimes, the marketing representative will have two numbers: one including skilled nursing and one without. Obviously, the older the residents, the more sedentary the activities are likely to be. The average age at move in is also helpful in painting a realistic picture of how active your new neighbors might be.

It is important for communities to have as low an average age as possible. Newly built communities, statistically, do not experience a wide turnover of their independent living homes for about ten years. Over this time, the average age of the community is mounting ever upward. This results in a slowly diminishing overall vitality of the community.

Marketing will have an ever increasingly difficult job of attracting younger residents. One of the best ways to combat this is for the community to build in stages. This should attract younger residents and/or more couples. If there are two or three phases that will open every three or so years, the average age of residents will, in theory, be kept lower.

Photo by Tim Schoon © 2004. Courtesy of SFCS, Inc.

Chapel.

Median Income and Median Assets

Other useful statistics are the median income and median assets of the residents. (Remember that median is the number where half of the figures are above a given number and half are below.) While statistics are not confidential information, many marketing reps will tell you they are and will not answer this question—yet others will volunteer the numbers. Sometimes the rep will at least tell you whether most residents readily met the financial requirements or barely qualified.

If the rep won't give you any of this information, then there are other ways to see if you will fit in with the crowd economically. Check out the cars in the parking lot; are they like yours? Notice the clothing and jewelry of the residents. In conversation, ask about second homes, the use of private duty aides, the trips they take, and other recreational activities.

Living with a group of people whose financial means are vastly different from yours can create tension and, perhaps, some disagreement. Residents with greater resources might pressure management to spend the community's money more freely because their values are different. Should this expenditure raise monthly fees, those in lower income brackets might find it hard to meet rising costs. They might also feel left out of expensive extracurricular social activities such as cruises and ski vacations. On the other hand, if these are the things you want to do with your neighbors, you will not want to feel restricted by living in a community with people of more modest means.

In life, our best friends are made from among our peers. In shopping for an FSRC, it is helpful to keep this in mind.

Living with the Aging

Looking at waves of grey hair in the dining room could bring thoughts that many dissenters often voice: "I don't want to live with all these old people." One resident pointed out the error of that viewpoint when she said, "These people are only old on the outside!"

We also shared the dissenters' opinions once, but we persevered in our search for our own FSRC because it was the practical thing to do. As we traveled and visited more communities, we soon came to be of the opinion that they really are only old on the outside.

CHARACTERISTICS

Usually you will meet the residents over a meal. Listen for lively chatter and laughter in the dining room. Congenial residents will table-hop, chatting with their friends.

At one FSRC we visited, the residents conversed gaily among themselves, creating a din in the dining room. They spoke to friends at other tables. They greeted us so warmly that we could not leave the dining room without speaking to the residents at each and every table on the way to the door. They stopped us, asking where we were from, hoping we liked the community and would choose to live there. They urged us to put our names on the waiting list.

In another FSRC's dining room, the scene was the same. We were pleased to note that it was a lively group—until we realized that not one person had spoken to us!

For the most part, FSRCs attract sociable people. However, when a community is made up of 90% or more of residents from the local area, new residents from out of town might have a hard time fitting into established cliques of many years.

As you talk to the residents, you can find out how they fill their time. Are they involved within the community or the local area? Do many travel a lot, leaving the community a ghost town? Friendly residents might invite you to their homes after dinner and even ask to exchange names and addresses so that they can answer future questions.

Billiards.

Communities who count among its residents attorneys, CPAs, doctors, and nurses can be proud. These residents brought their professional knowledge and judgments to choosing an FSRC for themselves.

You will want to surround yourself with active, open-minded people who have positive attitudes. Didn't your mother tell you that you are who your friends are? While every group has its crabs, it's preferable if they are in the minority.

OPINIONS OF THE RESIDENTS

Ask the residents their opinions of management. What do they like? What don't they like? What is management's reaction to abuse of privileges? If management addresses problems at all, does it come up with creative solutions or punish all? Are rules changed for the better?

Hopefully, you can chat with a member of the residents' association. The issues that they discuss the most will tell you a lot about the community.

The residents are full of information about the community and are usually eager to share quite candidly with visitors. You will find that virtually all of the residents are happy with their communities.

❊

This chapter has helped you determine if you might enjoy living among the residents in a full service retirement community. The next chapter offers hints on selecting your FSRC and your new home at that community.

11

FINDING, SCREENING, AND SELECTING YOUR NEW HOME

Nothing is more difficult and,
therefore, more precious,
than to be able to decide.

—Napoleon Bonaparte
French General and Emperor, 1769-1821

You might be looking for a community for yourself or a loved one. For most potential residents or the relatives of future residents of these communities, help evaluating full service retirement communities (FSRCs), also called continuing care retirement communities (CCRCs), is invaluable. Searching for your FSRC can be fun if you are not facing a critical time deadline. Whether or not you have any idea of what you are looking for, it is important that you are not settling for whatever community is down the street. As you begin your search, remember that when you have seen one FSRC, you have seen one FSRC.

STEPS to FINDING and SCREENING FSRCs
At a Glance
• selection of geographical areas • finding FSRCs • calling for information packets • reading information packets • phone screening FSRCs • visiting FSRCs • personal interview w/ rep/agent • dining with residents • researching outside sources • several return visits • speaking with the CEO • making your decision

Figure 11-1

Hopefully, your selected geographic regions will have a few FSRCs to choose from. Weeding some of them out before you start visiting is very helpful. You can determine a great deal from the information packets and the phone interviews.

Where are you going to retire? For some people, it is a simple decision; they will stay in the same town they have lived in for years. Others will move where their children, relatives, or friends are. Still, others will seek sun, snow, or water. The process has several steps, listed in Figure 11-1.

FINDING FSRCS

The first step to finding your FSRC is to determine what regions of the country you are considering. There are several factors to evaluate. Once that decision is made, you will need to locate FSRCs to choose from.

GEOGRAPHICAL LOCATION AND LOCAL AREA

The whole world is potentially available to you when it comes to where you will live in your retirement years. Your family, friends, interests, likes and dislikes, medical condition, finances, and a host of other things will narrow your choices.

Staying Where You Are

There is a lot to be said for staying where you are now. You probably have roots in the local area. You know people; your family might live there. You most likely have doctors and dentists you like. You know where to shop for the best bargains and you know where to get lamp shades custom made.

The more populated your local area is, the more likely it is to have an FSRC. Of course, many regions have multiple communities to choose from. If so, please do not move to the FSRC down the street just because it is there. Get out and look around; visit several.

As people age, their excursions will be closer and closer to home; the FSRC will ultimately become the center of their universe. A community that is compatible with who the residents are will be more comfortable.

Moving Elsewhere

For one reason or another you might not want to stay where you are. Life somewhere else might be cheaper. Many other reasons might tempt you to move.

Moving to the Region Where Relatives or Friends Live

How enjoyable it is to be able to move where you know people! There are several advantages. You have probably visited your children so many times that you are quite familiar with the area. You might even be comfortable in their churches and organizations and you might know some of your children's friends. In case of an emergency, you have the support of family and friends close by.

Choosing a Retirement Location

There are many books on places to retire. When there is that much to say, we really cannot do justice to the topic in this short chapter, but we can give you enough information to remind you of what you are undertaking. Should you decide to relocate, there are many things to consider in moving to another city and/or state.

Reasons for Moving

First of all, why are you moving? There are lots of understandable reasons why you would want to move. For example, our friend Don wants to sail his boat in warm waters. Peter loves to ski. Diane dreams of having lush tropical flower gardens. Eleanor loves the museums in the big city. Steve's lung problem is greatly improved in the desert Southwest. Bob is fed up with paying top dollar for a modest house in the city; his wife Phyllis longs for the simpler life of a small town. Anne loves the mountains and forests, while Orin is inspired by big sky country. They all have chosen to retire in places that suit what they want and need. Sometimes that meant leaving their homes of many years behind, in search of a new adventure. What is important to you?

Things to Consider

Whether you are driven by climate, terrain, health, activities, cost of living, or a simpler lifestyle, examine each location for a host of attributes that could possibly influence your happiness, security, and health. While the following discussion touches on the primary concerns, it is by no means complete.

Climate has an impact on lifestyle. Do you want four seasons? Do you mind an extremely hot or cold climate? The weather dictates something about everyone's daily life to some extent. Will residents need a heavy coat, light jacket, or sunscreen every time they leave home? As we age our bodies find it more difficult to adapt to extremes in weather. Outdoor activities are very much climate driven. Look for your favorites.

Quality of life is affected by all of the things listed below, but get the big picture first. Look for vitality in a town. Well-maintained neighborhoods and buildings reveal a concerned citizenry and a healthy economy. In addition, look for other things, such as noise, the amount of traffic, and the availability of parking downtown. How does the town feel?

The local economy needs to be stable. Nothing is drearier than a dying town. Look for a bright job forecast, not just for retirees, but for everyone. Prosperous businesses contribute to the town's economy. Only a healthy town can support the services seniors will need.

Cost of living is affected by many things. Housing is always the major expense in any area. Many lovely towns and cities are quite affordable. The cost of food varies from community to community, as does the cost of utilities. Taxes of all kinds cover a very broad range, from nearly nonexistent to quite high. Check out the state sales tax; personal property taxes; and state, county, and city income taxes; among others. Many states have exemptions for seniors or for pension income. It is very telling to fill out last year's tax form for the state you are considering and compare it with your actual state tax form from last year.

Goods and services must be readily available at prices that you can afford. Look not only at the basics, but also for the things that you need to indulge your passions. A large book store is essential for Andi, an avid reader. Jackie is a zealous needlepointer; how happy will she be without a shop in town? Bill wants to be sure that the town has mechanics who can work on his beloved foreign sports car. Donnie and her husband John are devoted antique collectors; they would love to be able to make regular rounds to several nearby shops.

Community services improve the quality of life. Libraries, hospitals, and schools offer possibilities for volunteerism and part time jobs. Small Business Development Centers are begging for help. Colleges and universities offer wonderful opportunities to expand one's horizons as a student and/or adjunct faculty. Workshops and seminars are probably offered by city, county, and religious community centers, as well.

It is a well-known fact that college and university towns have a wider range of goods and services *per capita* than other towns of similar population. They give their residents the perks of a city without many of its ills.

Public health and safety is always a concern. Nearby, heavy industry, toxic waste storage, nuclear reactors, high-power electric lines, and the local dump are probably not your idea of ideal neighbors.

As we age we are more vulnerable to crime. Statistics are readily available on how much property crime and violence is in each municipality. Some sections of towns have more problems than others and crime is very often confined to just those areas. It is not likely that retirement communities will be located in these neighborhoods, but you never know for sure until you check with the local police department.

Recreational activities will be more in demand in your retirement, for you will have more time to indulge in them. Seek your favorites. Do not overlook outdoor pursuits, including sports, both participatory and spectator, and picnicking in the park. Look for nearby restaurants, theaters, movies, golf courses, bowling alleys, and other activities that you enjoy. Look for the ease of accessing these diversions.

Cultural activities are more abundant in larger cities. However, enjoyable visual and performing arts and museums can be found in small towns.

Transportation to and from the airport is important if you like to travel. How much will it bother you to drive two hours to catch a flight at the nearest airport? If you like to take the train, it would be handy for it to be nearby. A public bus is indispensable for seniors who can no longer drive to get around town. Choosing a location without such a system might not be in your best interest.

Laws in a new state might alter the way you do things. They might even affect your life dramatically. For example, some states require only 20/40 vision in one eye to get a driver's license; others require that level of vision in two eyes. Some states have no income tax for all of its citizens; a few states exempt pensions. Inheritance and other laws also vary.

Emergency services that are nearby are necessary. An FSRC nestled between rolling green hills and surrounded by forests is peaceful and beautiful, but it might take the ambulance too long to get there. This is less of a problem for FSRCs that have their own ambulances. Emergency room physicians would remind you of the Golden Hour Rule: acute conditions have more successful outcomes if they are treated within the first hour of onset.

Other issues are also worthy of consideration. For instance, the neighbors of the FSRC can make a difference in the quality of life. Rundown property next door can, perhaps, mean security problems, rodents, and other pests. This could result in increased costs for combating them. Faltering businesses in close proximity to the FSRC pose similar threats. Seek an FSRC in a neighborhood that is not likely to deteriorate in the next twenty to thirty years. Ask the help of local police and planners at city hall in making this judgment. A check of the master plan will tell you whether the county or city is planning to build a major highway just outside the FSRC's property line in the next five to ten years.

Elementary and secondary schools bring traffic congestion, as does a college or university. Visitors to a shopping mall, tourist attractions, and a coliseum also clog the roads leading to them. Visit the FSRC of your choice during different times of the day, month, and year for the complete traffic story. Of course, you may ask the residents, as well.

Choosing the Immediate Area for Your FSRC

Having shopping and entertainment close by means our lives will be more enriched by availing ourselves of their benefits. Just outside your FSRC should be thriving businesses. They must offer basic needs, such as groceries and clothing, and basic services, e.g., dry cleaning, auto repair, and gas stations.

Health care is of paramount importance as we age. Unfortunately, we will, statistically, need doctors and hospitals more as we grow older. Equipment and personnel for physical therapy, medical testing, and other medical services should also be handy. Living far away from good medical care can be inconvenient at best.

✻

Our brief treatment of this subject in no way diminishes its importance. Selection of the perfect geographical area for you is a crucial decision. Figure 11-2 highlights issues to consider. Please explore it further. For more information, refer to any of several good books on the subject.

LOCATION CONSIDERATIONS
At a Glance
• climate • well-maintained town • thriving economy • cost of living • community services • goods & services • health care • emergency services • public safety • recreational activities • transportation • state & local laws

Figure 11-2

213

LOCATING FSRCs

Unfortunately, there is no national listing of FSRCs at this writing. Many businesses, especially those that advertise on the Internet, will do the searching for you. Some of the searches are personalized and others provide very little service beyond the phone book. However, your own resources for finding a wonderful FSRC that is well suited to your tastes and wallet are extensive!

Without the Internet

The local library has many resources to help you find the names and addresses of local government agencies and associations. Write or call to ask for lists of FSRCs in the selected areas. Look in the

RESOURCES
At a Glance
Commission on Aging, local office
State Legislator, County Supervisor, City Council member, or Mayor
Chamber of Commerce
Newspaper   Newspapers usually offer a month of Sundays for free or for a nominal charge to prospective residents of an area. Check for ads for FSRCs.
Yellow Pages   The phone company will also send the Yellow Pages to prospective residents for free or for a nominal charge.

Figure 11-3

Yellow Pages. Many libraries carry telephone books from out of town. Some newspapers will send you a month of Sundays for little or no charge. See Figure 11-3 for a list of resources to find FSRCs in distant towns without using the Internet. Also, refer to Appendices A and E in this book.

With the Internet

We Baby Boomers are more transient than our parents, and we will be more likely to move to new locations for our retirement years. Most of us are likely to be computer literate. The best way for FSRCs to reach this new batch of retirees across the country is the Internet. It promises to become the closest thing to a national listing that we will have any time soon.

Therefore, many FSRCs are turning to the information superhighway to get themselves known to potential residents. Having out-of-state people relocate to their FSRCs makes a community more well rounded and diverse. If a community is actively seeking a diverse population, its marketing efforts will be directed beyond ads in the local media and direct mail to its town's own residents.

If you have never used the Internet, this is the perfect project for which to learn this new skill. You may gain access to the Internet at your local library or through a friend if you do not have it yourself.

Figure 11-4 has a list of helpful Web sites for locating your retirement home. Of course, as time goes on, this list will grow. We have left blank rows for you to fill in your favorite sites.

Search engines are the equivalent of the card catalog at the library, only tremendously more efficient. Several might list some of the same sites, but each will not have all of them. To find Web sites through search engines, type in keywords and ask the computer to search for matches. Using quotation marks will tell the computer to search for a phrase instead of single, disconnected words. See Figure 11-5. These keywords should uncover the Web addresses of almost all of the FSRCs that have Web sites. Also add keywords that will be meaningful to you. Narrow your search by adding the name of the state and city that you are interested in or amenities that are important to you, such as "acres," "fitness," or "chaplain." Also, try the same keywords in different search engines.

Most of the sites have a mechanism by which you may contact the FSRC electronically. It is so easy to fill in your name and address to request an info packet. (Remember to ask for an "information packet," because asking for a "brochure" will often get you a one-sheet explanation of why FSRCs are a good thing.)

SEARCHING on the INTERNET	
Web Site Name	**Web Address**
Continuing Care Accreditation Commission	http://www.ccaconline.org
ElderNet.com	http://www.eldernet.com
Homestore.com	http://www.springstreet.com
Life Care Services	http://www.lcsnet.com
New Life Styles Online	http://www.newlifestyles.com
Nursing Home Compare	http://www.medicare.gov/NHcompare/home.asp
Retirement Net	http://www.retirenet.com
Total Living Choices for Seniors	http://www.tlchoices.com
Other	
Other	

Figure 11-4

Collect as many information packets from FSRCs as you are willing to read. The more you learn, the better a decision you will make. The next step is screening all of them and deciding which ones you want to visit.

SCREENING FSRCs

Once you have a stack of information packets before you, it is necessary to choose which ones to visit. It is true that you cannot judge a book by its cover; FSRCs whose brochures are modest do not always come from communities of modest means. Some come from popular, and possibly, luxurious communities that have long waiting lists and choose not to spend a lot of money on marketing.

FINDING FSRCs on the INTERNET	
Search Engines	
http://www.google.com	http://search.aol.com
http://www.yahoo.com	http://search.msn.com
http://www.metacrawler.com	http://search.netscape.com
http://searchenginewatch.com (for a list of search engines)	Other
Other	Other
Keywords to Use in Search Engines	
"continuing care retirement community"	lifecare retirement (no space between life & care)
"retirement community"	CCRC retirement
full-service "retirement community" (with hyphen)	"extended care" retirement
"full service" "retirement community" (with space)	continuum care retirement
"life care" retirement (with space)	"continuum of care" retirement
"life-care" retirement (with hyphen)	"continuous care" retirement
Other	Other
To Refine Your Search, Add:	
city & state	equity, endowment, lease, or rental
golf, ceramics, chapel, *e.g.*	condo, co-op, or membership
ethnic, religious, or fraternal	university-linked or college-linked
rural, wooded, or urban	Other

Figure 11-5

The initial step is to decide what basic features you want in an FSRC. You might not know exactly at first, but our guidelines will help you. As you visit the communities, your opinions will surface.

THE INFORMATION PACKETS

Examine each of the information packets carefully. In reading for facts and impressions, it is helpful to organize your findings. Keeping track of information is easier with the form in Figure 11-6; it can be typed with a word processor onto peel-and-stick shipping labels. Affix one to the outside of each envelope of the information packet and fill it in as you read about the community.

The label is a duplicate of the questions in the phone screening checklist in Chapter 12—but in much abbreviated form. Reading the questions will help clarify its brevity. We like using the labels because they give us the details about each community at a glance on the outside of the envelope.

Study the photographs and compare them with those in the other brochures. Look for signs that the residents could be active, such as a swimming pool, walking trails, and exercise equipment. Is the natural terrain the kind that you want? Look for bodies of water, mountains, desert, or beach in the photos. Check for landscaping and overall appearance. Is the atmosphere of the community focused on vibrant independent living and warm care? See Figure 11-7.

PHONE SCREENING

A call to the marketing representative is almost always necessary for a good preliminary screening effort. It is helpful to fill in the name of the marketing representative you spoke to on the phone rather than the one who sent you the information. Often the toll-free phone number is not advertised; but once a prospective resident calls for the first time, the marketing representative will usually give it to you. Record your first impression of the rep and the person who answers the phone. Most of the time, their personalities will give you the first hint as to the personality of the community.

PHONE SCREENING	
Fits 3 1/3" x 4" Peel-and-Stick Label	

Mkting rep: _____

First impression of rep: ☐ positive   ☐ neutral   ☐ negative

Phone # toll-free _____

Total # of residents: _____	**Age:** min _____
_____ # of IL ☐ HHC	☐ younger spouse accepted
_____ # of AL ☐ A/D:AL	☐ w/ additional fee
_____ # of SN ☐ A/D:SN	avg age: IL _____
☐ nonprofit ☐ for profit	avg age w/ SN _____
Occupancy: ☐ endowment	**Fee inc:** ____meal(s)/day or mo.
☐ equity ☐ lease	**Most popular meal:** ☐ brkfst
Refund plan ☐ no ☐ yes ___%	☐ noon ☐ evening
Mo. fee: ☐ LC ☐ MFFS ☐ FFS	**Meals at:** ☐ set times ☐ range
☐ plan X	**Visit?** ☐ yes ☐ no
Accredited ☐ yes ☐ no	**Guest rm:** ☐ free ☐ fee $_____
Property type: ☐ high rise	**Meals during visit:** ☐ free ☐ fee
☐ sm campus	dine w/ residents ☐ yes ☐ no
☐ lg campus # acres _____	coat/tie req'd ☐ yes ☐ no
on site: ☐ clinic ☐ doctor	**Appointment:** _____

Key:

IL = Independent Living homes
AL = Assisted Living homes
SN = Skilled Nursing homes
HHC = Home Health Care
X = Plan X (obsolete)
FFS = Fee for Service
MFFS = Modified FFS

LC = Life Care
A/D: AL = separate AL for
Alzheimer's/Dementia residents
A/D: SN = separate SN for
Alzheimer's/Dementia residents
inc = included in monthly fee
req'd = required

Figure 11-6

True FSRCs

Because there are so many FSRC look-alikes, it is necessary to check first to be sure that you are calling a true FSRC. By asking what levels of living it has, you can determine for yourself if it really has a continuum of care. Keep in mind that some reps will think their community is an FSRC when it is not. See page 29.

True Life Care

Some communities use the term "life care" to mean that they guarantee to take care of their residents for the rest of their lives, but they do not have an all-inclusive fee plan as do true life care communities, as defined by AAHSA (page 136). They are instead fee-for-service communities that provide continuing care to residents and guarantee access to it for the duration of each resident's life.

READING the INFO PACKET
Cues from Photos
• signs of active residents
▸ swimming pool
▸ walking trails
▸ exercise equipment
• natural terrain
▸ water
▸ mountains
▸ desert
▸ beach
▸ forest
• health care
▸ rehabilitation
▸ caring staff
• attractive buildings
• happy people
• local area

Figure 11-7

Size of the Community

The size of the community tells you a whole lot more than just how many people live there. Generally, an FSRC with more than 350 residents is large enough that it can generate enough money to stay afloat while providing a wide range of amenities and necessary services.

There are enough people to make life stimulating. They will have a variety of interests and will have had a wide range of experiences. A community of 100 people will get very small after a number of years; the variety of amenities will be limited. Knowing the number of residents and homes gives you an idea of not only how big the community is, but also how many couples and how many singles live there.

The larger the community, the more amenities it can offer. This can make the difference between having a single multipurpose room as opposed to a theater, a ballroom, and one or more multipurpose rooms. It might not have the cozy feel of a smaller community; however, some large FSRCs are broken down into smaller neighborhoods that are cozy. Larger communities are more likely to have at least one formal dining room in addition to one or more informal dining rooms.

The proportion of residents at each level also indicates where the energy of the community is concentrated. The percentage of homes in independent living (IL) versus assisted living (AL) and skilled nursing (SN) will tell you this. A large percentage of independent living homes tends to show a number of things. Among them is a focus on maintaining a healthy, vibrant, independent living population and a community that puts energy and money into the needs of these residents. This is not meant to imply that there is not a sufficient emphasis on assisted living and skilled nursing; although, we have found, indeed, that is the case in some communities.

It is vital that, no matter how frail residents are, they live in a community where the bulk of the population is independent. The spirit and mood of the community are vastly different when people are running around instead of sitting around. If they can't keep up physically, they can at least catch the spirit and enthusiasm for life.

Nonprofit and For Profit

Many for-profit FSRCs are now appearing on the market. The advantages of both nonprofit and for-profit communities are discussed on page 174.

Occupancy Options and Monthly Fees

This is the opportunity for you to record what types of occupancy options the community has. They will be either endowment, equity, or lease.

All of the occupancy options offer life care (LC), modified fee-for-service (MFFS), or fee-for-service (FFS) plans. Some endowment and equity communities might have a rental program as well. It is helpful to know how the fee structure is set up.

Some information packets are not clear as to whether the FSRC is life care or fee for service. Most often, the words, "life care," will be readily visible, but not always. The information packets seldom, if ever, say outright that the community is fee for service.

The best clue that a community has a fee-for-service payment structure is that it offers direct entry into health care and the marketing materials offer separate prices for assisted living (AL) and skilled nursing (SN). Often fee-for-service marketing departments have separate brochures for each level of living. They almost always point out that, in their communities, residents will never have to pay for more services than they use. (This is not always an advantage for everyone. See page 141.) See Figure 11-8.

READING the INFO PACKET
Clues to Fee for Service
• offers opportunity to order info about AL and/or SN separately • higher prices for AL & SN • "Don't pay for more services than you use."

Figure 11-8

Refund Plans

If you have determined that a refund plan is the only way to go (page 115), you will want that to be your own personal deal breaker. Knowing that up front will save you a lot of time. Do realize that the older you are on moving in, the more of an advantage a refund plan is.

Grounds

Knowing the grounds type will give you a good mental picture of the community. Looking at the pictures could also be meaningful. The size of the property is important, also.

Minimum and Average Age

If you are a young retiree, you will be interested in the minimum age for yourself and, if you are married, for your spouse. The average age of the residents gives you a vague idea of how active the residents are likely to be. See page 148 for warnings about minimum age policies.

Meals

The meal situation reveals a great deal about the activity level of the residents. FSRCs, where all three meals for independent living residents are included in the monthly fee, tend to cater to the more frail elderly. We have found that when the noon meal is well attended, the residents are often, but not always, less active than in other communities. The same conclusion holds for meals that are served at set times, even the evening meal. These are the communities where the emphasis is on care. Don't get us wrong; it's good for there to be a caring atmosphere, but disability cannot be the prevailing focus in a vibrant FSRC; ability should be.

Active residents like continuous dining (11:00 a.m. to 7:00 p.m., *e.g.*). That range of service exists, but is far from the norm. Without that option, active residents usually eat their main meals in the evening and they will be served over a period of time, for example 4:30 p.m. to 7:00 p.m.

Wellness Center in Independent Living

Be sure to ask about the medical care that is offered to residents in independent living. Look for a wellness center. Hopefully, it is staffed with a local doctor who has office hours at the FSRC. Sometimes the doctors are employees of the community and other times they are independent contractors who lease space from the FSRC.

Invitation to Visit

Most likely the marketing representative will ask you to visit. Residents of the local area are periodically invited to marketing events. Communities have luncheons and open houses to show themselves off. While these occasions are fun and informative, they will not replace your private appointment and tour with the marketing representative if you are seriously considering that FSRC.

Even if you want to retire in another locale, visit your local FSRCs and practice interviewing the marketing rep. This will help you learn what you want and don't want in your future home.

If you live out of state, the rep will very often offer you a one or two nights' complimentary stay in the guest room and meals in the dining room. While the guest rooms are quite nice, they do not come with the amenities of hotel rooms; they are more like lovely guest rooms in friends' homes. FSRCs do not provide hair dryers, as a rule, but the rooms sometimes have sample-size toiletries and a coffee pot with coffee.

Occasionally, you will be told that there are no guest rooms that marketing may offer to visitors. Sometimes the community will charge a fee that is often about the same as or less than a moderately priced hotel room. Most of the time meals are included in that fee. In either case, you surely must wonder how actively it is soliciting future residents from other regions. A diverse body of residents contributes variety to the quality of life and is highly desirable.

Wonder also about the community's approach to spending money. New residents are the life's blood of an FSRC. It is vital that the marketing department do all it can to attract prospective residents. Skimping at this level is not considered wise among business management experts.

Once newly built communities reach full occupancy, a few close their marketing departments, thinking that the administrative staff can field the future inquiries. This can be a mistake, for one never knows when a group of vacancies can occur suddenly. Without a waiting list to fill them quickly, FSRCs lose valuable dollars.

Also, in question are their budgets. Can they afford a good marketing effort? If not, it could be a sign of the beginning of their downward financial spirals. The less they spend on marketing, the fewer people they will attract. As bodies of residents become smaller, the communities will have less money coming in for expenses. They will become less competitive and, ultimately, less able to attract new residents.

SELECTING A FLOOR PLAN

The next step is choosing one or two of the many floor plans. FSRCs offer a wide variety of homes. The choices can be so attractive that picking just one might be difficult.

COTTAGE VERSUS APARTMENT

Some communities offer a choice between cottages (collective term for single family home, villa, duplex, quadraplex, and others) and apartments. Each has its pros and cons, just like everything else in life. (Figure 11-9.)

SELECTING YOUR NEW HOME			
Cottages		**Apartments**	
Pros	**Cons**	**Pros**	**Cons**
• more square feet • yard • more likely to have off-street parking • windows on 2-4 sides	• farther away from community center • more expensive • must go outdoors in bad weather	• no need to go outdoors in bad weather • closer to dining room & activities • panoramic views from higher floors • breeze more likely on higher floors • less expensive	• fewer square feet • no yard • home farther from parking • windows on 1-2 sides

Figure 11-9

Many residents prefer cottages because they can be similar to the single family home they just left. They might prefer the ready outdoor access (usually a yard that the community takes care of) and maybe a garage. As a rule, the cottages are larger than apartments. Some are as large as 3500 square feet, with four bedrooms, a den, and three baths. Cottages have windows on two to four sides of the structure, instead of the typical one wall of windows in an apartment (two in a corner home).

On the other hand, they are farther away from the community center and its activities. Residents will have to go that distance to eat in the dining room, sometimes coping with unpleasant weather. It is a longer distance to go back to fetch a forgotten item, as well.

Residents get around on campus by walking or driving their golf carts or cars. Some communities provide a small bus or open-air trolley to get about the campus. Less agile residents find a van difficult to get in and out of.

Apartment living cures most of the ills of cottage living. The apartments are close to the daily happenings, the dining room, and the mail boxes. Residents do not have to negotiate through wind, rain, snow, heat, or cold. High-rise apartment buildings usually have lovely views from the upper floors and they are more likely to catch the breeze.

The apartments are, as a rule, smaller than the cottages. Their outdoor access is limited. Some communities offer no outdoor access from each apartment. Others have a balcony or a patio.

First floor atrium and garden apartments (page 57-8) allow residents to walk out into a courtyard, with back yard or balcony access from the other side. There might be landscaping, benches, and, occasionally, a fountain.

EXPOSURE OF HOME

If you love fluttering curtains and the fresh scent and gentle feeling of cross ventilation, an atrium or garden apartment or a cottage will be important to you. Lorraine likes to open her windows to catch the prevailing breeze. This would be a dominant factor in selecting the location of her home. The wind usually comes from the west or southwest where she is, so she will want windows that face that direction.

Recessed balconies catch less of the summer breeze and warming sunlight than extended balconies. On the other hand, they offer privacy and shelter in the fringe seasons when the winds are chilly. They also do not overheat a room to the degree that the extended balcony might.

Which way your windows face affects how much light your home will get. Sunlight makes a room cheerier, but it also fades upholstery and draperies more quickly. The sun shines in the southern facing windows almost all day, and it can be too warm in the summertime, as can the western exposure. On the other hand, the beaming light is spiritually uplifting. The eastern sunrise is wasted on night owls. Apartments whose windows face north will never get the sun, but artists and many others love the northern light, especially residents whose eyes are sensitive to light. It will not fade the upholstery and draperies as quickly as direct sun, nor will it overheat a room as much in the summer.

In communities where there are no laundry facilities in each home, the distance to the community laundry room might be important to you. Equally deserving of your consideration is the

SELECTING the FLOOR PLAN and LOCATION of YOUR HOME WITHIN the FSRC
At a Glance

• number of bedrooms
• number of baths/half baths
• den?
• exposure to the sun
• exposure to prevailing breeze
• view
• noise
  ▸ air conditioner compressors
  ▸ highway
  ▸ dumpster
  ▸ service entrances/loading dock
•   outdoor access
  ▸ recessed balcony or patio
  ▸ extended balcony or patio
  ▸ screened-in balcony or patio
  ▸ enclosed balcony or patio
• parking arrangements
  ▸ off-street
  ▸ garage
  ▸ carport
  ▸ on-street at curb
  ▸ parking lot
• distance to community center

Figure 11-10

distance to the dining room and the community center. Martha wants to be sure she gets her daily exercise, so she chose an apartment as far away from the dining room as possible. An old injury causes Amy to limp a little when she overextends herself; consequently, she likes to be near the hub of activities. See Figure 11-10 for a summary of things to consider in selecting a home.

❧❧

By now you should have some feel for the character and personality of the communities you have investigated. The next step is a visit in person. It is fun to go and see FSRCs. The residents that you meet will, no doubt, be friendly, delightful people.

The more communities you visit, the better you will be able to make a well-informed decision. We were comparing notes with someone on an FSRC that we had all visited. When we asked if she liked it, she replied that she did—until she looked at others.

Please, do not move down the street without looking at other communities. Once you get to them, be sure to ask lots of questions and tour the whole community, not just independent living.

※※

Now that you are armed with the knowledge and reasons behind many of the questions in Part II, it is time to visit several communities. The questions will help you narrow your list to two or three communities that you might consider seriously.

As you continue to weigh the attributes of your favorite FSRCs, one is likely to rise to the top as your first choice. If two are fairly equal, you certainly may put your name on both waiting lists and move into the first one that becomes available.

PART II

THE QUESTIONS

Try to put well into practice what you already know;
in so doing, you will, in good time, discover
the hidden things which you now inquire about.

—Rembrandt Van Rijn
Dutch Painter and Engraver, 1606-1669

12

GETTING STARTED

Life is the art of drawing sufficient conclusions
from insufficient premises.

—Samuel Butler
British Author, 1835-1902

The best way to evaluate full service retirement communities (FSRCs), also referred to as continuing care retirement communities (CCRCs), is to visit as many as you can. The more you see and the more questions you ask, the better you will understand just what it is you want in retirement living. See Chapter 11, "Finding and Screening FSRCs," to help you decide which ones to visit.

THE QUESTIONS

After visiting many FSRCs, the facts might run together. It sometimes seems as if you are comparing apples with oranges because the communities are different in so many ways; yet, they really are alike in many other ways. In order to help you keep the facts straight, we have devised an easy-to-use workbook in which to record information. You may shorten the process by just answering the deal-breaking and red-flag questions, described below.

THE CHECKLIST

The checklist is arranged in the order the information will most likely be presented. Every question is worded so that a positive response would be marked in the "☺" column; a neutral, in the "☺" column; and a negative, in the "☺" column. Simply place a ✓ in the appropriate column.

Our suggested evaluations of the possible answers you might receive are **judged against an IDEAL** with the sole goal as **optimal health** and **quality of life** for the residents. For example, it is ideal that housekeeping comes in once a week, but once every other week is adequate for most people. So, weekly housekeeping is considered, therefore, a better answer than biweekly cleaning.

Some of the questions refer to issues on which reasonable people hold differing opinions as to what is best. For instance, some prospective residents would never consider moving to an FSRC that serves alcohol and others would not dream of moving to one that does not. For these types of questions, we have simply left a blank space in which you can write the answer.

Many of the questions address issues or concerns that might not be so readily apparent. For example, the absence or presence of flowers on site reveals several issues. If there are flowers throughout the community, who maintains them? If the residents do, then there must be an active group of gardeners living in the FSRC. Their efforts help keep costs down and improve the community. If the FSRC maintains the flowers, is it overextending its budget? If the flowers are just at the front entrance, is the community putting on a good front for company and not giving its full resources to their residents in other areas as well? If there are no flowers, why? Is it a cost-cutting measure? Are residents not interested in donating time to their own community? Are they too frail? Do they not care? Many of the questions we ask can reflect a similar line of reasoning that should alert you to look more closely at other areas of the community.

DEAL BREAKERS AND RED FLAGS

Deal breakers are those policies and situations that make the choice of a particular community too high a risk for financial, physical, and/or emotional security. These are things that could come to haunt you when it is too late to move elsewhere. The dark grey numbers are the deal breakers. A negative answer (☹) to any one deal breaker is enough alone to cross an FSRC off your list. We have found that these questions, when answered in the negative, reveal policies that, for the most part, do not work in your best interest over the long run.

We are particularly concerned that the community will be financially stable for years into the future. It is equally important that the care is of high quality and that the management is trying to keep residents in independent living for as long as possible. These questions also address policies that directly affect the quality of life. For instance, no matter how active prospective residents are, it is important that they live in an atmosphere of activity and positive attitudes.

The light grey numbers are the red flags. Too many negative answers (☹) to the red-flag questions will also eliminate a community. For the most part they reveal situations or policies that might, when they appear in great numbers, affect the same important points that the deal breakers do. Use your judgment and your values to determine how many red flags are too many for you.

Every one of our deal-breaking and red-flag questions addresses a concern, sometimes a hidden agenda or an underlying problem. Visiting a few communities first will help you firm up your perceptions of what you do or do not want.

If you would like to add deal breakers and red flags of your own, try color coding the rows with a highlighter. There is also space to write in your own issues, but don't be too hasty to add your own; because as the process unfolds, you might change your mind. For instance, Sherry was *sure* she wanted a single family house until she saw the atrium apartment she eventually moved into.

Bernice wants to move to an FSRC that has a very active needlepoint group. She can write that in. Jenny wants a large campus with mature trees; she can highlight that question. They are not deal breakers for every reader—or even red flags, but, for her, the lack of a wooded campus is a deal breaker.

THE VISIT

Your visit will allow you to ask questions, interact with the residents, and observe daily happenings. The information you get at this appointment can help you quickly screen out communities that don't suit your tastes. Pay particular attention to the deal breakers and red flags. You will arrive with the answers to the questions in Chapter 12 already filled out.

YOUR CONCLUSIONS

Once you have as many facts as you need, you can draw conclusions from what you have seen and heard. Most of the questions address issues, but many are simply a space to record information, so the communities you visit won't all run together. **How much diligence you put into recording that information is up to you.** Answering every question and taking the tour, except the resident and the CEO portions, takes only about three hours—time well spent, we think. The idea is to give you, at a glance, an idea of how well one FSRC holds up when compared with another.

Remember that every question has an issue behind it. The more questions you ask, the clearer a picture you will draw. There are things you don't want to learn after you move in—especially when you could have known beforehand.

We recommend several visits to the community before you sign on the dotted line. At one of these visits it would be wise to meet with the wellness coordinator and the nutritionist. Many prospective residents might also be interested in meeting with the chaplain, if there is one. We have provided no preset questions for them; you will probably have your own. They can at least tell you what their jobs entail.

Notice that many questions are subjective, but your opinion is the only one that counts. Keeping that in mind, draw your own conclusions and decide which three FSRCs will be on your short list of finalists. If the fee is refundable, put your name on the waiting lists of your favorite communities. Then visit them repeatedly at different hours of the day and on different days of the week until you can comfortably cross all of them off the list but one. If the fee is not refundable, think twice, of course.

FSRCs VISITED	
FSRC # 1	
Name	
Address	
Address	
City/State/Zip	
Phone	
Contact	
FSRC # 2	
Name	
Address	
Address	
City/State/Zip	
Phone	
Contact	
FSRC # 3	
Name	
Address	
Address	
City/State/Zip	
Phone	
Contact	

PHONE SCREENING										

Key: ☺ yes positive ideal many ☺ slightly neutral good some ☹ no negative poor few	FSRC #1			FSRC #2			FSRC #3		
☹ answer to question after dark grey numbers is a Deal Breaker. | ☹ answer to question after light grey numbers is a Red Flag	☺	☺	☹	☺	☺	☹	☺	☺	☹

SERVICES and SIZE of the FSRC

		FSRC #1	FSRC #2	FSRC #3
12-1	Do you have Independent Living (IL)[6]			
12-2	Assisted living area (AL) on site ☺ totally separate from skilled nursing area & Alzheimer's/dementia area ☺ separate wing ☹ mixed in with skilled nursing &/or Alzheimer's/dementia or no assisted living area			
12-3	Skilled nursing area (SN) on site ☺ totally separate from AL & Alzheimer's/dementia area ☺ separate wing ☹ mixed in with AL &/or Alzheimer's/ dementia or no skilled nursing area			
12-4	Alzheimer's/dementia area (A/D) on site ☺ two areas, one for AL & one for SN ☺ one area for AL & SN ☹ no Alzheimer's/dementia area			
12-5	Number of homes in each section[7]	IL= AL= SN=	IL= AL= SN=	IL= AL= SN=
12-6	Number of acres			

---

[6] Because there are many FSRC look-alikes, the first four questions will remind you to double check that all four levels of care are on-site.

[7] These figures show how active and vibrant the community is.

PHONE SCREENING *(continued)*					
12-7	Type of property: mid-/high rise, small campus, large campus (marketing rep's opinion)				
12-8	Other				
ACCREDITATION					
12-9	Accredited by CARF/CCAC ☺ accredited ☺ in progress or not eligible yet ☹ not accredited				
RESIDENTS					
12-10	Total number of residents[8] ☺ 350 & up, if well over 500, multiple community centers ☺ well over 500 & not divided into neighborhoods ☹ far fewer than 350				
12-11	Average age of residents at move in ☺ sixties ☺ seventies ☹ eighties				
12-12	Average age of residents in independent living ☺ sixties to mid-seventies ☺ late seventies to early eighties ☹ mid-eighties or older				
12-13	Average age of residents, including skilled nursing residents ☺ seventies ☺ early eighties to mid-eighties ☹ late eighties or older				
12-14	Other				

---

[8] A minimum of 350 residents is likely to be needed to support an array of amenities, services, medical care, and recapitalization without reducing quality.

PHONE SCREENING *(continued)*									

ENTRANCE REQUIREMENTS

12-15	Minimum age: 55, 62, 65, or other (insert age) ☺ only one spouse need be the minimum age ☺ both spouses minimum age ☹ N/A								
12-16	For couples with one spouse younger than the minimum age, younger spouse accepted into community ☺ unconditionally ☺ with conditions for health program (other than reaching minimum age) ☹ ousted on older spouse's leaving IL, AL, SN &/or A/D before reaching minimum age								
12-17	Younger spouse accepted into health care program ☺ without younger spouse fee ☺ with younger spouse fee ☹ not accepted until reaching minimum age & still healthy								
12-18	Other								

FISCAL INFORMATION

12-19	Type of occupancy: endowment (EN), equity (EQ), lease (LE)				
12-20	Nonprofit or for profit				
12-21	Fee structures Plan A life care (LC) AH life care hybrid Plan B modified fee for service (MFFS) BH modified FFS hybrid Plan C fee for service (FFS) CH FFS hybrid Plan X assign assets				

PHONE SCREENING *(continued)*									
12-22	Other								

FOOD

12-23	Meals included in monthly fee ☺ flexible meal plan ☺ 1 ☹ 2-3								
12-24	Most popular meal of the day[9] ☺ evening meal ☺ split between the midday meal & the evening meal ☹ breakfast or noon								
12-25	Meal times[9] ☺ continuous dining (*e.g.* 11 a.m. to 7 p.m.) ☺ range of times (*e.g.* 11 a.m. -1 p.m. &/or 5-7 p.m.) ☹ set times								
12-261	Coat & tie required in the dining room								
12-27	Other								

HEALTH CARE

12-28	Wellness center for IL residents								
12-29	Other								

MARKETING POLICIES for OUT-OF-TOWNERS

12-30	Dining with the residents ☺ as guest of marketing department ☺ you pay ☹ not invited								

---

[9] Residents' participation in meals and the times they are offered shows how active the population of the community is.

	PHONE SCREENING *(continued)*									
12-31	Toll-free phone number ☺ given in the information packet ☺ given upon your request ☹ no toll-free phone number									
12-32	Guest room stays for out-of-town prospective residents[10] ☺ as their guest ☺ you pay ☹ not invited or no guest room for marketing									
12-33	Other									
AFTER the PHONE CALL, RECORD:										
12-34	Impression of receptionist[11]									
12-35	Impression of marketing representative[11]									

[10] The extent to which management is seeking a diverse resident population is shown by how easy they make it for out-of-town prospective residents to visit.

[11] This will be your first indication of the warmth and friendliness of the community.

13

THINGS TO NOTICE
ON ARRIVAL

In the fields of observation,
chance favors only the prepared mind.

—Louis Pasteur
French Scientist, 1822-1895

Riding around the neighborhood and property before you park will give you an opportunity to record the answers to the questions in this chapter. There will be a number of items to assess while you're waiting in the lobby for the marketing representative.

THINGS TO NOTICE ON ARRIVAL					FSRC #1			FSRC #2			FSRC #3		
Key: ☺ yes ☺ slightly ☹ no	positive neutral negative	ideal good poor	many some few										
☹ answer to question after dark grey numbers is a Deal Breaker.		☹ answer to question after light grey numbers is a Red Flag			☺	☺	☹	☺	☺	☹	☺	☺	☹
PROPERTY/CAMPUS													
13-1	Traffic approaching the FSRC												
13-2	Attractive surrounding properties												
13-3	Curb appeal												
13-4	Well-maintained grounds												
13-5	Well-maintained roads & parking lots												
13-6	Well-maintained buildings[12]												
13-7	Cars in parking lots similar to mine[13]												
13-8	Attractive landscaping throughout, not just at front entrance[14]												
13-9	Flowers throughout[14]												
13-10	Shady places to sit outdoors												
13-11	Water ☺ lake, pond, river, etc. ☺ fountain ☹ no water												

---

[12] The community has enough reserves to fund capital improvement projects.

[13] The residents' economic level might be similar to yours.

[14] Attractive landscaping throughout is an indicator that all levels of care receive equal attention to detail.

	THINGS TO NOTICE ON ARRIVAL *(continued)*									
13-12	Hilly terrain[15]									
13-13	Mature trees									
13-14	Type of property: high rise, small campus, large campus									
13-15	Attractive front entrance									
13-16	Other									

LOBBY

13-17	Easily opened doors									
13-18	Receptionist[16] ☺ warm & friendly ☺ polite, but not friendly ☹ none of the above									
13-19	Decor I am comfortable with									
13-20	Clean & tidy lobby									
13-21	Flowers &/or plants (real or silk) ☺ many attractive bouquets or pots ☺ token amount ☹ none or not attractive									
13-22	Mission & vision statements on display									
13-23	Awards from the local area on display									
13-24	First impression ☺ WOW! ☺ OK ☹ Let's leave									
13-25	Other									

---

[15] Hills help to stretch muscles and retain range of motion.

[16] The receptionist is the first clue as to the community's personality.

14

QUESTIONS FOR THE MARKETING REPRESENTATIVE

*A question not to be asked
is a question not to be answered.*

—Robert Southey
British Poet, 1774-1843

Next you will meet with the marketing representative in his/her office for an hour or so. This is your opportunity to ask lots of questions. The checklist will be easier to manage if you request that the conversation follow its order, rather than having the marketing rep follow his/her plan. Any questions that the rep cannot answer can be answered by the CEO on another visit. It will be easier to find the unanswered questions later if you highlight the answer column's box for that community.

QUESTIONS FOR THE MARKETING REPRESENTATIVE

Key:	☺	yes	positive	ideal	many	FSRC #1			FSRC #2			FSRC #3		
	☺	slightly	neutral	good	some									
	☹	no	negative	poor	few									
☹ answer to question after dark grey numbers is a Deal Breaker.			☹ answer to question after light grey numbers is a Red Flag			☺	☺	☹	☺	☺	☹	☺	☺	☹

Ask rep/agent to follow this order for an easier time recording the answers. Highlight the questions that the rep cannot answer. Ask CEO on another visit.

LOCAL AREA

14-1	Mode of transportation to local hospital ☺ community's own ambulance ☺ nearby ambulance service ☹ distant ambulance service											
14-2	Ambulance response time ☺ fewer than 10 minutes ☺ 10 to 20 minutes ☹ more than 20 minutes											
14-3	Medical offices nearby											
14-4	Goods & services readily available											
14-5	Religious facilities nearby											
14-6	University or college nearby											
14-7	Other											

PROPERTY/CAMPUS

14-8	AL easily accessible to IL											
14-9	SN easily accessible to IL											
14-10	A/D easily accessible to IL											
14-11	Measured indoor walking course											

	QUESTIONS FOR THE MARKETING REPRESENTATIVE *(continued)*										
14-12	Measured outdoor walking course										
14-13	Paved, outdoor walking/biking paths ☺ lighted path with benches ☺ benches only ☹ neither or no path										
14-14	Easily accessible nature trail or park[17]										
14-15	Space for expansion										
14-16	Buffer between the community & the neighboring properties ☺ permanent park or protected wildlife area ☺ community-owned ☹ no buffer										
14-17	Fenced property										
14-18	Gated property										
14-19	Gate ☺ guarded 24/7 ☺ guarded at night ☹ not guarded										
14-20	Security on duty ☺ 24/7 ☺ nights only ☹ fewer hours or no security										
14-21	Security personnel ☺ EMTs or CPR-trained ☺ no medical training ☹ no security										
14-22	Number of square feet of common area										
14-23	Other										

---

[17] Proprioceptor nerves (balance control) are lost without stimulation. See page 94.

	QUESTIONS FOR THE MARKETING REPRESENTATIVE *(continued)*								
SERVICES									
14-24	Ratio of staff/residents (insert number)[18] ☺ 1:1.5 to 2.5 ☺ 1:1 only with an extraordinary number of services being provided ☹ too low (3:1) or too high (1:1)								
14-25	Housekeeping ☺ weekly ☺ biweekly ☹ not available								
14-26	Heavy housecleaning ☺ every six months ☺ yearly ☹ not available								
14-27	On-site transportation (for campuses only) ☺ continuous or property so small it's not needed ☺ meal times only ☹ none even though campus is large								
14-28	Off-site transportation ☺ wide radius ☺ limited radius ☹ not available								
14-29	Additional transportation for hire ☺ wide radius ☺ limited radius ☹ not available								
14-30	Mode of transportation available ☺ bus ☺ car or limo ☹ van								

---

[18] This addresses the staff's ability to deliver needed services.

	QUESTIONS FOR THE MARKETING REPRESENTATIVE *(continued)*								
14-31	Receptionist on duty ☺ 24/7 ☺ fewer than 24/7 ☹ no receptionist								
14-32	FSRC accepts packages for residents								
14-33	Administrator or representative available 24/7 ☺ on site ☺ on call ☹ not available								
14-34	Activities director ☺ full time ☺ part time ☹ no activities director								
14-35	Social worker ☺ full time ☺ part time ☹ none								
14-36	Chaplain ☺ full time ☺ part time ☹ none								
14-37	Support groups								
14-38	Other								
RESIDENTS									
14-39	Professions represented in resident population[19] ☺ doctors, nurses, attorneys, CPAs ☺ children of residents are doctors, nurses, attorneys, CPAs ☹ few or none of these professions represented								

[19] The community stands up to professional scrutiny.

QUESTIONS FOR THE MARKETING REPRESENTATIVE *(continued)*

14-40	Most common profession of residents				
14-41	Percentage of residents from local area[20] ☺ Fewer than 70% ☻ 70-85% ☹ more than 85%				
14-42	Average age at move-in ☺ sixties ☻ seventies ☹ eighties				
14-43	Percentage of couples		%	%	%
14-44	Percentage of men		%	%	%
14-45	Percentage of women		%	%	%
14-46	Residents' absence from community ☺ moderate amount of travel ☻ minimal amount of travel ☹ large number gone half of the year				
14-47	Other				

ACTIVITIES

14-48	Resident-planned activities[21]				
14-49	My favorite activity				
14-50	My spouse's favorite activity				
14-51	Outings scheduled by activities director				
14-52	Opportunities for volunteerism				

---

[20] A diverse population gives new residents a better chance of fitting in.

[21] Residents who sponsor a wide variety of activities create a sense of community.

QUESTIONS FOR THE MARKETING REPRESENTATIVE *(continued)*										
14-53	Opportunities for diverse activities ☺ physical, intellectual, cultural, and spiritual activities ☺ three of the above ☹ one or two of the above									
14-54	Diverse special interest groups									
14-55	Dancing									
14-56	Outdoor activities, other than swimming									
14-57	Tennis court									
14-58	Putting green									
14-59	Golfer's chipping area									
14-60	Shuffleboard									
14-61	Croquet court									
14-62	Horseshoe pit									
14-63	Bocce ball court (lawn bowling)									
14-64	Other									
FOOD										
14-65	Nutritionist/dietitian for IL ☺ full time ☺ part time ☹ none									
14-66	Special diets in IL ☺ custom, doctor ordered ☺ standardized only; *e.g.* diabetic, low salt, low fat, vegetarian, etc. ☹ no special diets available									
14-67	Special diets in AL, SN, & A/D ☺ custom, doctor ordered ☺ standardized only; *e.g.* diabetic, low salt, low fat, vegetarian, etc. ☹ no special diets available									

QUESTIONS FOR THE MARKETING REPRESENTATIVE *(continued)*

14-68	Cost to add meals ☺ less than the cost of a fast food meal ☺ about the same cost as a fast food meal ☹ more than the cost of a fast food meal												
14-69	Dining room ☺ 3 meals served daily ☺ 2 meals served daily ☹ 1 meal served daily												
14-70	Café ☺ 2 or 3 meals served daily ☺ 1 meal served daily ☹ no café												
14-71	Number of meals available in community on Saturday & Sunday ☺ 6 ☺ 4-5 ☹ 0-3												
14-72	Menu rotation ☺ 6 weeks & up ☺ 4-5 weeks ☹ 3 or fewer weeks												

14-73	Policy on serving alcohol	FSRC # 1
		FSRC # 2
		FSRC # 3

14-74	Take-out meals												
14-75	Catering services												
14-76	Box lunches												
14-77	Other												

QUESTIONS FOR THE MARKETING REPRESENTATIVE *(continued)*									
POLICIES									
14-78	Credit for missed meals ☺ fewer than 30 ☺ 30 or greater ☹ no credit								
14-79	Make up missed meals before end of month								
14-80	Walkers allowed in IL[22]								
14-81	Wheelchairs allowed in IL[22]								
14-82	Wheelchairs allowed IL dining room[22]								
14-83	AL residents welcome in IL dining room, *if able* ☺ any time ☺ by invitation of spouse & friends only ☹ not welcome								
14-84	AL residents welcome in IL community center & activities								
14-85	Residents of IL apartments ☺ open to all IL residents ☺ N/A ☹ open only to the very frail; others *must* live in cottages								
14-86	Renovation/refurbishment of common areas ☺ 5-7 years ☺ 8-9 years ☹ 10 or more years or as needed								
14-87	Refurbishment of homes (carpet, paint) ☺ 5-7 years ☺ 8-10 years or upon request ☹ 11 or more years, as needed, or between residents only								

[22] Residents should not be pushed into assisted living prematurely.

	QUESTIONS FOR THE MARKETING REPRESENTATIVE *(continued)*										
14-88	Extent of renovation of each home *between* residents ☺ paint, replace carpet, appliances & kitchen cabinets ☺ paint, replace carpet, & others as needed ☹ clean & paint only										
14-89	Move walls during renovation										
14-90	Cost of small-scale custom modifications to residents on move-in: ☺ no extra charge ☺ nominal to moderate amount ☹ all										
14-91	Cost of reversal of custom modifications to residents on move-out ☺ no extra charge or not necessary to reverse modifications ☺ nominal amount ☹ all or most										
14-92	Fees associated with move to *smaller* home in the community ☺ none or renovation of previous *or* new home ☺ renovation of previous & new home ☹ new entrance fee										
14-93	Fees associated with move to *larger* home in the community ☺ difference in entrance fees plus renovation of previous *or* new home ☺ difference in entrance fees plus renovation of previous & new home ☹ new entrance fee										
14-94	Move to another community in family										

	QUESTIONS FOR THE MARKETING REPRESENTATIVE *(continued)*										
14-95	Fees associated with move to same home in another community in family ☺ renovation of previous *or* new home ☺ renovation of previous & new home ☹ new entrance fee										
14-96	Pet policy at move-in	FSRC # 1									
		FSRC # 2									
		FSRC # 3									
14-97	Policy for replacing a pet after move-in	FSRC # 1									
		FSRC # 2									
		FSRC # 3									
14-98	Guest rooms for residents' guests										
14-99	Staff welcome in fitness room ☺ any time[23] ☺ limited hours ☹ not welcome										
14-100	Smoking policy	FSRC # 1									
		FSRC # 2									
		FSRC # 3									
14-101	Other										
MANAGEMENT											
14-102	Name of the owner	FSRC # 1									
		FSRC # 2									
		FSRC # 3									
14-103	Number of communities owned										

---

[23] The mood of the community is one of family, rather than a "them" and "us" feeling.

QUESTIONS FOR THE MARKETING REPRESENTATIVE *(continued)*					
14-104	Name of the sponsor	FSRC # 1			
		FSRC # 2			
		FSRC # 3			
14-105	Number of communities sponsored				
14-106	Name of the management company	FSRC # 1			
		FSRC # 2			
		FSRC # 3			
14-107	Experienced management				
14-108	Tenure of current management team				
14-109	Year opened				
14-110	CEO's managing style: autocratic, participative, or *laissez faire*				
14-111	Occupancy rate ☺ waiting list or 90+% ☺ 80-90% ☹ below 80%				
14-112	Emergency power generator ☺ whole property or health care plus limited access for IL ☺ health care only ☹ none				
14-113	Changes to attract the Baby Boomers?[24] ☺ plan in place ☺ plan on paper ☹ no plan				
14-114	Residents' association/council				
14-115	Resident on the board of directors				

[24] Plans should address issues such as bigger homes, more amenities, state-of-the-art fitness room, healthier diet, and choice of financial plans.

	QUESTIONS FOR THE MARKETING REPRESENTATIVE *(continued)*								
14-116	Town meetings								
14-117	Other								
WELLNESS									
14-118	Aerobic activities								
14-119	Classes in wellness								
14-120	Yoga or stretching exercises								
14-121	*Tai Chi* or balance exercises								
14-122	Strength training exercises								
14-123	Other								
HEALTH CARE									
14-124	System for residents' daily check ☺ automatic, noninvasive system or staff checks on each resident daily ☺ resident checks in with staff ☹ residents check in with designated resident or no check								
14-125	Daily check system notes if resident is attending meals in dining room								
14-126	Person who calls 911 in emergency ☺ RN or EMT ☺ security ☹ resident or no policy								
14-127	Person who answers call for help in IL[25] ☺ EMT ☺ RN or CPR-trained security ☹ no medically-trained person								

---

[25] Management has residents' well being in mind.

	QUESTIONS FOR THE MARKETING REPRESENTATIVE *(continued)*								
14-128	Rehabilitation facilities on site ☺ extensive ☺ minimal ☹ none on site								
14-129	Physical therapist on site ☺ full time ☺ part time ☹ none on site								
14-130	Occupational therapist on site ☺ full time ☺ part time ☹ none on site								
14-131	Speech therapist on site ☺ full time ☺ part time ☹ none on site								
14-132	Help with medications for IL residents ☺ dispensed in IL ☺ dispensed in AL or SN ☹ community requires residents to move into AL								
14-133	Help with filling out insurance forms for independent living residents								
14-134	Adult day care for residents who live in independent living with spouse ☺ without extra fee ☺ with extra fee ☹ service not available								
14-135	Respite care for residents who live in independent living with spouse ☺ without extra fee ☺ with extra fee ☹ service not available								
14-136	Home health care								
14-137	Number of IL residents receiving tray service on a regular basis								

	QUESTIONS FOR THE MARKETING REPRESENTATIVE *(continued)*									
14-138	Guaranteed space in AL, SN, A/D ☺ in this community ☺ temporarily outside the community ☹ no or not in this community									
14-139	If beds *guaranteed* & not available in AL, SN, & A/D & if outside facility is more expensive, difference paid by ☺ FSRC ☺ N/A ☹ resident									
14-140	Policy on moving residents to AL, SN, or A/D ☺ case-by-case basis, guided by written policy ☺ case-by-case basis ☹ written policy									
14-141	Insurance required: medical; long-term care; Medicare, Part B; other Medicare, etc.	FSRC # 1								
		FSRC # 2								
		FSRC # 3								
14-142	Documents to be on file in office ☺ Advance directives (living wills & durable powers of attorney for health care, etc.) ☺ N/A ☹ will									
14-143	Other									
ASSISTED LIVING										
14-144	AL residents' allowable range of travel ☺ off site, if able ☺ on site only, if able ☹ confined to AL									

	QUESTIONS FOR THE MARKETING REPRESENTATIVE *(continued)*								
14-145	Non-community persons admitted to assisted living ☺ yes, but hold *x* beds for residents ☺ no or residents have priority ☹ yes, without regard for the community's residents								
14-146	Other								
SKILLED NURSING									
14-147	Levels of care offered ☺ sub-acute, skilled, & intermediate ☺ skilled & intermediate ☹ intermediate only								
14-148	SN residents' allowable range of travel ☺ off site, if able ☺ on site only, if able ☹ confined to SN								
14-149	Non-community persons admitted to skilled nursing ☺ yes, but hold *x* beds for residents ☺ no or residents have priority ☹ yes, without regard for the community's residents								
14-150	Medicare certified								
14-151	Medicaid certified								
14-152	Other								
ALZHEIMER'S/DEMENTIA/MEMORY SUPPORT									
14-153	Non-community persons admitted to A/D ☺ yes, but hold *x* beds for residents ☺ no or residents have priority ☹ yes, without regard for the community's residents								
14-154	Other								

QUESTIONS FOR THE MARKETING REPRESENTATIVE *(continued)*					
FINANCES					
14-155	Rescission period (100% refund) ☺ 6 to 12 months ☺ 1 to 5 months (30 to 150 days) ☹ fewer than 30 days				
14-156	Monthly fees raised reasonably in past				
14-157	Guaranteed residency if I outlive my money and draw-down of refund ☺ with help from benevolence fund ☺ with help from community ☹ no, asked to leave				
14-158	Audited financial statements regularly available to residents				
14-159	Homestead exemption				
14-160	Other				
For Endowment Communities Only					
14-161	Switch to another fee plan after moving in (enter cut-off date)				
14-162	Refund plans available (insert % of refund)	%	%	%	
14-163	For non-refundable entry fees, rate of refund on declining balance	%/mo	%/mo	%/mo	
14-164	Conditions for refund	FSRC # 1			
		FSRC # 2			
		FSRC # 3			
14-165	Refund payable ☺ on move out ☺ on resale of home ☹ to resident's estate only				

	QUESTIONS FOR THE MARKETING REPRESENTATIVE *(continued)*				
14-166	Refund not subject to tax on imputed interest				
14-167	Percentage of entrance fee tax deductible		%	%	%
14-168	Percentage of monthly fee tax deductible		%	%	%
14-169	Other				
For Equity Communities Only					
14-170	Condo, co-op, or membership				
14-171	Property tax amount		$	$	$
14-172	Developer retains some control				
14-173	Any payments refundable				
14-174	Conditions for refund	FSRC # 1			
		FSRC # 2			
		FSRC # 3			
14-175	Limitations on resale				
14-176	Percentage of transfer fees		%	%	%
14-177	Percentage of equity kept by community		%	%	%
14-178	Other				
For Lease Communities Only					
14-179	Duration of lease[26]				

---

[26] Communities may escape being controlled by laws that protect residents of FSRCs if their contract renews for only one year at a time or, if more than one year, it renews only at the sole discretion of the management.

	QUESTIONS FOR THE MARKETING REPRESENTATIVE *(continued)*							
14-180	Renewal of lease for more than one year ☺ at resident's discretion or automatic renewal (without good cause for management to cancel the contract) ☺ N/A ☹ at community's *sole* discretion							
14-181	Amount of security deposit							
14-182	Any payments refundable							
14-183	Conditions for refund	FSRC # 1						
		FSRC # 2						
		FSRC # 3						
14-184	Other							

For Communities under Construction Only

14-185	Deposit ☺ refundable ☺ refundable less a fee (insert % or $) ☹ not refundable							
14-186	Restrictions on refund of deposit							

ENTRANCE REQUIREMENTS

14-187	Must be independent to put name on waiting list for IL							
14-188	Provisional acceptances for disorders such as COPD, Parkinson's disease, matastisized cancer, congestive heart failure, etc.							
14-189	Must be independent to put name on ready list							
14-190	Must be independent to move-in							

	QUESTIONS FOR THE MARKETING REPRESENTATIVE *(continued)*				
14-191	Required monthly fee to income ratio ☺ 1.5 to 2 times the monthly fee in income ☺ 2.5 to 3 times ☹ greater than 3 or fewer than 1.5				
14-192	Assets to entrance fee ratio ☺ 1.5 to 2 times the entrance fee in assets ☺ 2.5 or 3 ☹ greater than 3 or fewer than 1.5				
14-193	Other				

FEES FOR HOMES

			FSRC # 1	FSRC # 2	FSRC # 3
14-194	Name of my favorite floor plan		FSRC # 1	FSRC # 2	FSRC # 3
14-195	Number of bedrooms (BR) & baths (BA) in my favorite floor plan		BR	BR	BR
			BA	BA	BA
14-196	Den				
14-197	Square footage of my favorite floor plan				
14-198	Entrance fee for my favorite floor plan	one person	$	$	$
14-199		second person	$	$	$
14-200		couple (add two figures above)	$	$	$
14-201	Monthly fee for my favorite floor plan	one person	$	$	$
14-202		second person	$	$	$
14-203		couple (add two figures above)	$	$	$

	QUESTIONS FOR THE MARKETING REPRESENTATIVE *(continued)*				
14-204	Name of my second favorite floor plan	FSRC # 1			
		FSRC # 2			
		FSRC # 3			
14-205	Number of bedrooms (BR) & baths (BA) in my favorite floor plan		BR	BR	BR
			BA	BA	BA
14-206	Den				
14-207	Square footage of my second favorite floor plan				
14-208	Entrance fee for second favorite floor plan	one person	$	$	$
14-209		second person	$	$	$
14-210		couple (add two figures above)	$	$	$
14-211	Monthly fee for second favorite floor plan	one person	$	$	$
14-212		second person	$	$	$
14-213		couple (add two figures above)	$	$	$
14-214	No road usage fee				
14-215	One time parking fee ☺ garage ☺ covered parking ☹ uncovered parking		$	$	$
14-216	Other				
WAITING LIST POLICY					
14-217	Waiting-list fee	per person	$	$	$
		per couple/home	$	$	$

QUESTIONS FOR THE MARKETING REPRESENTATIVE *(continued)*						
14-218	Waiting-list fee refundable if I don't move in ☺ fully ☺ less fee (insert % or $) ☹ no					
14-219	Waiting-list fee is refunded, interest on waiting list fee goes to ☺ potential resident ☺ community (for processing fee) ☹ N/A					
14-220	Average length of wait on the waiting list for my favorite floor plan					
14-221	Average length of wait on the waiting list for my second favorite floor plan					
14-222	Ready-list fee	per person	$	$	$	
		per couple/unit	$	$	$	
14-223	Ready-list fee refundable if I don't move in ☺ fully ☺ less fee (insert % or $) ☹ no					
14-224	If ready-list fee is refunded, interest on ready list fee goes to ☺ resident ☺ community (for processing fee) ☹ N/A					
14-225	Average length of wait on the ready list for my favorite floor plan					
14-226	Average length of wait on the ready list for my second favorite floor plan					
14-227	If waiting list or ready list fee is applied to entry fee, interest goes to ☺ resident ☺ community ☹ N/A					

QUESTIONS FOR THE MARKETING REPRESENTATIVE *(continued)*									
14-228	Waiting list refusal policy ☺ I specify what date to start calling & stay at the top of list if I refuse offer ☺ stay at top of list if I refuse offer ☹ go to the bottom of list upon refusal								
14-229	Moves within the IL homes possible ☺ residents have priority over those on waiting or ready list ☺ yes, but no priority ☹ not allowed								
14-230	Other								

FEE QUESTIONS FOR MARKETING REPRESENTATIVE		FSRC #1			FSRC #2			FSRC #3		
Key: ☺ included in fee ☺ available for extra cost ☹ not available										
This list includes expenditures that might be eliminated if you live in a FSRC.		☺	☺	☹	☺	☺	☹	☺	☺	☹

INCLUDED in MONTHLY FEE

14-231	House payment/rent									
14-232	Homeowner's insurance (not personal articles insurance)									
14-233	Renter's insurance									
14-234	Homeowners' association/condo fees									
14-235	Other fees									
14-236	Real estate taxes									
14-237	Other taxes									
14-238	Electric									
14-239	Gas									
14-240	Water & sewer									

FEE QUESTIONS FOR MARKETING REPRESENTATIVE *(continued)*											
14-241	Trash removal										
14-242	Exterior maintenance										
14-243	Snow removal										
14-244	Interior maintenance										
14-245	Security system										
14-246	Housekeeping service										
14-247	Flat linen laundered										
14-248	Flat linens furnished										
14-249	Scheduled transportation										
14-250	Transportation on request										
14-251	Parking fee										
14-252	Parking, reserved &/or covered										
14-253	Meal(s)										
14-254	Special diets										
14-255	Tray service when ill										
14-256	Take-out meals										
14-257	Long-term care insurance premium										
14-258	Spa/health club dues										
14-259	Personal trainer										
14-260	Activities (class fees, concerts, lectures)										
14-261	Basic telephone										
14-262	Intra-community phone system										
14-263	Basic cable										
14-264	Computer access										

FEE QUESTIONS FOR MARKETING REPRESENTATIVE *(continued)*

14-265	Social services									
14-266	Minor services in wellness center									
14-267	Assisted living									
14-268	Skilled nursing									
14-269	Alzheimer's/dementia									
14-270	Other									

DOCUMENT QUESTIONS FOR MARKETING REPRESENTATIVE

Key: ☺ received document ☺ document coming in the mail ☹ document not available	FSRC #1			FSRC #2			FSRC #3		
	☺	☺	☹	☺	☺	☹	☺	☺	☹

DOCUMENTS to REQUEST

14-271	Application									
14-272	Waiting list contract									
14-273	Residential agreement/contract									
14-274	Resident handbook									
14-275	Fee schedule for extra charges in IL, AL, SN, & A/D									
14-276	Disclosure statement									
14-277	Five-year history of fees									
14-278	Tax letter									
14-279	Audited financial statement									
14-280	Inspection reports (government, others)									
14-281	List of members of Board of Directors & their biographies									
14-282	Mission statement									

	DOCUMENT QUESTIONS FOR MARKETING REPRESENTATIVE *(continued)*									
14-283	Philosophy									
14-284	Calendar of events for IL, AL, SN, A/D									
14-285	Menus for IL, AL, SN, A/D									
14-286	Site map									
14-287	Other									

15

TOUR QUESTIONS

*Accuracy of observation is the
equivalent of accuracy of thinking.*

—Wallace Stevens
American Poet, 1879-1955

꙳꙳꙳

The tour is your chance to observe things that will tell you volumes about the community. Observe and ask questions. While touring the FSRC, feel free to read the bulletin boards; you can learn much from them. While you are visiting, take time to talk to the residents and their families. Find out what they like and don't like.

The tour usually begins with the common areas, the activities areas, and the amenities. The kitchen is not usually on the tour, but the marketing representative will probably take you in, if you ask. You will most likely see the apartments and/or cottages next.

Be sure to request the documents listed. In order to evaluate a community seriously and completely, information needs to be gathered from researching other sources.

Assisted living (AL), skilled nursing (SN), and Alzheimer's/dementia (A/D) areas are usually last. If you are uncomfortable touring these sections, at the very least, send a friend or relative to be sure that they pass muster. You certainly don't want any surprises here later.

TOUR QUESTIONS										

Key: ☺ yes positive ideal many	FSRC #1			FSRC #2			FSRC #3		
☺ slightly neutral good some									
☹ no negative poor few									

☹ answer to question after dark grey numbers is a Deal Breaker.	☹ answer to question after light grey numbers is a Red Flag	☺	☻	☹	☺	☻	☹	☺	☻	☹

INDEPENDENT LIVING (IL) COMMON AREAS										
15-1	Well-maintained									
15-2	Clean & tidy									
15-3	Community center									
15-4	Lots of places to sit indoors									
15-5	People up & about									
15-6	Easily opened doors									
15-7	Wheelchair friendly									
15-8	Decor I am comfortable with									
15-9	Flowers &/or plants (real or silk) ☺ many attractive bouquets or pots ☻ token amount ☹ none or not attractive									
15-10	Fireplace in common area									
15-11	Cocktail lounge									
15-12	Formal dining room									
15-13	Informal dining room									
15-14	Patio dining area									
15-15	Private dining room									

TOUR QUESTIONS *(continued)*											
15-16	Spotless kitchen										
15-17	Spotless public restrooms										
15-18	Windows or glass walls into activities rooms, lounge, & other common areas										
15-19	All-purpose room										
15-20	Separate ballroom										
15-21	Separate theater										
15-22	Separate chapel										
15-23	Separate buildings connected with covered walkways										
15-24	Climate-controlled walkways between buildings										
15-25	Staff ☺ warm & friendly ☻ polite, but not friendly ☹ none of the above										
15-26	Other										
AMENITIES											
15-27	Bank ☺ full service ☻ visiting representative ☹ no banking services										
15-28	Safety deposit boxes										
15-29	ATM										
15-30	Beauty/barber shops ☺ hair, manicures, & pedicures ☻ pedicures not available ☹ no shop										
15-31	Dry cleaning										

	TOUR QUESTIONS *(continued)*									
15-32	Shoe repair									
15-33	U.S. Post Office									
15-34	Mailing services (FedEx, UPS)									
15-35	Convenience store									
15-36	Gift shop									
15-37	Thrift shop									
15-38	Other									
COMMUNITY HEALTH CARE										
15-39	Wellness center for use of IL residents ☺ doctor or nurse practitioner on staff ☺ RN or LPN on staff ☹ no wellness center									
15-40	Hours of wellness center ☺ 24/7 or may go to SN after hours ☺ 40 hours/week ☹ fewer than 40 hours/week									
15-41	Local doctors hold office hours in wellness center ☺ full time ☺ part time ☹ no doctor's office hours									
15-42	Length of appointments ☺ 30 or more minutes ☺ 20-25 minutes ☹ fewer than 20 minutes									
15-43	Defibrillator on site									
15-44	In-clinic X-rays									
15-45	In-clinic mammograms									
15-46	Dentist									
15-47	Geriatrician									

	TOUR QUESTIONS *(continued)*											
15-48	Gynecologist											
15-49	Ophthalmologist											
15-50	Optometrist											
15-51	Podiatrist											
15-52	Psychiatrist											
15-53	Psychologist											
15-54	Pharmacy ☺ community or commercial on site ☺ pick-up-and-delivery service ☹ none of the above											
15-55	Other											
ACTIVITIES												
15-56	Library ☺ extensive, with current magazines, newspapers, video tapes, & books ☺ limited library ☹ no library											
15-57	Low vision equipment for reading											
15-58	Business center ☺ with fax, copy machine, & computer ☺ some of the above ☹ no business center											
15-59	Conference room											
15-60	Computer room											
15-61	Music room											
15-62	Card room											
15-63	Billiards											

	TOUR QUESTIONS *(continued)*									
15-64	Arts & crafts room[27] ☺ makes projects for the community ☺ active group ☹ no room or minimal activity									
15-65	Garden club[27] ☺ tends flower beds for the community ☺ active group ☹ no club or minimal activity									
15-66	Greenhouse &/or gardening room									
15-67	Garden plots or flower beds									
15-68	Dance floor ☺ permanent ☺ portable ☹ none									
15-69	Photo lab									
15-70	Closed circuit TV station ☺ resident run ☺ staff run ☹ no station									
15-71	Woodworking shop[27] ☺ makes projects for the community ☺ active group ☹ no shop or inactive									
15-72	Signs of lively participation in activities									
15-73	Some activities off site									
15-74	Other									
WELLNESS										
15-75	Fitness room									

[27] This shows residents' involvement in the community.

	TOUR QUESTIONS *(continued)*										
15-76	Strength-training equipment ☺ air pressurized equipment ☺ lead weight equipment ☹ no strength-training equipment										
15-77	Free weights										
15-78	Trainer ☺ full time ☺ part time ☹ someone just shows residents how to use the equipment										
15-79	Fitness room amenities ☺ TV/VCR, water cooler, & mats ☺ some of the above ☹ none of the above										
15-80	Jacuzzi/whirlpool										
15-81	Swimming pool ☺ indoor & outdoor pool ☺ indoor or outdoor pool ☹ no pool										
15-82	Indoor pool disinfectant ☺ ultraviolet light ☺ chlorine with good ventilation ☹ chlorine with poor ventilation										
15-83	Pool for water aerobics										
15-84	Pool for swimming laps										
15-85	Ramp or lift to help disabled residents into the pool										
15-86	Other										

HALLS in INDEPENDENT LIVING APARTMENT BUILDING

15-87	Well maintained										
15-88	Clean & tidy										
15-89	Decor I am comfortable with										

	TOUR QUESTIONS *(continued)*									
15-90	Flowers &/or plants (real or silk) ☺ many attractive bouquets or pots ☺ token amount ☹ none or not attractive									
15-91	Handrails in halls[28]									
15-92	Halls well lit[29] ☺ recessed lighting ☺ non-recessed lighting ☹ poorly lit or glaring light									
15-93	Seating in long halls									
15-94	Climate controlled halls									
15-95	Public restrooms in long halls									
15-96	Attractive halls									
15-97	Architecturally interesting halls									
15-98	Seating by the elevators									
15-99	Common areas on each floor									
15-100	Other									
INDEPENDENT LIVING APARTMENTS										
15-101	Wheelchair accessible ☺ yes ☺ willing to retrofit ☹ unable or unwilling to retrofit									
15-102	Door levers, not knobs									
15-103	Electric or gas stove									

---

[28] Handrails in halls show management's interest in keeping residents in independent living as long as possible.

[29] This shows management's concern for the residents' well being.

	TOUR QUESTIONS *(continued)*								
15-104	Refrigerator provided ☺ & serviced by community ☻ by resident; serviced by community ☹ & serviced by resident								
15-105	Ice maker								
15-106	Microwave oven								
15-107	Dishwasher								
15-108	Garbage disposer								
15-109	Pullout shelves in lower kitchen cabinets								
15-110	Lazy susans in corner kitchen cabinets								
15-111	Fireplace								
15-112	Type of window treatments provided								
15-113	Window screens								
15-114	Insulated windows								
15-115	Storm windows								
15-116	Screen door								
15-117	Storm door								
15-118	Individual, *central* heat & air								
15-119	Maximum number of bedrooms in community[30] ☺ 3 or 2 with den ☻ 2 or 1 with den ☹ 1								

[30] Communities that offer larger apartments and cottages are preparing for the Baby Boomers.

	TOUR QUESTIONS *(continued)*									
15-120	Emergency call system in home ☺ mobile within home ☺ fixed within home ☹ none									
15-121	Emergency call system on property ☺ mobile, individualized ☺ fixed on property ☹ none in common areas									
15-122	Walk-in closet									
15-123	Bathtub									
15-124	Walk-in shower									
15-125	Seat in shower									
15-126	Raised toilets vs. standard-height toilets ☺ community pays for change ☺ resident pays for change ☹ no change allowed									
15-127	Washer & dryer location ☺ in resident's home ☺ convenient location outside resident's home ☹ inconvenient location outside resident's home									
15-128	Free use of community washer & dryer									
15-129	Washer & dryer provided ☺ & serviced by community ☺ by resident; serviced by community ☹ & serviced by resident									
15-130	Washer & dryer size ☺ full sized, side-by-side ☺ large capacity stackable ☹ small capacity stackable									

	TOUR QUESTIONS *(continued)*						
15-131	Patio ☺ with a pleasant view &/or private ☺ no view & not private ☹ no patio						
15-132	Patio: screened in, glassed in, enclosed						
15-133	Balcony ☺ with a pleasant view &/or private ☺ no view & not private ☹ no balcony						
15-134	Balcony: screened in, glassed in, enclosed						
15-135	Storage area						
15-136	Other						
INDEPENDENT LIVING HOUSES/COTTAGES/VILLAS/DUPLEXES, etc.							
15-137	Wheelchair accessible ☺ yes ☺ willing to retrofit ☹ no or not willing to retrofit						
15-138	Door levers, not knobs						
15-139	Electric or gas stove						
15-140	Refrigerator provided ☺ & serviced by community ☺ by resident; serviced by community ☹ & serviced by resident						
15-141	Ice maker						
15-142	Microwave						
15-143	Dishwasher						
15-144	Garbage disposer						
15-145	Pullout shelves in lower kitchen cabinets						
15-146	Lazy susans in corner kitchen cabinets						

TOUR QUESTIONS *(continued)*											
15-147	Fireplace										
15-148	Window treatments provided										
15-149	Window screens										
15-150	Storm windows										
15-151	Screen door										
15-152	Storm door										
15-153	Insulated windows										
15-154	Individual, *central* heat & air										
15-155	Maximum number of bedrooms in community ☺ 3 or 2 with den ☺ 2 or 1 with a den ☹ 1										
15-156	Emergency call system ☺ mobile in home ☺ fixed in home ☹ none										
15-157	Walk-in closet										
15-158	Bathtub										
15-159	Walk-in shower										
15-160	Seat in shower										
15-161	Raised toilets vs. standard-height toilets ☺ community pays for change ☺ resident pays for change ☹ no change allowed										
15-162	Washer & dryer location ☺ in resident's home ☺ convenient location ☹ inconvenient location										
15-163	Free use of community washer & dryer										

	TOUR QUESTIONS *(continued)*							
15-164	Washer & dryer provided ☺ & serviced by community ☺ by resident; serviced by community ☹ & serviced by resident							
15-165	Washer & dryer size ☺ full sized, side-by-side ☺ large capacity stackable ☹ small capacity stackable							
15-166	Patio ☺ with a pleasant view &/or private ☺ no view & not private ☹ no patio							
15-167	Patio: screened in, glassed in, enclosed							
15-168	Deck ☺ with a pleasant view &/or private ☺ no view & not private ☹ no deck							
15-169	Deck: screened in, glassed in, enclosed							
15-170	Parking ☺ garage ☺ covered ☹ no covered parking							
15-171	Storage area							
15-172	Other							
ASSISTED LIVING (AL)								
15-173	No odor on entry							
15-174	Well maintained							
15-175	Clean & tidy							
15-176	People up & about							
15-177	Easily opened doors							
15-178	Wheelchair friendly							

	TOUR QUESTIONS *(continued)*									
15-179	Decor I am comfortable with									
15-180	Flowers &/or plants (real or silk) ☺ many attractive bouquets or pots ☺ token amount ☹ none or not attractive									
15-181	Wide halls									
15-182	Halls well lit									
15-183	Handrails in halls									
15-184	Attractive halls									
15-185	Architecturally interesting halls									
15-186	Spotless public restrooms									
15-187	Seating by the elevators									
15-188	Seating in long halls									
15-189	Pleasant common areas									
15-190	Music playing in common areas									
15-191	Comfortable-looking chairs									
15-192	Big screened TV									
15-193	Quality activities									
15-194	Participation in activities									
15-195	Size of largest home in AL ☺ one or two bedroom apartment ☺ studio ☹ hospital-like room									
15-196	Private rooms ☺ all or most ☺ some ☹ none or very few									

	TOUR QUESTIONS *(continued)*											
15-197	Resident's furniture allowed ☺ all ☻ some ☹ none											
15-198	Emergency call system ☺ mobile in home ☻ fixed in home ☹ none											
15-199	Kitchens in homes ☺ complete kitchen, even if small ☻ tea kitchen (sink, microwave, refrigerator) ☹ no kitchen											
15-200	Window treatments provided											
15-201	View from most home windows (trees, gardens, mountains, parking lots, etc.)											
15-202	Private full baths ☺ all or most ☻ some ☹ none or very few											
15-203	Private half baths ☺ all or most ☻ some ☹ none or very few											
15-204	Phone line in each room											
15-205	Individual, *central* heat & air											
15-206	Washer & dryer location ☺ in each home ☻ on each hall ☹ inconvenient location											
15-207	Washer & dryer size ☺ full sized, side-by-side ☻ large capacity stackable ☹ small capacity stackable											

	TOUR QUESTIONS *(continued)*										
15-208	Laundry service provided ☺ flat & personal ☺ flat only ☹ no service										
15-209	Use of community washer & dryer ☺ no charge ☺ N/A ☹ coin operated										
15-210	Same menu as IL dining room[31]										
15-211	Nutritious meals										
15-212	Food served hot without re-warming										
15-213	Fresh fruit readily available										
15-214	Open seating at meals										
15-215	Tablecloths on dining room tables										
15-216	Easily accessible garden										
15-217	Community dog										
15-218	Community cat										
15-219	Community birds										
15-220	Community fish										
15-221	Staff ☺ warm & friendly ☺ polite, but not friendly ☹ none of the above										
15-222	No odor throughout										
15-223	Other										

---

[31] From our observations, residents who eat the same menu as independent living, are seemingly and arguably more alert and vital.

	TOUR QUESTIONS *(continued)*								
SKILLED NURSING (SN)									
15-224	No odor on entry								
15-225	Well maintained								
15-226	Clean & tidy								
15-227	Easily opened doors								
15-228	Wheelchair friendly								
15-229	Decor I am comfortable with								
15-230	Flowers &/or plants (real or silk) ☺ many attractive bouquets or pots ☺ token amount ☹ none or not attractive								
15-231	Halls well lit								
15-232	Handrails in halls								
15-233	Attractive halls								
15-234	Architecturally interesting halls								
15-235	Spotless public restrooms								
15-236	Pleasant common areas								
15-237	Music playing in common areas								
15-238	Comfortable-looking chairs								
15-239	Big screened TV								
15-240	Most residents out of bed, except at nap time								
15-241	Most residents dressed in street clothes								
15-242	Quality activities								
15-243	Participation in activities								

	TOUR QUESTIONS *(continued)*								
15-244	Emergency call system ☺ mobile in home ☺ fixed in home ☹ none								
15-245	Private rooms ☺ all or most ☺ some ☹ none or very few								
15-246	Resident's furniture allowed ☺ some ☺ N/A ☹ none								
15-247	Window treatments provided								
15-248	View from most home windows (trees, gardens, mountains, parking lot, etc.)								
15-249	Private full baths ☺ all or most ☺ some ☹ none or very few								
15-250	Private half baths ☺ all or most ☺ some ☹ none or very few								
15-251	Phone line in each room								
15-252	Individual, *central* heat & air								
15-253	Same menu as IL dining room[32]								
15-254	Nutritious meals								
15-255	Food served hot without re-warming								
15-256	Fresh fruit readily available								

---

[32] From our observations, residents who eat the same menu as independent living, are seemingly and, arguably, more alert and vital.

	TOUR QUESTIONS *(continued)*								
15-257	Tablecloths on dining room tables								
15-258	Easily accessible garden								
15-259	Community dog								
15-260	Community cat								
15-261	Community birds								
15-262	Community fish								
15-263	Staff ☺ warm & friendly ☺ polite, but not friendly ☹ none of the above								
15-264	No odor throughout								
15-265	Other								

ALZHEIMER'S/DEMENTIA (A/D)

15-266	No odor on entry								
15-267	Well maintained								
15-268	Clean & tidy								
15-269	Wheelchair friendly								
15-270	Decor I am comfortable with								
15-271	Flowers &/or plants (real or silk) ☺ many attractive bouquets or pots ☺ token amount ☹ none or not attractive								
15-272	Halls well lit								
15-273	Handrails in halls								
15-274	Attractive halls								
15-275	Architecturally interesting halls								

	TOUR QUESTIONS *(continued)*									
15-276	Curio cabinet for personal items at each door									
15-277	Spotless public restrooms									
15-278	Pleasant common areas									
15-279	Music playing in common areas									
15-280	Comfortable-looking chairs									
15-281	Big screened TV									
15-282	Most residents dressed in street clothes									
15-283	Most residents out of bed, except at nap time									
15-284	Quality activities									
15-285	Participation in activities									
15-286	Emergency call system ☺ mobile in home ☺ fixed in home ☹ none									
15-287	Private rooms ☺ all or most ☺ some ☹ none or very few									
15-288	Resident's furniture allowed ☺ all ☺ some ☹ none									
15-289	Window treatments provided									
15-290	View from most home windows (trees, gardens, mountains, parking lot, etc.)									
15-291	Individual, *central* heat & air									

	TOUR QUESTIONS *(continued)*									
15-292	Private full baths ☺ all or most ☺ some ☹ none or very few									
15-293	Private half baths ☺ all or most ☺ some ☹ none or very few									
15-294	Type of home ☺ home-like studio apartment ☺ home-like room ☹ hospital-like room (except for end-stage patients)									
15-295	Same menu as IL dining room[33]									
15-296	Nutritious meals									
15-297	Food served hot without re-warming									
15-298	Fresh fruit readily available									
15-299	Wandering safeguards									
15-300	Easily accessible garden									
15-301	Community dog									
15-302	Community cat									
15-303	Community birds									
15-304	Community fish									
15-305	Staff ☺ warm & friendly ☺ polite, but not friendly ☹ none of the above									

---

[33] From our observations, residents who eat the same menu as independent living, are seemingly and, arguably, more alert and vital.

TOUR QUESTIONS *(continued)*										
15-306	No odor throughout									
15-307	Other									

16

DINING WITH THE RESIDENTS

Without a sense of caring,
there can be no sense of community.

—Anthony J. D'Angelo
American Author

❧❦

If you are invited to stay for a meal (out of town visitors usually are), the marketing representative will very often select two residents to eat with you. This is your opportunity to find out more about the personality of the community.

Eating lunch or dinner with the residents is a wonderful chance to confirm what you have been told and to learn things from another perspective. This is also an opportunity to observe the menus and the quality of the food, among other things. Your resident hosts will answer questions from a different viewpoint than a staff member will. It is best if the marketing rep does not join you so that the responses that you receive may be given more freely.

DINING WITH THE RESIDENTS					FSRC #1			FSRC #2			FSRC #3		
Key: ☺ yes positive ideal many ☻ slightly neutral good some ☹ no negative poor few													
☹ answer to question after dark grey numbers is a Deal Breaker.			☹ answer to question after light grey numbers is a Red Flag		☺	☻	☹	☺	☻	☹	☺	☻	☹

YOUR MEAL IN THE DINING ROOM

		FSRC #1			FSRC #2			FSRC #3		
16-1	Dining companions ☺ residents ☻ residents with marketing rep or other staff present at table ☹ not invited to dinner or with marketing rep alone									
16-2	No waiting to be seated in dining room ☺ ample seating for all ☻ occasional short wait ☹ routine waiting or first & second sittings									
16-3	Seating in dining room ☺ no assigned seating ☻ friendship table ☹ assigned seating									
16-4	Casters on chairs in dining room ☺ 4 ☻ 2 ☹ none									
16-5	Tablecloths on dining room tables									
16-6	Style of main food service: restaurant style, family style, buffet, or cafeteria									
16-7	Daily menu ☺ permanent & daily specials ☻ daily specials only ☹ limited entrées									

DINING WITH THE RESIDENTS *(continued)*							
16-8	Daily specials ☺ beef, chicken, fish, & vegetarian ☺ 3 dissimilar choices ☹ limited or similar choices							
16-9	Menu at noon & evening meals ☺ Evening menu different from noon menu ☺ Same menus at both meals, but several choices ☹ Few or no choices							
16-10	Salad bar							
16-11	Healthy salad bar ☺ dark leafy greens with fresh fruits & many brightly colored raw vegetables ☺ some of the above ☹ iceberg lettuce with canned fruits & vegetables							
16-12	Primarily nutritious meals							
16-13	Whole pieces of fruit available							
16-14	Lively chatter & laughter							
16-15	Table hopping by residents							
16-16	Other							
CONVERSATION WITH RESIDENTS							
16-17	Active residents ☺ physically & mentally ☺ either ☹ neither							
16-18	Residents involved within community							
16-19	Residents involved in the local area							

	DINING WITH THE RESIDENTS *(continued)*									
16-20	Dining companions ☺ officer(s) on residents' council ☺ active members of residents' council ☹ neither									
16-21	Residents visit sick friends in AL & SN									
16-22	Welcoming committee for new residents									
16-23	Resident's timing on moving in: ☺ just right ☺ too early ☹ too late									
16-24	Residents' presence on site ☺ moderate amount of travel ☺ minimal amount of travel ☹ large number gone half of the year									
16-25	CEO's managing style: autocratic, participative, or *laissez faire*									
16-26	Residents' opinions of management									
16-27	Management & staff reasonably flexible in applying rules									
16-28	Management's reaction to abuse of privileges ☺ satisfactory solutions ☺ no problems noted by residents ☹ punish all or no action									
16-29	Management's changes in rules ☺ resulted in improved conditions ☺ questionably effective or no rule changes noted by residents ☹ ineffective									
16-30	No-tipping policy ☺ residents adhere to it ☺ residents tip anyway ☹ no policy									

	DINING WITH THE RESIDENTS *(continued)*										
16-31	Price of guest meal ☺ reasonably priced ☻ moderately priced ☹ too highly priced										
16-32	Doggie bags allowed (from restaurant-style dining)										
16-33	Minimal take out (desserts, fruit, muffins, etc.)										
16-34	Homes (guest room) reasonably soundproof										
16-35	Other										
YOUR OBSERVATIONS about the RESIDENTS											
16-36	Residents ☺ warm & friendly ☻ polite, but not friendly ☹ none of the above										
16-37	Residents spontaneously stopped to greet me in dining room & halls										
16-38	Residents with positive attitudes										
16-39	Open-minded residents										
16-40	Residents invited me into their homes										
16-41	Clothing & jewelry of residents similar to mine										
16-42	Economic level of residents seemingly similar to mine										
16-43	Interests of residents similar to mine										
16-44	Other										

17

OUTSIDE SOURCES TO CHECK

*It is an immutable law in business that words are words;
explanations are explanations; promises are promises,
but only performance is reality.*

—Harold Geneen
American Businessman, 1910-1997

❧❧❧

Even though you are diligent in asking questions and fortunate in getting complete answers, there is still more to know. A number of easily found sources can tell you about the reputation and past performance of the communities that you are interested in. In doing a little research, you could uncover information that you might not learn any other way. This step is especially important for communities that are not accredited.

OUTSIDE SOURCES TO CHECK		FSRC #1			FSRC #2			FSRC #3		
Key: ☺ positive ☻ neutral ☹ negative		☺	☻	☹	☺	☻	☹	☺	☻	☹	
Use a highlighter to mark your own deal breakers and red flags.											
INFO SOUGHT	**SOURCE**										
17-1	FSRC's reputation for stability & high quality in the local area	Back issues of local newspapers, Better Business Bureau, & the Internet									
17-2	Sponsor's &/or owner's reputation for stability & high quality in the local area	Back issues of newspapers in the sponsor's &/or owner's hometown, Better Business Bureau, & the Internet									
17-3	Management's reputation	Better Business Bureau, old newspapers, articles from the library, & the Internet									
17-4	Management's track record at other FSRCs	Better Business Bureau, old newspapers, articles from the library, & the Internet									
17-5	Owner's credit rating	*Dun & Bradstreet, Standard & Poor's* (in the library), attorney, & CPA									

OUTSIDE SOURCES TO CHECK *(continued)*												
17-6	Bond ratings	*Moody's, Standard & Poor's* (in the library), attorney, & CPA										
17-7	Financial stability of community	CPA & audited financial statements from FSRC, *Financial Ratios & Trend Analysis of the CCAC Accredited Organizations* from CARF/CCAC (Appendix A), IRS form 990										
17-8	Interpretation of contract, lawsuits, bankruptcies	Attorney & the Internet										
17-9	State laws (*e.g.* driver's license, taxes [inheritance, personal property, income])	Attorney & the Internet										
17-10	Fee structure best for you	Financial advisor										
17-11	Inspection reports, State Department of Health	State Department of Health & the FSRC										
17-12	Inspection reports, other	Licensing agencies, other inspection bodies, Appendix C										
17-13	Usage of agency employees	Temporary employment agencies in area										

	OUTSIDE SOURCES TO CHECK *(continued)*									
17-14	Complaints of elder abuse	Nursing Home Ombudsman, Appendix B								
17-15	Protection available by law	State laws, the Internet, & attorney								
17-16	Quality of local hospital	*Places Rated Almanac*, library								
17-17	Quality of local ambulance service	Commission of Accreditation of Ambulance Services, the Internet								
17-18	Religious community	Personal visits to churches								
17-19	Viability of neighborhood	City hall								
17-20	Crime rate	Police								
17-21	Other									

18

QUESTIONS FOR THE CEO

Where there is no vision, the people perish.

—Proverbs 29:18

    The CEO can answer many questions about the finances and day-to-day operations of the community. Meeting with him or her will give you better insight into how things are run. We strongly recommend that you make an appointment to meet the CEOs of the communities on your very short list. Meeting them and hearing their answers can be very educational.

QUESTIONS FOR THE CEO										

Key: ☺ yes positive ideal many ☺ slightly neutral good some ☹ no negative poor few		FSRC #1			FSRC #2			FSRC #3		
☹ answer to question after dark grey numbers is a Deal Breaker.	☹ answer to question after light grey numbers a Red Flag	☺	☹	☺	☺	☹	☺	☺	☹	☺

MANAGEMENT

18-1	Sponsor's obligation to community ☺ financial & legal ☺ advisory only ☹ in name only									
18-2	Allocation of entrance fees ☺ capital improvements, medical care, benevolence fund ☺ capital improvements & medical care ☹ overhead &/or services									
18-3	Allocation of monthly fees ☺ overhead & services ☺ N/A ☹ capital improvements									
18-4	Benevolence fund ☺ funded from entrance fees & other sources ☺ funded from donations only ☹ no fund									
18-5	Amount of benevolence fund	$			$			$		
18-6	Ethics committee									
18-7	For nonprofits, membership in AAHSA (American Association for Homes & Services for the Aging) ☺ member & attend conferences ☺ attend conferences ☹ do not attend conferences									

	QUESTIONS FOR THE CEO *(continued)*									
18-8	Membership in ASHA (American Senior Housing Association) ☺ member & attend conferences ☺ attend conferences ☹ do not attend conferences									
18-9	Efforts to keep nurses ☺ special program in place ☺ plan rolled in with other employee retention efforts ☹ no plan									
18-10	Low employee turnover									
18-11	Use of few agency employees									
18-12	Management style of CEO: autocratic, participative, *laissez-faire*									
18-13	Eden Alternative, philosophy of management									
18-14	Legal minimum for nursing hours per patient per day (NHPPD)									
18-15	FSRC's nursing hours per patient per day (NHPPD)									
18-16	Legal minimum for ratio of Nurse Managers to residents in SN									
18-17	Community's ratio of Nurse Managers to residents in SN									
18-18	Legal minimum for ratio of RNs to residents in SN									
18-19	Community's ratio of RNs to residents in SN									
18-20	Legal minimum for ratio of LPNs to residents in SN									
18-21	Community's ratio of LPNs to residents in SN									

colspan="5"	**QUESTIONS FOR THE CEO *(continued)***
18-22	Legal minimum for ratio of CNAs to residents in SN			
18-23	FSRC's ratio of CNAs to residents in SN			
18-24	Amount reserve fund	$	$	$
18-25	Alternate sources of income for FSRC			
18-26	Raw food per plate cost (not per *day*)	$	$	$
18-27	Cost to purchase additional meals ☺ raw food per plate cost + 15-20% ☺ N/A ☹ more			
18-28	Deficiencies in state inspections			
18-29	Most challenging change made by CEO — FSRC # 1			
	FSRC # 2			
	FSRC # 3			
18-30	Other			

	**IF FSRC IS NOT ACCREDITED BY CARF/CCAC**
18-31	If not accredited, why? ☺ not eligible yet ☺ in progress ☹ not necessary			
18-32	Properly licensed & certified			
18-33	Compliant w/ laws: federal, state, & local			
18-34	Loan payments made on time			
18-35	Cash flow ☺ positive ☺ negative, but a new community ☹ negative			
18-36	Strong sources of non-operating income			
18-37	Predicted generation of future non-operating income by outside source			

	QUESTIONS FOR THE CEO *(continued)*									
18-38	Written 5 year integrated strategic plan									
18-39	Written marketing plan									
18-40	Written budget for next fiscal year									
18-41	Five-year written cash flow projections									
18-42	Written risk management plan									
18-43	Written emergency preparedness plan									
18-44	Other									
FOR NEW COMMUNITIES										
18-45	Payments to subcontractors up to date									
18-46	Construction loan payments up to date									
18-47	All monies spent on this community only									
18-48	Adequate fiscal reserves									
18-49	Licensing in order									
18-50	Sales targets being met									
18-51	Plan to attend AAHSA or AHSA conferences									
18-52	Plan to be CARF/CCAC accredited									
18-53	Phase II being planned									
18-54	Other									
FOR COMMUNITIES under CONSTRUCTION										
18-55	Payments to subcontractors up to date									
18-56	Construction loan payments up to date									
18-57	All monies spent on this community only									
18-58	Adequate fiscal reserves									
18-59	Licensing in order									

	QUESTIONS FOR THE CEO *(continued)*										
18-60	Experienced team: financial, actuarial, lender, construction, management, etc.										
18-61	High bond ratings										
18-62	Sales targets being met										
18-63	Deposit ☺ refundable ☺ refundable less a fee (insert % or $) ☹ not refundable										
18-64	Restrictions on refund of preconstruction deposit										
18-65	Other										

19

CONCLUSIONS

*The art of being wise
is the art of knowing what to overlook.*

—William James
American Philosopher, 1842-1910

No community and/or its homes will have all the features you want. The house you bought and neighborhood it's in probably didn't either.

We do not recommend sending this list of questions ahead of your visit. Doing so will deprive you of the unspoken messages gained. from the demeanor of the people you meet. This is not a test that each community must pass; it is a fact-finding mission for you. Reading and becoming familiar with the questions before you visit any FSRCs will help speed the process along.

Keep in mind that NO community will earn all "☺" answers in all categories. We are not judging; we are comparing each community against an ideal. You can judge for yourself what is most important to you in your retirement years.

MY CONCLUSIONS									
Study the answers to the questions in the previous chapters, the documents you were given at the FSRC, and the information you discovered checking your outside resources. Remember, there is no perfect FSRC.	FSRC #1			FSRC #2			FSRC #3		
	☺	☻	☹	☺	☻	☹	☺	☻	☹
19-1 Surroundings I am comfortable with									
19-2 Residents I am comfortable with									
19-3 Management I am comfortable with									
19-4 Staff I am comfortable with									
19-5 Policies I am comfortable with									
19-6 Services I am comfortable with									
19-7 Food I am comfortable with									
19-8 Financial structure I am comfortable with									
19-9 Quality wellness program									
19-10 Proven management track record									
19-11 Services equitably allocated to all levels of care									
19-12 Activities I am interested in									
19-13 Future direction of this FSRC ☺ progressive ☻ improving steadily ☹ moving toward becoming all AL &/or SN or stagnant									
19-14 Cost vs. ideal ☺ a good value for the money ☻ worth the money ☹ too expensive									
19-15 Other									
19-16 Is this FSRC for me?									

APPENDICES

The next best thing to knowing something is knowing where to find it.

—Samuel Johnson
English Author, 1709-1784

Appendix A

National Organizations for the Aging
http://www.asaging.org

Note: In using the Web sites, it will, most likely, be necessary to search a little through the site to find the information that you seek. If the site features a "Search" box, enter your main or keywords to get a good start. To print a more complete address is a violation of the copyrights of these organizations.

American Association of Homes and Services for the Aging
901 E Street NW, #500
Washington, DC 20004
202-783-2242

American Association of Retired Persons
601 E Street NW
Washington, DC 20049
202-434-2277
202-434-6563 (TTY)

American Seniors Housing Association
5100 Wisconsin Avenue NW, #307
Washington, D.C. 20016
202-237-0900

Continuing-Care Accreditation Commission
2519 Connecticut Avenue NW
Washington, DC 20008-1520
(202)783-7286
Order books at 800-508-9472

Joint Commission on Accreditation of Healthcare Organizations
One Renaissance Blvd.
Oakbrook Terrace, IL 60181
708-916-5600

National Association of Area Agencies on Aging
927 15th Street NW
Washington, DC 20005
202-926-8130

National Association of Boards
of Examiners for Nursing
Home Administrators
808 17th Street NW, #200
Washington, DC 20006
202-223-9750

National Association
of Insurance Commissioners
120 W. 12th Street, #1100
Kansas City, MO 64105
816-842-3600

National Council of Senior
Citizens
8403 Colesville Road, #1200
Silver Spring, MD 20910-3314
301-578-8800

National Senior Citizens Law
Center
Washington, DC Office
1101 14th Street NW, #400
Washington, DC 20005
202-289-6976

National Council on the Aging
300 D Street SW
Washington, DC 20024
202-479-1200
800-424-9046

See http://www.elderweb.com for more resources.

APPENDIX B

STATE LONG-TERM CARE OMBUDSMEN
http://www.ltcombudsman.org

Alabama
Commission on Aging
RSA Plaza, #470
770 Washington Avenue
Montgomery, AL 36130
334-242-5743
800-243-5463

Alaska
Older Alaskans Commission
3601 C Street, #260
Anchorage, AK 99503-5209
907-563-6393

Arizona
Aging and Adult
Administration
Dept. of Economic Security
1789 West Jefferson, 950A
Phoenix, AZ 85007
602-542-4446

Arkansas
Arkansas Division of Aging
and Adult Services
P.O. Box 1437, Slot 1412
Little Rock, AR 72201-1437
501-682-2441

California
State Long Term Care
Ombudsman
1600 K Street
Sacramento, CA 95814
916-323-6681

Colorado
The Legal Center
455 Sherman Street, #130
Denver, CO 80203
303-722-0300

Connecticut
Dept. on Aging
25 Sigourney Street, 10th
Floor
Hartford, CT 06106-5033
860-424-5200, ext. 5221

Delaware
Delaware Services for Aging-
Disabled
Health and Social Services
Oxford Bldg.
256 Chapman Road, #200
Newark, DE 19702
302-453-3820

District of Columbia
AARP, Legal Counsel for the
Elderly
601 E Street NW,
4th Floor, Bldg. A
Washington, DC 20049
202-434-2188

Florida
Florida State LTC
Ombudsman Council
600 South Calhoun Street,
#270
Tallahassee, FL 32301
850-488-6190

Georgia
Division of Aging Services
2 Peachtree Street NW, #36-385
Atlanta, GA 30303-3176
404-657-5258
888-454-5826

Hawaii
Executive Office on Aging
Office of the Governor
250 South Hotel Street, #107
Honolulu, HI 96813-2831
808-586-0100

Idaho
Office on Aging
P.O. Box 83720
3380 American Terrace, #1
Boise, ID 83720-0007
208-334-3833

Illinois
Illinois Dept. on Aging
421 E. Capitol Avenue, #100
Springfield, IL 62701-1789
217-785-3143

Indiana
Indiana Division of Aging and
Rehabilitation Services
402 W. Washington Street
Indianapolis, IN 46204-7083
317-232-1750

Iowa
Dept. of Elder Affairs
Clemens Bldg.
200 10th Street, 3rd Floor
Des Moines, IA 50309-3609
515-281-8643

Kansas
Office of the State Long-Term
Care Ombudsman
610 SW 10th Street, 2nd Floor
Topeka, KS 66612-1616
785-296-3017

Kentucky
Division of Family/Children
Services
275 E. Main Street, 5th Floor
Frankfort, KY 40621
502-564-6930

Louisiana
Louisiana Governor's Office of
Elderly Affairs
412 N. 4th Street, 3rd Floor
P.O. Box 80374
Baton Rouge, LA 70802
225-342-7100

Maine
Maine State Long-Term-Care
Ombudsman Program
1 Weston Court
P.O. Box 126
Augusta, ME 04332
207-621-1079

Maryland
Office on Aging
301 West Preston Street,
#1007
Baltimore, MD 21201
410-767-1074

Massachusetts
Executive Office of Elder
Affairs
1 Ashburton Place, 5th Floor
Boston, MA 02108-1518
617-727-7750

Michigan
Citizens for Better Care
6105 W. St. Joseph Highway,
#211
Lansing, MI 48917-3981
517-886-6797

Minnesota
Office of Ombudsman for
Older Minnesotans
121 East 7th Place, #410
St. Paul, MN 55101
651-296-0382

Mississippi
Division of Aging and Adult
Services
750 North State Street
Jackson, MS 39202
601-359-4929

Missouri
Division on Aging
Dept. of Social Services
P.O. Box 1337
615 Howerton Court
Jefferson City, MO 65102-
1337
573-526-0727

Montana
Office on Aging
Dept. of Health & Human
Services
Senior & LTC Division
P.O. Box 4210
111 Sanders
Helena, MT 59604-4210
406-444-4077

Nebraska
Dept. of Aging
P.O. Box 95044
301 Centennial Mall South
Lincoln, NE 68509-5044
402-471-2306

Nevada
Division of Aging Services
Dept. of Human Resources
340 North 11th Street, #203
Las Vegas, NV 89101
702-486-3545

New Hampshire
Division of Elderly and Adult
Services
129 Pleasant Street
Concord, NH 03301-3857
603-271-4375

New Jersey
State Long-Term-Care
Ombudsman for
Institutionalized Elderly
P.O. Box 807
Trenton, NJ 08625-0807
609-588-3614

New Mexico
State Agency on Aging
228 East Palace Avenue
Santa Fe, NM 87501
505-827-7640

New York
Office for the Aging
2 Empire State Plaza
Agency Bldg., #2
Albany, NY 12223-0001
518-474-7329

North Carolina
Division of Aging
693 Palmer Drive
Caller Box #29531
Raleigh, NC 27626-0531
919-733-8395

North Dakota
Aging Services Division
Dept. of Human Services
600 South 2nd Street, #1C
Bismarck, ND 58504
701-328-8910

Ohio
Dept. of Aging
50 West Broad Street
9th Floor
Columbus, OH 43215-5928
614-644-7922

Oklahoma
Aging Services Division
Dept. of Human Services
312 NE 28th Street, #109
Oklahoma City, OK 73105
405-521-6734

Oregon
Office of the Long-Term-Care
Ombudsman
3855 Wolverine NE, #6
Salem, OR 97310
503-378-6533

Pennsylvania
Dept. of Aging
555 Walnut Street, 5th Floor
P.O. Box 1089
Harrisburg, PA 17101
717-783-7247

Puerto Rico
Governor's Office for Elder
Affairs
Call Box 50063
Old San Juan Station
San Juan, Puerto Rico 00902
787-725-1515

Rhode Island
Alliance for Better Long-Term
Care
422 Post Road, #204
Warwick, RI 02888
401-785-3391

South Carolina
Division on Aging
1801 Main Street
P.O. Box 8206
Columbia, SC 29202-8206
803-253-6177

South Dakota
Office of Adult Services and
Aging
700 Governors Drive
Pierre, SD 57501-2291
605-773-3656

Tennessee
Commission on Aging
Andrew Jackson Bldg.
500 Deaderick Street, 9th
Floor
Nashville, TN 37243-0860
615-741-2056

Texas
Dept. on Aging
4900 North Lamar Boulevard,
4th Floor
P.O. Box 12786
Austin, TX 78751-2316
512-424-6890

Utah
Division of Aging and Adult
Services
Dept. of Social Services
120 North, 200 West, #401
Salt Lake City, UT 84103
801-538-3924

Vermont
Vermont Legal Aid, Inc.
P.O. Box 1367
Burlington, VT 05402
802-863-5620

Virginia
Virginia Association of Area
Agencies on Aging
530 East Main Street, #428
Richmond, VA 23219
804-644-2923

Washington
South King County Multi-
Service Center
1200 South 336th Street
P.O. Box 23699
Federal Way, WA 98093
253-838-6810

West Virginia
Commission on Aging
1900 Kanawha Boulevard
East Charleston, WV 25305-
0160
304-558-3317

Wisconsin
Board of Aging and Long-
Term Care
214 North Hamilton Street
Madison, WI 53703-2118
608-266-8945

Wyoming
Wyoming Senior Citizens, Inc.
756 Gilchrist
P.O. Box 94
Wheatland, WY 82201
307-322-5553

Appendix C

State Licensing and Certification Programs
http://www.hospicepatients.org

Alabama
Division of Provider Services
Dept. of Public Health
P.O. Box 303017
Montgomery, AL 36130-3017
334-206-5219

Alaska
Health Facilities Licensing
and Certification
Dept. of Health and Social
Services
4730 Business Park
Boulevard
#18, Bldg. H
Anchorage, AK 50399-503
907-561-3011

Arizona
Division of Assurance and
Licensure Services
Arizona Dept. of Human
Services
1647 E. Morten Avenue, #130
Phoenix, AZ 85020-4610
602-674-9705

Arkansas
Division of Medical Services
Office of Long-Term Care
Arkansas Dept. of Human
Services
P.O. Box 8059, Mail Slot 400
Little Rock, AR 72203-8059
501-682-8430

California
Licensing and Certification
Program
Dept. of Health Services
P.O. Box 942732
1800 Third Street, #210
Sacramento, CA 94234-7320
916-445-1054

Colorado
Health Facilities Division
Colorado Dept. of Public
Health and Environment
4300 Cherry Creek Drive S.
Denver, CO 80246
303-692-2835

Connecticut
State of Connecticut Dept. of
Public Health
410 Capitol Avenue, Mail Slot
12 HSR
P.O. Box 340308
Hartford, CT 06134
860-509-7406

Delaware
Division of Long-Term-Care
Residents Protection
Delaware Dept. of Health and
Social Services
3 Mill Road, #308
Wilmington, DE 19806
302-577-6672

District of Columbia
Health Regulation
Administration
Dept. of Health
825 N. Capitol Street NE
Washington, DC 20002
202-442-9430

Florida
Long Term Care Unit
Florida Agency for Health
Care
Mail Station 33
2727 Mahan Drive
Tallahassee, FL 32308
850-448-5861

Georgia
Office of Regulatory Service of
Long-Term Care
Dept. of Human Resources
Two Peachtree Street NW,
#31-447
Atlanta, GA 30303
404-657-8935

Hawaii
Office of Health Care
Assurance
Dept. of Health
State of Hawaii
P.O. Box 3378
Honolulu, HI 96801
808-692-7447

Idaho
Bureau of Facility Standards
P.O. Box 83720
Boise, ID 83720-0036
208-334-6626

Illinois
Office of Quality Assurance
Illinois Dept. of Public Health
525-535 W. Jefferson Street
Springfield, IL 62761-0001
217-782-5180

Indiana
Bureau of Aging and In-Home
Services
P.O. Box 7083
402 W. Washington Street
Room W-454
Indianapolis, IN 46204-7083
317-232-7020

Iowa
Health Facilities Division
Dept. of Inspection and
Appeals
Lucas State Office Bldg.
Des Moines, IA 50319-0083
515-281-4115

Kansas
Health Facilities
Landon State Office Bldg.
900 SW Jackson, #1001
Topeka, KS 66612
785-296-1240

Kentucky
Licensing and Regulation
Office of the Inspector
General
275 E. Main Street, Mail Stop
SE
Frankfort, KY 40621
502-564-6786

Louisiana
State of Louisiana Health
Standards
P.O. Box 3767
Baton Rouge, LA 70821-3767
225-342-0138

Maine
Bureau of Medical Services
Division of Licensing and
Certification
Dept. of Human Services
35 Anthony Avenue
11 State House Station
Augusta, ME 04333-0011
207-624-5443

Maryland
Office of Health Care Quality
Spring Grove Hospital Center
BB Bldg.
55 Wade Avenue
Baltimore, MD 21228
410-402-8000

Massachusetts
Licensure and Certification
Division of Health Care
Quality
10 West Street, 5th Floor
Boston, MA 02111
617-753-8000

Michigan
MDCIS
Bureau of Health Systems
Division of Nursing Home
Monitoring
P.O. Box 30664
Lansing, MI 48909
517-241-2506

Minnesota
Long-Term Care and
Certification
Division of Facility and
Provider Compliance
85 E. Seventh Place, #300
St. Paul, MN 57101
651-215-8701

Mississippi
Licensure and Certification
570 E. Woodrow Wilson, #200
Jackson, MS 39215
601-576-7300

Missouri
Division of Aging
615 Howerton Court
P.O. Box 1337
Jefferson City, MO 65102
573-751-3082

Montana
State Aging Coordinator
Quality Assurance Division
Dept. of Public Health and
Human Services
2401 Colonial Drive
Helena, MT 59620
406-444-0231

Nebraska
Regulation and Licensure
Credentialing Division
Dept. of Health and Human
Services
301 Centennial Mall S.
P.O. Box 95007
Lincoln, NE 68509-5007
402-471-2946

Nevada
Bureau of Licensure and
Certification
1550 E. College Parkway,
#158
Carson City, NV 89706
775-687-4475

New Hampshire
Office of Program Support
Health Facilities
Administration
Dept. of Health and Human
Services
129 Pleasant Street
Concord, NH 03301-3857
603-271-4592

New Jersey
Division of Long-Term Care
Systems
New Jersey Dept. of Health
Services
P.O. Box 367
Trenton, NJ 08625
609-633-9034

New Mexico
Health Facilities Licensing
and Certification Bureau
525 Camino de los Marquez,
#2
Santa Fe, NM 87501
505-827-7640

New York
Office of Continuing-Care
New York State Dept. of
Health
166 Delaware Avenue
Delmar, NY 12054
518-474-1000

North Carolina
Division of Facilities Services
Licensure and Certification
Section
Dept. of Health and Human
Services
2711 Mail Service Center
Raleigh, NC 27699-2711
919-733-7461

North Dakota
Division of Health Facilities
North Dakota Dept. of Health
600 E. Boulevard Avenue
Bismarck, ND 58505-0200
701-328-2352

Ohio
Licensure Program
Ohio Dept. of Health
246 N. High Street
Columbus, OH 43215-2412
614-466-7713

Oklahoma
Special Health Services
Oklahoma State Health Dept.
1000 N.E. Tenth Street
Oklahoma City, OK 73117
405-271-6868

Oregon
Long-Term Care Quality
Section
Senior and Disabled Services
Divisions
500 Summer Street N.E.
Salem, OR 97310
503-945-5853

Pennsylvania
Bureau of Facility Licensure
and Certification
Division of Nursing Care
Facilities
Pennsylvania Dept. of Health
Room 526, Health and
Welfare Bldg.
Harrisburg, PA 17120
717-787-1816

Rhode Island
Rhode Island Dept. of Health
Division of Facilities
Regulation
3 Capitol Hill, Room 306
Providence, RI 09908
401-222-2566

South Carolina
Office of Senior and Long-
Term Care Services
Division of Health Licensing
Dept. of Health and
Environmental Control
2600 Bull Street
Columbia, SC 29201-8206
803-737-7370

South Dakota

Licensure and Certification
South Dakota Dept. of Health
615 E. Fourth Street
Pierre, SD 57501-3357
605-773-3357

Tennessee

Office of Health Licensure
and Regulation
Division of Health Care
Facilities
Tennessee Dept. of Health
425 Fifth Avenue N
Cordell Hull Bldg., First Floor
Nashville, TN 37247
615-741-7221

Texas

Long-Term Care Regulatory
Mail Code E-342
Texas Dept. of Human
Services
P.O. Box 149030
Austin, TX 78714-9030
512-438-2633
in-state: 800-458-9858

Utah

Bureau of Licensing
Dept. of Health
288 North 1460 West
P.O. Box 142003
Salt Lake City, UT 84116
801-538-6152

Vermont

Division of Licensing and
Protection
Dept. of Aging and
Disabilities
103 S. Main Street, Ladd Hall
Waterbury, VT 05671-2306
802-241-2345

Virginia

Division of Long-Term Care
Services
Center for Quality Health
Care Services and Consumer
Protection
Virginia State Dept. of Health
3600 W. Broad Street, #216
Richmond, VA 23230-4920
804-367-2100

Washington

Residential Care Services
Dept. of Social and Health
Services
P.O. Box 45600
Olympia, WA 98504-5600
360-725-2300

West Virginia

Licensure and Certification
Office of Health Facilities
350 Capitol Street, Room 206
Charleston, WV 25301-3718
304-558-0050

Wisconsin
Bureau of Quality Assurance
Dept. of Health and Family
Services
One W. Wilson Street, Room
950
Madison, WI 53701
608-266-8847

Wyoming
Office of Health Quality
Dept. of Health
2020 Carey Avenue, 8th Floor
Cheyenne, WY 82002
307-777-7123

APPENDIX D

AREA AGENCIES ON AGING
http://www.eldercare.gov

Alabama
Commission on Aging
P.O. Box 301851
770 Washington Avenue,
#470
Montgomery, AL 36130-1851
334-242-5743
800-243-5463

Alaska
Division of Senior Services
Dept. of Administration
P.O. Box 110209
Juneau, AK 99811-0209
907-465-4879

Arizona
Aging and Adult
Administration
Dept. of Economic Security
1789 W. Jefferson, #950A
Phoenix, AZ 85007
602-542-6575

Arkansas
Division of Aging and Adult
Services
Arkansas Dept. of Human
Services
P.O. Box 1437, Mail Slot
1412
7th and Main Streets
Little Rock, AR 72203
501-682-2441

California
Dept. of Aging
1600 K Street
Sacramento, CA 95814
916-324-1903

Colorado
Division of Aging and Adult
Services
Dept. of Human Services
110 16th Street, #200
Denver, CO 80202-5202
303-620-4147

Connecticut
Elderly Services Division
Dept. of Social Services
25 Sigourney Street
Hartford, CT 06106
860-424-5277

Delaware
Division of Services for Aging
Adults with Physical
Disabilities
Dept. of Health & Social
Services
1901 N. Du Pont Highway
New Castle, DE 19720
302-577-4791

District of Columbia
Office on Aging
One Judiciary Square
441 4th Street NW, 9th Floor
Washington, DC 20001
202-724-4979

Florida
Dept. of Elder Affairs
Building B, #152
4040 Esplanade Way
Tallahassee, FL 32399
850-414-2000

Georgia
Division of Aging Services
2 Peachtree Street NW #36-
385
Atlanta, GA 30303-3176
888-454-5826
404-657-5258

Hawaii
Executive Office on Aging
No 1 Capitol District
250 S. Hotel Street, #109
Honolulu, HI 96813-2831
808-586-0185

Idaho
Commission on Aging
3380 Americana Terrace,
#120
P.O. Box 83720
Boise, ID 83720-0007
208-334-2423

Illinois
Dept. of Aging
421 E. Capitol Avenue
Springfield, IL 62701
217-785-2870

Indiana
Bureau of Aging and In-Home
Services
402 W. Washington Street
P.O. Box 7083
Indianapolis, IN 46204-7083
317-232-7020

Iowa
Dept. of Elder Affairs
Clemens Bldg., 3rd Floor
200 10th Street
Des Moines, IA 50309-3609
515-281-5187

Kansas
Dept. on Aging
New England Bldg.
503 S. Kansas
Topeka, KS 66603-3404
785-296-4986

Kentucky
Office of Aging Services
Cabinet for Health Services
275 E. Main Street, 5 West
Frankfort, KY 40621
502-564-6930

Louisiana
Office of Elderly Affairs
Elderly Protective Services
P.O. Box 80374
412 N. 4th Street
Baton Rouge, LA 70898-0374
225-342-7144

Maine
Bureau of Elder & Adult
Services
Dept. of Human Services
#11 State House Station
Augusta, ME 04333-0011
207-624-5335

Maryland
Dept. of Aging
State Office Bldg., #1007
301 W. Preston Street
Baltimore, MD 21201
410-767-1100

Massachusetts
Executive Office of Elder
Affairs
1 Ashburton Place, 5th Floor
Boston, MA 02108
617-222-7470

Michigan
Office of Services to the Aging
P.O. Box 30676
Lansing, MI 48909-8176
517-373-8230

Minnesota
Board on Aging
444 Lafayette Road
St. Paul, MN 55155-3843
651-296-2770

Mississippi
Council on Aging
Division of Aging & Adult
Services
750 N. State Street
Jackson, MS 39202
601-359-4929

Missouri
Division of Aging
Dept. of Social Services
P.O. Box 1337
615 Howerton Court
Jefferson City, MO 65102-
1337
573-751-3082

Montana
Senior Long Term Division
111 Sanders Street
P.O. Box 4210
Helena, MT 59604
406-444-7788

Nebraska
Division of Aging Services
Dept. of Health and Human
Services
P.O. Box 95044
301 Centennial Mall-South
Lincoln, NE 68509
402-471-2307

Nevada
Division of Aging Services
Dept. of Human Resources
3416 Goni Road, Bldg. D-132
Carson City, NV 89706
775-687-4210

New Hampshire
Division of Elderly & Adult
Services
State Office Park South
129 Pleasant Street
Concord, NH 03301-3843
603-271-4394

New Jersey
Division of Senior Affairs
Dept. of Health and Senior
Services
P.O. Box 807
Trenton, NJ 08625-0807
609-588-3141

New Mexico
State Agency on Aging
La Villa Rivera Bldg.
228 E. Palace Avenue,
Ground Floor
Santa Fe, NM 87501
505-827-7640

New York
Office for the Aging
New York State Plaza
Agency Bldg. #2
Albany, NY 12223
518-474-5731

North Carolina
Division of Aging
CB 29531
693 Palmer Drive
Raleigh, NC 27626-0531
919-733-3983

North Dakota
Aging Services Division
Dept. of Human Services
600 S. 2nd Street, #1C
Bismarck, ND 58504
701-328-8910

Ohio
Dept. of Aging
50 W. Broad Street, 9th Floor
Columbus, OH 43215-5928
614-466-5500

Oklahoma
Aging Services Division
Dept. of Human Services
P.O. Box 25352
312 N.E. 28th Street
Oklahoma City, OK 73105
405-521-2327

Oregon
Senior & Disabled Services
Division
500 Summer Street NE, 2nd
Floor
Salem, OR 97310-1015
503-945-5811

Pennsylvania
Dept. of Aging
Forum Place
555 Walnut Street, 5th Floor
Harrisburg, PA 17101-1919
717-783-1550

Rhode Island
Dept. of Elderly Affairs
160 Pine Street
Providence, RI 02903-3708
401-222-2858

South Carolina
Dept. of Health and Human
Services
P.O. Box 8206
1801 Main Street
Columbia, SC 29202-8206
803-898-2501

South Dakota
Office of Adult Services &
Aging
700 Governors Drive
Pierre, SD 57501
605-773-3656

Tennessee
Commission on Aging
Andrew Jackson Bldg.
500 Deaderick St., 9th Floor
Nashville, TN 37243-0860
615-741-2056

Texas
Dept. on Aging
4900 N. Lamar, 4th Floor
Austin, TX 78751-2316
512-424-6840

Utah
Division of Aging & Adult
Services
Dept. of Social Services
Box 45500
120 North-200 West
Salt Lake City, UT 84145-
0500
801-538-3910

Vermont
Aging & Disabilities
103 S. Main Street
Waterbury, VT 05671-2301
802-241-2400

Virginia
Dept. for the Aging
1600 Forest Avenue
Preston Bldg., #102
Richmond, VA 23229
804-662-9354

Washington
Aging & Adult Services
Administration
Dept. of Social & Health
Services
P.O. Box 45050
Olympia, WA 98504-5050
360-902-7797

West Virginia
West Virginia Bureau of
Senior Services
1900 Kanawha Blvd., East
Holly Grove Bldg 10
Charleston, WV 25305-0160
304-558-5609

Wisconsin
Bureau of Aging & LTC
Resources
Dept. of Health and Family
Services
One West Wilson Street
P.O. Box 7851
Madison, WI 53707-7851
608-266-2536

Wyoming
WDH, Division on Aging
Hathaway Bldg., #139
Cheyenne, WY 82002-0710
307-777-7986
800-442-2766

Appendix E

Other Resources on Aging

Center for Consumer Health
Choices
Consumers Union
http://www.consumersunion.org
101 Truman Avenue
Yonkers, NY 10703
914-378-2000

Consumer Reports Nursing
Home Watch List
http://www.consumerreports.org
/health
914-378-2000

Eldercare Locator
http://www.eldercare.gov
800-677-1116

ElderWeb
http://www.elderweb.com
1305 Chadwick Drive
Normal, Illinois 61761
309-451-3319

Health Policy Center
Brandeis University
The Heller School for Social
Policy and Management
P.O. Box 549110/MS 035
Waltham, MA 02454
781-736-3800

Medicare
http://www.medicare.gov
800-MEDICARE
(800-633-4227)

National Institute on Aging
http://www.nia.nih.gov
Building 31, Room 5C27
31 Center Drive, MSC 2292
Bethesda, MD 20892
301-496-1752

U.S. Administration on Aging
http://www.aoa.gov
330 Independence Avenue SW
Washington, DC 20201
202-619-0724

U.S. Office of Disability, Aging,
and Long Term Care Policy
http://aspe.hhs.gov
Room 424E
200 Independence Avenue SW
Washington, D.C. 20201
202-619-0257
877-696-6775

U.S. Senate Special Committee
on Aging
http://www.senate.gov/~aging
G-31 Dirksen Building
Washington, D.C. 20510

202-224-5364

INDEX

Note: Page numbers in *italic type* refer to charts and tables.

Printed in the United States
132032LV00001B/87/A